A NATURAL SYSTEM
OF HOUSE DESIGN

THE WHOLE DIFFERENCE
BETWEEN CONSTRUCTION AND
CREATION IS EXACTLY THIS: THAT A
THING CONSTRUCTED CAN ONLY BE
LOVED AFTER IT IS CONSTRUCTED; BUT
A THING CREATED IS LOVED
BEFORE IT EXISTS.

—GILBERT KEITH CHESTERTON

A NATURAL SYSTEM OF HOUSE DESIGN

AN ARCHITECT'S WAY

CHARLES G. WOODS, A.I.A.

INTRODUCTION BY VINCENT VAN DE VENTER, R.A

ILLUSTRATED BY MALCOLM WELLS, R.A.

McGraw-Hill

New York   San Francisco   Washington, D.C.   Auckland   Bogotá
Caracas   Lisbon   London   Madrid   Mexico City   Milan
Montreal   New Delhi   San Juan   Singapore
Sydney   Tokyo   Toronto

LIBRARY OF CONGRESS CATALOGING-IN-PUBLICATION DATA

WOODS, CHARLES G.
    A NATURAL SYSTEM OF HOUSE DESIGN / CHARLES G. WOODS ; INTRODUCTION
BY VANCE VAN DE VENTER ; ILLUSTRATED BY MALCOLM WELLS.
        P.   CM.
    INCLUDES BIBLIOGRAPHICAL REFERENCES AND INDEX.
    ISBN 0-07-071736-2
    1. MODULAR COORDINATION (ARCHITECTURE)   2. ARCHITECTURE. DOMESTIC—
UNITED STATES.   I. TITLE
    NA7115.W68   1996
    728'.37'0973—DC21   96-48319
                                                       CIP

McGraw-Hill

A Division of The McGraw-Hill Companies

1 2 3 4 5 6 7 8 9 0   KGP/KGP   9 0 1 0 9 8 7 6

ISBN 0-07-071736-2

THE SPONSORING EDITOR FOR THIS BOOK WAS WENDY LOCHNER,
THE EDITING SUPERVISOR WAS VIRGINIA CARROLL, AND THE PRODUCTION
SUPERVISOR WAS PAMELA A. PELTON. IT WAS SET IN HERCULANUM BY
NORTH MARKET STREET GRAPHICS.

PRINTED AND BOUND BY QUEBECOR/KINGSPORT.

I dedicate this book to some of the important men in my life: my father, Mr. Sid Woods; my late stepfather, Mr. Robert Orloski; my grandfather, Mr. Bill Polzin; my late grandfather, Mr. Charles Poklacki; and to my father-in-law, Mr. Herman Gundlach.

CONTENTS

CONTENTS

EVEN FOR WHAT MIGHT SEEM LIKE A SIMPLE BOOK, I HAVE A LOT OF PEOPLE TO THANK.

FIRST, THANKS TO MY WIFE JULIE KETTLE GUNDLACH, WITHOUT WHOM I COULD NOT HAVE DONE ALL THIS WORK, PERSONALLY OR EMOTIONALLY. SHE WAS ENDLESSLY SUPPORTIVE, EVEN WHEN SHE DIDN'T AGREE WITH ALL MY "CRAZY" IDEAS. I ALSO THANK HER FOR HER PHOTO OF ME. NEXT, AND IN A CLOSE TIE FOR FIRST, THANKS TO ARCHITECT MALCOLM WELLS. MAC HAS DONE AN UNBELIEVABLE JOB ON ALL THESE DRAWINGS (AND SOME NOT SHOWN) IN JUST THREE YEARS—AND OVER HALF IN LESS THAN A YEAR! OUR METHOD OF WORKING LONG DISTANCE ON HOUSE DESIGNS AND THE EXIGENCIES OF BOOK DEADLINES NECESSITATED SEEMINGLY ENDLESS PHONE CALLS TO MAC FROM ME. CONSIDERING THAT MAC DISLIKES THE PHONE, HE WAS PATIENT INDEED. I WOULD ALSO LIKE TO THANK HIM FOR TEACHING ME SO MUCH THESE LAST TEN YEARS AND FOR BEING MY FRIEND.

THANKS TO ARCHITECT VINCE VAN DE VENTER FOR A GREAT INTRODUCTION AND FOR HIS WORK ON RECENT PROJECTS (SUCH AS OUR CATHEDRAL) AT A TIME OF GREAT PERSONAL PRESSURE AS A RESULT OF MOVING HIS RESIDENCE.

I WOULD LIKE TO THANK NOTED ARCHITECTS CHARLES GWATHMEY, F.A.I.A.; BART PRINCE; JOHN BAKER; FRANCIS CHING; AND JOHN C. LAHEY FOR TAKING TIME OUT OF THEIR VERY BUSY SCHEDULES TO REVIEW AND SUPPORT A JUNIOR PEER'S WORK. THIS WAS ESPECIALLY GENEROUS SINCE I HAVE MET ONLY JOHN LAHEY.

I AM ALSO GRATEFUL TO MY DOCTORAL TEACHER, NOTED PHILOSOPHER/THEOLOGIAN ROBERT C. NEVILLE, AND MY FRIEND, FAMOUS TRANSPERSONAL PSYCHOLOGIST KEN WILBER, FOR COMMENTING ON MY WORK.

THOUGH THEY DID NOT REVIEW MY WORK, I AM GRATEFUL TO NOTED ARCHITECTS MOSHE SAFDIE, GUNNAR BIRKERTS, PAOLO SOLERI, AND THE OFFICE OF YAMASAKI FOR PLEASANT NOTES OR CALLS.

THANKS TO ARCHITECTS DAVID WRIGHT AND ALFREDO DE VIDO FOR CRITICAL COMMENTS AT AN EARLIER STAGE OF THIS BOOK'S DEVELOPMENT.

I WOULD LIKE TO THANK ARCHITECT JOHN J. MARTIN, SENIOR PARTNER OF OUR FORMER FIRM, NATURAL ARCHITECTURE, FOR FIVE YEARS OR SO, FOR WORKING WITH ME ON SOME OF THESE PROJECTS. ALSO,

ACKNOWLEDGMENTS

THANKS TO ARCHITECT GLEN STRAIGHT FOR HIS ASSOCIATE WORK ON THE COOPER PROJECT.

THANKS TO FINE ARCHITECTS DONALD PASSMAN, JAY AND TRACY BOYLES, AND ELIZABETH DAVIDSON FOR THEIR GREAT WORK AND SUPPORT ON MANY OF THESE PROJECTS.

I WOULD LIKE TO THANK ALL MY FAMILY, ESPECIALLY MY BROTHER MICHAEL, MY MOTHER, MY SISTER DEBBIE, MY AUNTS JENNY AND JO, FRIENDS, AND CLIENTS (ESPECIALLY THE SISSONS, WEBERS, STULTZES, COOPERS, COBB, AND AUGELLO). SO MUCH OF THIS BOOK WAS DONE BY MAIL, OFTEN IN DIFFERENT PARTS OF THE COUNTRY, THAT I WOULD LIKE TO THANK KINKO'S, MARTIN-PRATT'S PHOTOGRAPHY, ROYAL BLUEPRINT, FEDERAL EXPRESS, THE U.S. POSTAL SERVICE, AND ESPECIALLY QUALITY PRINTING.

THANKS TO MY LANDLORD, MARK OSTRANDER, THE TOWN HOUSE DINER, AND LINDA AND JOE CANZONERI'S FOR RECEIVING ENDLESS PACKAGES.

THANKS TO EDITORS LARRY ERICKSON, BOB WILSON (AND STACEY!) FOR PUBLISHING SO MANY (NINETEEN) OF THESE HOUSES IN BETTER HOMES AND GARDENS BUILDING IDEAS MAGAZINE DURING THE PAST FOUR YEARS.

I WOULD LIKE TO THANK ALL MY FRIENDS (ESPECIALLY DAVID HUSTON) AND FAMILY—IN PARTICULAR, MY BROTHER, ROBERT A. WOODS, THE NOTED ASTROLOGER, WHO PREDICTED MY MOST CREATIVE WORK YET. I DON'T KNOW IF I ALWAYS BELIEVE IN ASTROLOGY, BUT I DO BELIEVE IN HIM.

THANKS TO MY FRIENDS DANA AND ERIC FOR COMPANY AND SUPPORT ON MY LONG STAYS IN CHICAGO.

AND ALMOST LAST, BUT NOT LEAST, THANKS TO MCGRAW-HILL AND SENIOR ARCHITECTURE EDITOR JOEL STEIN (THANKS, JOEL, FOR GETTING THE BOOK IN COLOR AND SEEING IT TO ALMOST PRESS TIME), TO EDITOR WENDY LOCHNER AND HER ASSISTANTS FOR SEEING THE BOOK THROUGH TO PRESS IN A HIGH-QUALITY WAY (WENDY WAS ALSO THE EDITOR OF MY PREVIOUS THREE BOOKS AT VNR), TO MAGGIE WEBSTER-SHAPIRO FOR COVER WORK, AND TO ROGER KASUNIC FOR KEEPING IT ALL TOGETHER. ALSO, THANKS TO MARY LAWSON OF OPUS DESIGN FOR THE BOOK DESIGN, GINNY CARROLL AND THE GANG AT NORTH MARKET STREET GRAPHICS FOR THE EXCELLENT COPYEDITING, AND DAVID ERB FOR FINE LAYUP WORK.

TO MY GREAT TYPIST/SECRETARY, WHO REQUESTED ANONYMITY, MANY THANKS!

FINALLY, THANKS TO GOD AND FLW—IN HEAVEN (IN THAT ORDER!) FOR ALL THEIR INSPIRATIONS. AFTER ALL MY EXPLANATIONS, I'M NOT REALLY TOO SURE HOW I DO DO IT MYSELF!

IN <u>A NATURAL SYSTEM OF HOUSE DESIGN,</u> I HAVE TRIED TO SHOW THE READER A MODULE SYSTEM OF DESIGN THAT I HAVE DEVELOPED OVER TWENTY-FIVE YEARS. THIS SYSTEM, THOUGH NOT COMPLETELY UNIQUE TO ME, SHOULD PROVE USEFUL TO ARCHITECTS, DESIGNERS, STUDENTS, DRAFTSMEN/WOMEN, RENDERERS, ENGINEERS, BUILDERS, AND, OF COURSE, CLIENTS/HOMEOWNERS.

IN ADDITION TO AN EXPLANATION OF THIS SYSTEM, AS WELL AS ITS DESIGN POSSIBILITIES, THIS BOOK SHOWS THE SYSTEM AS APPLIED TO 25 HOUSE DESIGNS AND INCLUDES AN APPENDIX ON NONRESIDENTIAL DESIGN. THE SYSTEM IS SHOWN THROUGH ALL STAGES OF WORK, FROM PRELIMINARY DESIGN TO CONSTRUCTION. THERE IS ALSO AN ABSTRACT (AND POSSIBLY RAMBLING) ESSAY ON MY DESIGN PHILOSOPHY.

MY EARLIER BOOKS INCLUDED ALLUSIONS TO PHILOSOPHY/RELIGION AND CULTURE IN GENERAL. I ALSO USED HUMOR TO HELP LIGHTEN UP WHAT IS TOO OFTEN WRITTEN ABOUT IN A "SAWDUST" WAY. I CONTINUE THAT STYLE IN THIS BOOK.

I HAVE ALSO BEEN HONEST ABOUT THE (USUALLY ONLY TANGENTIAL) INFLUENCE OF OTHER ARCHITECTS AND THE PERSONALITIES OF MY CLIENTS AND ASSOCIATES—NOTABLY THIS BOOK'S ILLUSTRATOR/ARCHITECT, MALCOLM WELLS. I HAVE ALSO BEEN OPEN ABOUT CRITICISMS I HAVE OF MY OWN WORK AND OCCASIONAL PROBLEMS WITH THE BUILDING PROCESS OR CLIENTS. THIS GOES ON ALL THE TIME AMONG ARCHITECTS, CLIENTS, AND BUILDERS. I THOUGHT THAT BEING OPEN ABOUT IT AND OFFERING SUGGESTIONS WOULD HELP OTHERS TO AVOID THESE SAME PROBLEMS.

NO DOUBT, THESE ADMISSIONS WILL MAKE ME SEEM LESS OLYMPIAN AND MORE HUMAN, BUT THAT, AFTER ALL, IS ALL I AM. I HAVE DONE MY BEST IN MY OWN BY TURNS SYSTEMATIC AND HAPHAZARD WAYS. I HOPE YOU ENJOY THIS BOOK AND FIND AT LEAST SOME OF IT USEFUL.

CHARLES G. WOODS, AIA, ARCHITECT

MAC AND I: HOW WE WORKED TOGETHER

WITH MAC DOING MY RENDERINGS, I HAVE FELT MYSELF TO BE IN AN ODD SITUATION SIMILAR TO THAT OF A YOUNG FRANK LLOYD WRIGHT (AS IT WERE) WITH LOUIS SULLIVAN DOING MY DESIGNS. IT WAS A HUMBLING EXPERIENCE, AS MAC IS A MASTER ARCHITECT AND RENDERER. I ALWAYS WANTED TO HAVE A WHOLE BOOK DONE BY ONE GREAT RENDERER, AND MAC SAID THAT SINCE HE ENJOYED MY WORK, HE WOULD DO IT. I DON'T THINK EITHER OF US REALIZED HOW MUCH WORK THIS WOULD BE, SINCE I ORIGINALLY PLANNED TEN TO TWELVE HOUSES, AND WE'VE DONE OVER FIFTY.

MOST OF MY DESIGNS WERE DONE ON 24" BY 36" SHEETS (GRID PAPER) USUALLY IN PENCIL (THUMBNAIL PERSPECTIVE SKETCHES WERE OFTEN SENT, TOO). SOME WERE DONE FREEHAND AT ⅛" SCALE ON 11" BY 17" GRID PAPER (MAC'S FAVORITE SIZE) AND THIS IS THE SIZE AT WHICH THESE RENDERINGS WERE ORIGINALLY DRAWN. ONLY A FEW WERE SCRIBBLED ON 8½" BY 11" LINED PAPER WITH ONLY A ROUGH SCALE—ABOUT 1⁄16".

I PICKED THE PERSPECTIVE ANGLES, COLOR, LIGHTING, AND MANY DETAILS. MAC, OF COURSE, ADDED MANY NIFTY DETAILS HIMSELF, BUT HE TRIED TO KEEP WITHIN THE SPIRIT OF MY WORK. OUR DESIGN WORK IS AT LEAST HARMONIOUS, BUT HIS ORIENTATION IS EVEN MORE UNDERGROUND AND ENERGY-EFFICIENT THAN MINE AND WE HAVE, OF COURSE, OTHER STYLISTIC AND PHILOSOPHIC DIFFERENCES.

EVEN WITH THE MOST DETAILED PLANS SUBMITTED, WE WOULD GO BACK AND FORTH FROM 8½" BY 11" ROUGH SKETCHES TO 11" BY 17" ROUGH PERSPECTIVES TO FINAL DRAWINGS. MOST HOUSES INVOLVED THREE OR FOUR STAGES, SOME FIVE OR SIX, AND A FEW ONLY ONE OR TWO. THERE WERE ALSO NUMEROUS (MORE THAN MAC LIKED AT TIMES!) PHONE CALLS AND ENDLESS EXPRESS MAIL, AS WELL AS A FEW FAXES EXCHANGED. IT'S BEEN A TRULY CREATIVE PARTNERSHIP—ESPECIALLY SINCE WE NEVER MET UNTIL THE BOOK WAS FINISHED.

ALL THIS WAS DONE LONG DISTANCE. I DO NOT THINK IT COULD HAVE BEEN DONE WITHOUT THE MODULE SYSTEM. THE DESIGNS ARE LARGELY MINE, BUT FROM TIME TO TIME MAC WOULD SUGGEST A NEAT DETAIL OR THE LIKE, AND I WOULD ACCEPT SOME. ALL IN ALL, THE DESIGNS ARE 90 PERCENT MINE AND THE RENDERINGS 90 PERCENT MAC'S. ALL THE BOOK REVIEWERS MENTIONED THE EXTRA DIMENSION THE COLOR ADDED, SO I AM

GRATEFUL TO MCGRAW-HILL FOR GIVING
US SOME PAGES IN COLOR. SOME PEOPLE
HAVE ASKED ME WHY I DIDN'T RENDER
THESE MYSELF. MY OWN RENDERING
STYLE IS <u>HIGHLY</u> TIME CONSUMING AND,
THOUGH GOOD, IS NOT AS GREAT AS MAC'S.
ALSO, WHEN IN DESIGN MODE IT IS HARD
FOR ME TO SLOW DOWN FOR RENDERINGS,
SO WITH THE BUSINESS, MY PH.D.
DISSERTATION, AND 20 HOUSES IN THE PAST
YEAR, IT WOULD HAVE BEEN IMPOSSIBLE—
BUT POSSIBLY I WILL RENDER MY NEXT
BOOK.

A WORD FROM MALCOLM WELLS

CHARLES WOODS WAS KIND ENOUGH TO ASK ME TO DO THE ILLUSTRATIONS FOR THIS BOOK. HE DID IT IN SPITE OF THE FACT THAT ILLUSTRATORS FAR MORE GIFTED THAN I WERE AVAILABLE. HE DID IT BECAUSE WE'RE FRIENDS, BECAUSE I RESPOND QUICKLY, BECAUSE I SHARE HIS ADMIRATION OF FRANK LLOYD WRIGHT, AND BECAUSE HE SEEMS TO LIKE MUDDY-COLORED, HEAVY-HANDED PERSPECTIVES. SO PLEASE REMEMBER THAT ANY VISUAL MISTAKES, ANY TASTELESS COLOR COMBINATIONS, AND ALL THE MISREPRESENTATIONS OF HIS IDEAS ARE MINE.

MALCOLM WELLS, UNDERGROUND ON CAPE COD

A NOTE FROM THE BOOK DESIGNER

JUST AS CHARLES' ARCHITECTURE IS INFLUENCED BY THE WORK OF FRANK LLOYD WRIGHT, SO THIS BOOK WAS DESIGNED TO INCORPORATE MR. WRIGHT'S ESSENCE. THE NATURAL COLORS, SOFTLY TEXTURED CREAMY PAPER, AND SEPIA INKS REFLECT A HARMONY WITH NATURE; THE GRID THEME SPEAKS TO THE MODULAR SYSTEM THE ARCHITECT EMPLOYS. THE BOOK WAS ENTIRELY TYPESET IN HERCULANUM, COPYRIGHTED IN 1990 BY ADRIAN FRUTIGER, A MODERN ARTIST OF FONT DESIGN. THIS TYPEFACE INFERS AN ART DECO SENSIBILITY PAIRED WITH THE NATURAL SENSUALITY OF CELTIC WRITINGS.

MARY NICHOLS LAWSON, OPUS DESIGN

I KNOW OF NO ONE ELSE DOING WORK QUITE LIKE WOODS. HE REALLY
KNOWS HOW TO BALANCE ONE GEOMETRIC SHAPE AGAINST ANOTHER. . . .
MASTERFUL.
>   —MALCOLM WELLS, ARCHITECT,
>   "THE FATHER OF UNDERGROUND ARCHITECTURE,"
>   AND AUTHOR OF INFRASTRUCTURE

I AM IMPRESSED BY MANY OF [WOODS] DESIGNS . . . [AND HIS]
PHILOSOPHY OF AN ORGANIC ARCHITECTURE. . . . VERY WELL SAID!
>   —JOHN HOWE, ARCHITECT,
>   "THE HAND OF FRANK LLOYD WRIGHT"

WOODS HAS ALWAYS IMPRESSED ME AS A FREE THINKER IN A PROFESSION
THAT SEEMS TO BE FALTERING WITH UNCERTAINTY AND ONE-
UPMANSHIP. HE IS GENEROUS WITH HIS TALENTS AND HAS WORKED HARD
TO DEVELOP A PRACTICAL SYSTEM OF ARCHITECTURE THAT UPHOLDS HIS
HIGHEST PRINCIPLES AND THAT CAN BE APPLIED BY OTHERS.
>   —ELIZABETH DAVIDSON, ARCHITECT

OVER THE PAST TEN YEARS, BOTH AS A BUILDER AND A CONSULTANT, I
HAVE WORKED WITH CHARLES WOODS. HE HAS TAKEN THE MODULAR
SYSTEM OF DESIGN AND PUSHED ITS LIMITS TO CREATE SOME VERY
INTERESTING AND PLEASING HOUSES. WHEN I STARTED OUT WORKING
WITH THE MODULAR SYSTEM, MY ATTITUDE WAS SOMEWHAT NEGATIVE.
I THOUGHT IT WOULD BE TOO CONFINING AND LIMITING. HOWEVER,
AFTER BUILDING ONE OF HIS HOUSES AND CONSULTING WITH HIM ON
MANY MORE OVER THE YEARS, I HAVE GAINED A NEW RESPECT FOR THE
SYSTEM.
>   —LARRY WILSON,
>   GENERAL CONTRACTOR/CONSULTANT

WOODS' MODULAR SYSTEM APPROACH TO ARCHITECTURE HAS MADE IT SO
MUCH EASIER FOR US TO DESIGN OUR HOUSE. IT'S A LOT EASIER TO STAY
INSIDE A BASIC "FRAMEWORK" THAN TO JUST SHUFFLE ROOMS AROUND
AT WILL, AND THE END RESULT WILL BE A COHESIVE, UNIFIED,
COMPLEMENTARY ARRANGEMENT.
> —WELMOED B. SISSON,
> WOODS' CLIENT

CHARLES G. WOODS IS A TRULY GIFTED ARCHITECT WHOSE EXTRAORDINARY
DESIGNS INSPIRE US ALL TO APPRECIATE THE TEXTURE OF SPACE, TIME, AND
AWARENESS, AND THUS COME RADICALLY ALIVE TO THE WORLD WE
INHABIT . . . A WONDERFUL, WACKY GENIUS.
> —KEN WILBER, AUTHOR,
> THE EINSTEIN OF CONSCIOUSNESS

CHARLES G. WOODS IS AN OUTSTANDING ARCHITECT WITH ORIGINALITY
AND CLARITY OF VISION . . . HE IS ALSO A PHILOSOPHER . . . I COMMEND
THIS BOOK FOR REFLECTION AS WELL AS PLEASURE.
> —PROFESSOR ROBERT C. NEVILLE, AUTHOR,
> DEAN OF THEOLOGY, BOSTON UNIVERSITY

THE DISCIPLINED ORDER IMPLICIT IN WOODS' SYSTEM OF BUILDING IS
CONSISTENT AND SIMPLE . . . SHOULD BECOME A STANDARD REFERENCE
FOR . . . THE DESIGN OF HOUSES.
> —JOHN BAKER, A.I.A.
> ARCHITECT/AUTHOR

WEBER SCHEME C   CHARLES G. WOODS, AIA, ARCHITECT

INTRODUCTION: GEOMETRY AND EARTH—
THE ARCHITECTURE OF CHARLES G. WOODS

VINCE VAN DE VENTER, ARCHITECT

THIS INTRODUCTION WILL, I HOPE, BETTER SITUATE ARCHITECT CHARLES G. WOODS INTO ARCHITECTURAL HISTORY—OR INTO A "TRADITION." OUR INTRODUCTION WAS MADE BY ARCHITECT DENNIS BLAIR, WHO WAS AN APPRENTICE OF FRANK LLOYD WRIGHT, AND I ALSO KNEW MR. WRIGHT.

I STARTED SERVING A WORKING APPRENTICESHIP WITH DENNIS BLAIR IN BARRINGTON, ILLINOIS, IN 1962, PROMPTED BY MY STUDIES WITH ARCHITECT BRUCE GOFF AT THE UNIVERSITY OF OKLAHOMA. IN THE MID-FIFTIES, BRUCE GOFF WAS ONE OF THE FEW ARCHITECTS RESPECTED BY MR. WRIGHT AND IS AN IMPORTANT FIGURE IN THE ORGANIC TRADITION, WITH THEIR FOLLOWERS CREATING WHAT IS NOW BEING CALLED THE "AMERICAN SCHOOL" IN ARCHITECTURE.

I WAS ASSOCIATED WITH DENNIS BLAIR FOR OVER 30 YEARS, FIRST AS A DRAFTSMAN/ DESIGNER, LATER AS AN ASSOCIATE, AND LATER STILL, AS A COLLABORATOR AFTER STARTING MY OWN FIRM.

IN 1987, MR. BLAIR BROUGHT THE YOUNGSTER "CHARLIE" (AS WE CALLED HIM THEN) TO MY CRYSTAL LAKE, ILLINOIS,

STUDIO TO INTRODUCE US, AS HE WAS AWARE OF OUR COMMON INTERESTS, AND TO FURTHER OUR OWN WRIGHT/GOFF CONNECTIONS. FOR WOODS ALSO APPRENTICED (ON AND OFF) FOR OVER TEN YEARS UNDER DENNIS BLAIR (WHOM WOODS HAS CALLED "A GENIUS") AND LATER COLLABORATED WITH HIM ON TWO PROJECTS (THE CASHIN RESIDENCE AND THE ARCHITERRA CONDOMINIUMS). WOODS HAS PAID HOMAGE TO ONLY THREE REAL TEACHERS IN ARCHITECTURE, FIRST AND PRIMARILY TO MR. WRIGHT, WHOM WOODS NEVER MET (AS WOODS WAS ONLY SIX WHEN MR. WRIGHT DIED) BUT WHOSE WORKS HE HAS STUDIED INTENSELY. SECOND, TO MR. BLAIR HIMSELF FOR HIS TEN YEARS OF TEACHING AND FRIENDSHIP, SUPPORT, AND CRITICISM. AND LAST, TO "THE FATHER OF UNDERGROUND ARCHITECTURE," ARCHITECT MALCOLM (MAC) WELLS, FOR ANOTHER TEN YEARS OF TEACHING HIM AS A SENIOR MENTOR, AS WOODS NEVER ACTUALLY WORKED FOR WELLS. WELLS INFLUENCED HIM MOST, NO DOUBT, REGARDING EARTH-SHELTERING AND ENVIRONMENTAL ISSUES, BUT ALSO IN DESIGN.

WE NEVER ACTUALLY WORKED TOGETHER FOR MR. BLAIR AT THE SAME TIME, BUT WE

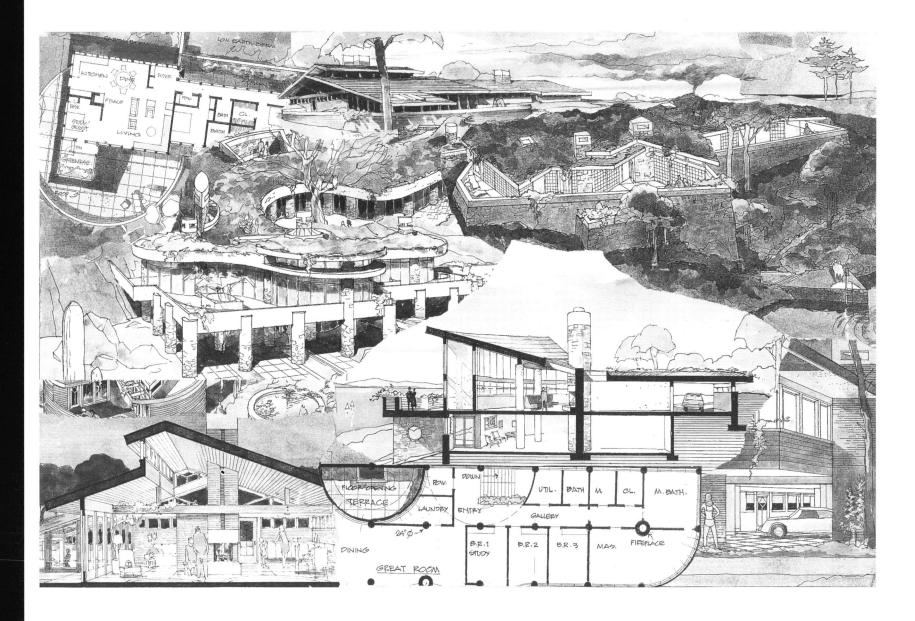

Raphael

CHARLES G. WOODS, AIA, ARCHITECT 1996

WORKED ON THE SAME PROJECTS BETWEEN 1972 AND 1984—I AS RENDERER, AND WOODS OFTEN ON CONSTRUCTION DRAWINGS.

THE WORK OF DENNIS BLAIR (NOW 74 YEARS OF AGE) HAS ALWAYS DEMONSTRATED AN INTEGRITY OF MATERIALS AND CONSISTENT DETAILING, RESULTING IN A DECEPTIVELY SIMPLE AND "NATURAL" LOOK. HIS WORK HAD A STYLE ALL HIS OWN AND WAS VERY SATISFYING TO MY DESIGN SENSE. HIS DESIGNS WERE RELATIVELY SIMPLE AND SPARSE (COMPARED TO GOFF'S, THAT IS!) AND, BECAUSE OF BUDGET LIMITATIONS, WERE NOT OVERLY DRAMATIC, BY WAY OF AN OSTENTATIOUS USE OF EXPENSIVE MATERIALS OR UNUSUAL STRUCTURAL EXPERIMENTS—ALTHOUGH BLAIR WAS A CREATIVE DETAILER WITHIN HIS CONSTRAINTS.

AFTER EXPERIENCING A NUMBER OF BLAIR HOUSES FIRSTHAND, I CAME TO THE CONCLUSION THAT A STRICT ADHERENCE TO A BUILDING "MODULE" GAVE A SENSE OF UNITY THAT WAS NOT READILY APPARENT AND, COMBINED WITH STRONG "SCULPTURAL" SHAPES AND NATURAL MATERIALS, GAVE A VERY SATISFYING FEELING OF BEING JUST RIGHT.

THERE IS NO DOUBT THAT THE USE OF MODULES BY WRIGHT AND BLAIR INFLUENCED ARCHITECT WOODS. HOWEVER, WOODS' "MODULE SYSTEM" IS DIFFERENT FROM BOTH WRIGHT'S AND BLAIR'S. IT IS DIFFERENT FROM BLAIR'S IN THAT BLAIR'S MODULES (LIKE WELLS') CHANGED WITH DIFFERENT WINDOW/SLIDING GLASS DOOR SIZES AND STRUCTURAL SYSTEMS. BLAIR'S MODULES ALSO OFTEN INCLUDED "FRACTIONS," AND THE WALLS WERE NOT USUALLY CENTERED ON HIS MODULES. WOODS' WINDOWS AND STRUCTURAL SYSTEMS, HOWEVER, ALWAYS ADAPT TO HIS MODULE, NOT THE OTHER WAY AROUND— THOUGH WINDOWS AND STRUCTURAL BAYS STILL WORK WELL ON THIS BASIS. WOODS' MODULE IS ALSO CLOSER TO ONLY ONE OF WRIGHT'S MODULES; IN FACT, WRIGHT ALSO USED A 4'0" BY 4'0" SQUARE MODULE MOST OF THE TIME (AS WELL AS OTHER MODULES). WOODS HAS ALSO EXPERIMENTED WITH OTHER MODULES BUT HAS FOUND THAT HE IS NOT LIMITED WITH JUST THIS ONE MODULE.

WRIGHT OFTEN VARIED FROM HIS OWN MODULES, WHERE WOODS IS ALMOST A FANATIC ABOUT STICKING TO HIS MODULE. HE IS LIKE THE PAINTER MONDRIAN, CREATING SEEMINGLY ENDLESS VARIATIONS ON A SIMPLE AND UNIFORM "SYSTEM."

ON CURVED DESIGNS, WOODS HAS, OF NECESSITY, JOINED A 5 OR 10 DEGREE OF ARC RADIAL MODULE TO HIS SQUARE MODULE. FOR EXAMPLE, WOODS ANGULAR FREEMAN HOUSE NEARS THE COMPLEXITY OF WRIGHT'S FAR MORE EXPENSIVE HANNA HOUSE BUT WITHOUT RESORTING TO AN ANGULAR MODULE. WOODS' NAUTILUS ALSO IS AN EXCELLENT EXAMPLE OF WOODS' USE OF DEGREE AND SQUARE MODULES, AND RED ROCKS AND CRAGGED ROCK ARE EXCELLENT EXAMPLES OF SEEMINGLY ASYMMETRICAL (REDROCKS) OR CHAOTIC (CRAGGED ROCK) DESIGNS THAT ARE STILL BASED ON JUST THE 4'0" SQUARE MODULE.

ANOTHER WAY WOODS ADMITS BLAIR'S INFLUENCE IS IN THE USE OF LARGE REPETITIVE MODULES OR SHAPES—WHOLE BUILDING-BLOCK SECTIONS. THIS IDEA CAME TO WOODS EARLY IN HIGH SCHOOL WHEN STUDYING MOSHE SAFDIE'S "HABITAT," BUT IT WAS WORKING WITH BLAIR THAT TRIGGERED WOODS TO TRY TO GET COMPLEX OR ASYMMETRICAL DESIGNS FROM SYMMETRICAL BUILDING BLOCKS, AS IT WERE. THOUGH HIGHLY DIFFERENT FROM BLAIR'S WORK, WOODS' CRYSTAL (THE KANDEL BEACH HOUSE) IS A GOOD EXAMPLE OF THIS USE OF LARGE AS WELL AS SMALL MODULES. THOUGH ALREADY

earth covered
multi-level
underg. parking

A Residence
for Mr. and Mrs. Small

present in the work of Wright and others, Woods gratefully declares he received this broad idea from Blair. This influence, however, did not show up in Woods' own work until he left Blair's office.

Dennis Blair's houses resulted in a special look and feel demonstrated by resale values that vastly exceeded any normal appreciation, and were so

noted by amazed realtors. This was later to prove the case again in Woods' own work. The work of this great artistic soul (Blair) should not be overlooked as a major influence on Charles G. Woods. Since Blair's work, though known, is not known well enough, Woods and I both wanted to emphasize his influence as well as the primary influence of Wright and the later Wellsian ones.

The experiencing of actual buildings is difficult to recreate in words, graphics, or photos. But Woods has done an exceedingly credible job of doing just this. This was accomplished with the help of the uniquely deft hand and guiding pen and brush of Malcolm Wells.

Architect Wells is known not only as the Father of Underground

LILY-PAD   CHARL... ...G. WOODS, AIA, ARCHITECT. 1996

ARCHITECTURE BUT AS A MASTER RENDERER. THOUGH WOODS' OWN INK RENDERINGS ARE QUITE FINE THEMSELVES IN THE INK STYLE OF A RUDOLPH OR A JACOBI, THEY ARE VERY TIME CONSUMING AND NOT QUITE AS FANTASY-LIKE AS WELLS' OWN FAST, SKETCHY STYLE—OR WOODS' OWN FANTASY-LIKE <u>DESIGN</u> STYLE! WOODS WAS WISE, THEN, TO CHOOSE HIM TO RE-PRESENT HIS OWN WORK. A GREAT CREATIVE SYNERGISTIC RELATIONSHIP HAS DEVELOPED BETWEEN WOODS AND WELLS IN THE LAST TWELVE YEARS, AS SHOWN IN THEIR PREVIOUS BOOK. THIS HAS RESULTED IN AN EXCEPTIONALLY DIVERSE AND EXPRESSIVE STATEMENT OF DESIGN.

THE ELOQUENCE OF THE JAPANESE ARTIST—NOTABLY IN HIROSHIGE'S WOODBLOCK PRINTS—IS WELL CAPTURED BY WELLS' WATERCOLOR-SKETCH TECHNIQUE. THE SHEER ESSENCE OF WOODS' DESIGNS AND THE ATMOSPHERIC AMBIANCE CREATED EXCEEDS ANYTHING POSSIBLE WITH HARD LINE DRAWINGS (WOODS' OWN STYLE) OR COMPUTERS AND PHOTOGRAPHS. THERE IS A QUALITY IN WELLS' DRAWINGS THAT I HAVE SEEN ONLY IN SOME JAPANESE PRINTS AND MAXFIELD PARRISH PAINTINGS, WHERE ONE CAN ACTUALLY "FEEL" THE WETNESS OF RAIN OR THE CRYSTALLINE, PURE AIR OF A SNOWCAPPED MOUNTAIN.

AND THOUGH WOODS WISHES TO TAKE NO CREDIT FOR WELLS' DRAWING ABILITY, WELLS HIMSELF HAPPILY ADMITS THE INFUSION OF WOODS' TALENTS AND DESIGN SKILLS, EVEN IN THE RENDERINGS. WOODS CHOSE MOST OF THE PERSPECTIVE ANGLES; THE CHOICES OF LIGHTING, THE EXTREMES OF WEATHER CONDITIONS (RAIN, LIGHTNING, EVEN A TORNADO), THE COLORS, AND DETAILS ARE ALL WOODSIAN INFLUENCES. LIKE THE YIN/YANG SYMBOL (WITH THE TOUCH OF BLACK ON WHITE AND VICE VERSA), "THE RENDERINGS ARE 10 PERCENT WOODS AND THE DESIGNS ARE 10 PERCENT WELLS." THIS IS EVEN MORE AMAZING WHEN ONE REALIZES THAT WOODS AND WELLS HAVE NEVER PHYSICALLY MET (UNTIL RECENTLY)! ALL THIS HAS BEEN DONE BY MAIL, TELEPHONE, AND FAX—A FURTHER TESTIMONY TO WOODS' MODULE SYSTEM. WOODS HAS PUSHED MAC TO THE LIMIT, AND WELLS HAS CREATED SOME OF HIS MOST POWERFUL DRAWINGS TO DATE. OF COURSE, THESE DESIGNS ALSO ARE NOT EASY TO DRAW CORRECTLY WITHOUT A COMPUTER—FOR INSTANCE, CRYSTAL HAD SIXTEEN VANISHING POINTS!

WOODS' DESIGNS EXHIBIT CHARACTERISTICS THAT REMIND ME OF THE WORKS OF NOTED ORGANIC ARCHITECTS, LLOYD WRIGHT, AARON GREEN, CHARLES MONTOOTH, AND JOHN RANDALL MCDONALD, WHICH IS

SURPRISING, SINCE WOODS IS ONLY BARELY FAMILIAR WITH SOME OF THEIR WORK. THE WORK OF THESE ARCHITECTS CLEARLY SHOWS THE POWERFUL INFLUENCE OF FRANK LLOYD WRIGHT'S VOCABULARY, BUT AT THE SAME TIME, THEY CREATED A MORE CONTEMPORARY, CLEAN, CRISP, AND FRESH FEEL. THIS FEELING IS ESPECIALLY EXEMPLIFIED IN THE MORE RECENT WORK OF E. FAY JONES, WHO RECEIVED THE 1990 A.I.A. GOLD MEDAL AWARD, SHOWING THAT

POSTMODERNISM AND DECONSTRUCTIONISM DO NOT YET RULE EXCLUSIVELY.

JONES WON HIS GOLD MEDAL FOR HIS DESIGN OF THORNCROWN CHAPEL NEAR EUREKA SPRINGS, ARKANSAS. A CLASSIC DESCRIPTION OF THORNCROWN BY A CRITIC WAS "THAT GREAT LATTICE STORM IN THE ARKANSAS WILDERNESS." THORNCROWN CHAPEL IS CERTAINLY THAT AND MORE, BUT AT THE SAME TIME, IT HAS A CRYSTALLINE

CLARITY AND A SERENE SIMPLICITY THAT I HAVE ONLY RARELY EXPERIENCED IN MY FORTY YEARS OF ARCHITECTURE TRAVEL. THORNCROWN SEEMS TO ME TO BE THE ULTIMATE EXPRESSION—IN THE PUREST FORM—OF THE LEGACY OF FRANK LLOYD WRIGHT'S WORK, AS PREVIOUSLY REFINED BY LLOYD WRIGHT AND HARWELL HAMILTON HARRIS, WHOSE WORK WAS OBVIOUSLY A GREAT INFLUENCE ON JONES. I HAVE SPENT MANY HOURS IN DIFFERENT

TERRASOL CORPORATE OFFICE
COMPLEX "ROUGH"

SEASONS EXPERIENCING THE QUIETING, PEACEFUL EFFECT CREATED BY THIS MANMADE STRUCTURE IN PERFECT HARMONY WITH THE BEAUTY OF NATURE (WITH A CAPITAL "N"). AN ALL TOO RARE TREAT—THE SPIRIT, MIND, AND BODY OF MAN.

NOTED ARCHITECT JOHN CAMPBELL LAHEY, THE PRESIDENT OF SOLOMEN, CORDWELL,

AND BUENZ, ALSO SPENT TIME AT THORNCROWN CHAPEL, SO IT IS HIGH PRAISE INDEED WHEN HE SAYS OF WOODS' RECENT WORK THAT IT SHOULD "BE REFRESHING TO ARCHITECTS IN MUCH THE SAME WAY AS E. FAY JONES' WORK HAS APPEALED TO THE ARCHITECTURAL COMMUNITY." BECAUSE OF WOODS' CREATIVE AND PRODIGIOUS PRODUCTIVITY (OVER 150 BUILDINGS), FIFTY PUBLICATIONS, AND NUMEROUS

AWARDS, WITH THREE PREVIOUS BOOKS ON ARCHITECTURE, (AND A RECENT WORK IN PHILOSOPHY STILL TO BE PUBLISHED) ALL AT ONLY FORTY-THREE YEARS OF AGE, I THOUGHT IT TIME TO SITUATE WOODS CLEARLY IN A TRADITION. THE PROBLEM WITH THIS IS THE POSSIBILITY OF DROWNING WOODS' OWN CREATIVITY IN THESE "PAST" FORMS. WOODS' OWN WORK IS <u>NOT</u> SIMPLY ORGANIC BUT A CREATIVE SYNTHESIS OF THE

ORGANIC, MODERN, AND EXPRESSIONIST TRADITIONS. HIS WORK, THOUGH, IS NOT EVERYTHING TO EVERYONE, FOR HE IS STRONGLY OPPOSED TO NEOCLASSICAL (THOUGH APPRECIATING HISTORY) POSTMODERNISM, AND MOST FORMS OF DECONSTRUCTIONIST ARCHITECTURE.

WOODS HIMSELF HAS SPOKEN OF THE TEACHING INFLUENCES OF WRIGHT, BLAIR, AND WELLS. IS HE THEN SYNCRETISTIC OR A MERE MANNERIST FOLLOWER OF WRIGHT? HE IS NOT! WOODS IS A CREATIVE DEVELOPER, NOT JUST A CONTINUATOR OF THE ORGANIC (HE CALLS IT "NATURAL" ARCHITECTURE) TRADITION. ALREADY IN 1983, FAMED ARCHITECT JOHN HOWE— POSSIBLY WRIGHT'S CLOSEST AND MOST CREATIVE DISCIPLE (KNOWN AS "THE HAND OF FRANK LLOYD WRIGHT")—WROTE TO WOODS THAT HE WAS "OVERWHELMED" AND TOLD WOODS THAT HE HAD "GREAT CREATIVE CAPABILITY" AND THAT HE WAS "IMPRESSED BY MANY OF [HIS] DESIGNS" AND WISHED HIM "EVEN SUCCESS." THIS WAS AS CLOSE AS WOODS WOULD EVER COME TO TOUCHING "THE HAND OF FRANK LLOYD WRIGHT," AND THIS MEANT MUCH TO HIM.

BY PHONE, ARCHITECT HOWE SAID HE THOUGHT WOODS' DESIGNS WERE VERY "ORGANIC" BUT NOT ESPECIALLY "WRIGHTIAN." AT THE TIME (1983), THE YOUNG WOODS WAS SADDENED BY THIS, THOUGH NOW HE LARGELY IS RELIEVED.

MORE RECENTLY, NOTED ARCHITECT AND AUTHOR JOHN BAKER ASSURED WOODS (BY PHONE) THAT HIS WORK WAS NOT "MANNERIST," AND ARCHITECT LAHEY AGAIN WROTE THAT "[WOODS] HAS CONSISTENTLY PURSUED THE NATURAL, ORGANIC-CRAFTSMAN TRADITION FOR OVER TWENTY YEARS. HE HAS STUCK TO HIS GUNS AND NOW IT IS PAYING OFF. HIS WORK IS AT A POINT WHERE IT IS ALL COMING TOGETHER. THE STRAIGHTFORWARD SIMPLICITY OF THE TREEHOUSE, THE BROAD APPEAL OF THE CRAFTSMAN-STYLE HOUSE, THE MODULAR COMPLEXITY OF CRYSTAL, AND THE STRENGTH OF NAUTILUS SHOW A MATURITY AND RICHNESS WHILE RETAINING THE PRAGMATIC SIMPLICITY CONSISTENT WITH HIS THOROUGHLY RATIONAL FOUNDATION. HE HAS GONE PAST . . . BEING A DERIVATIVE OF WRIGHT TO NOW HAVING HIS OWN PERSONAL STATEMENT." WORLD-RENOWNED ARCHITECT CHARLES GWATHMEY, F.A.I.A., SECONDS THIS, DECLARING OF WOODS' WORK, "THOUGH THERE IS NO QUESTION THAT IT REFLECTS THE INFLUENCES OF FRANK LLOYD WRIGHT AND DENNIS BLAIR, WOODS INTERPRETS AND CLARIFIES THE SOURCE." [EMPHASIS MINE.]

WOODS IS HIS OWN MAN, BUT HE INSISTS THAT THIS CAME FROM LISTENING TO WRIGHT'S OWN ADVICE—TO FOLLOW HIS "PRINCIPLES" NOT HIS DETAILS. WOODS ALSO INSISTS THAT, THOUGH NOT NEARLY AS PRIMARY AS WRIGHT, SULLIVAN, MIES, AALTO, CORBU, NEUTRA, SCHINDLER, AND MENDELSOHN WERE ALL MINOR INFLUENCES—ESPECIALLY NEUTRA, WHOM HE "RELATES TO" A LOT.

RECENT ARCHITECTURAL WORKS HE APPRECIATES ARE THOSE OF GWATHMEY, GOLDFINGER, HOWE, MEIERS, PRINCE, BAKER, CALATRAVA, JOSEPH N. BIONDO, VAN DE VENTER (SO HE TELLS ME!), AND ALSO THE "LATE GREATS," JOHN LAUTNER, NORMAN JAFFE, AND FRANK ISRAEL. HE ALSO THINKS HIS WORK HAS MUCH IN COMMON WITH ANOTHER TALIESIN APPRENTICE, WALLACE CUNNINGHAM. WOODS AT FORTY-THREE IS STILL YOUNG TO BE A "NOTED" DESIGNER ON THE EDGE OF FAME—MOST ARCHITECTS TRULY COME INTO THEIR OWN ONLY AROUND FIFTY OR LATER, SO WOODS' FUTURE IS PROMISING INDEED, AS SOME NOTED SENIOR ARCHITECTS

WOLLENBERG ADDITION/REMODELING, 1992

SCHEME "B"
THE RAMIREZ HOUSE at TINKWIG, PENNSYLVANIA

1996
CHARLES GREGORY WOODS, AIA, ARCHITECT

CRYSTAL HOUSE

AND HUMANISTS BOTH AGREE. HOWE POINTED OUT THAT WOODS IS "FULL OF IDEAS" AND GWATHMEY COMMENTED ON "THE ARCHITECT'S VISION . . . WHICH IS BOTH PASSIONATE AND DISCIPLINED," AND SAID HE ADMIRED THE "CLARITY AND CONSCIOUSNESS" OF HIS LAST BOOK. ARCHITECT JOHN BAKER ALSO WROTE OF THE "<u>DISCIPLINED</u> ORDER IMPLICIT IN WOODS' SYSTEM OF BUILDING." [EMPHASIS MINE.]

BART PRINCE HAS WRITTEN OF WOODS' WORK AS "EXCEPTIONAL FOR ITS QUALITY AND VARIETY" AND THAT IT "OFFERED SUPERIOR ALTERNATIVES TO <u>MOST</u> ARCHITECT-DESIGNED HOUSES BEING

DESIGNED THESE DAYS!" [EMPHASIS MINE.] HIGH PRAISE FROM GREAT ARCHITECTS, BUT SOME GREAT HUMANISTS ALSO AGREE. THE FAMOUS PHILOSOPHER/THEOLOGIAN ROBERT C. NEVILLE WRITES THAT, THOUGH "WOODS IS AN OUTSTANDING ARCHITECT WITH ORIGINALITY [AND] CLARITY OF VISION, HE IS ALSO A 'PHILOSOPHER' STEEPED IN THE CLASSICAL WESTERN TRADITION OF PHILOSOPHY." ALSO, THE GREAT TRANSPERSONAL PSYCHOLOGIST KEN WILBER WROTE OF WOODS' "EXTRAORDINARY DESIGNS" AND SIMPLY OF HIS "GENIUS." FINALLY, MALCOLM WELLS HAS COMMENTED ON WOODS' "MASTERFUL DESIGNS."

I CONCUR AND SECOND THESE GENEROUS JUDGMENTS. WOODS' WORK IS A DAZZLING BUT SIMPLE BLEND OF GEOMETRICAL SHAPES, HARMONIOUSLY WEDDED TO NATURAL MATERIALS. HENCE THE TITLE OF THIS INTRODUCTION. WOODS IS A WONDERFULLY CREATIVE SPIRIT AND I HAVE WORKED WITH HIM DIRECTLY AS RENDERER AND MODEL MAKER ON TWO PROJECTS, AND AS ASSOCIATE DESIGNER AND MODEL MAKER ON OUR NOTRE DAME CATHEDRAL (ALL OF THIS LONG DISTANCE ALSO). I HAD WONDERED AT TIMES WHETHER A SECRET "ELF" WAS DOING HIS DESIGNING FOR HIM, BUT THEN LAST YEAR, WHILE VISITING CHICAGO, WOODS ASKED ME IF HE COULD USE MY OFFICE FOR "A FEW

HOURS" AT A TIME TO REDESIGN SNOWFLAKE (THE SISSON RESIDENCE). WHILE KEEPING THE OVERALL SHAPE, HE WAS TO INCORPORATE PAGES OF SUGGESTIONS BY THE CLIENTS INTO THE DESIGN. I WAS GOING OUT AND I SAW HIM TAPE DOWN THE PAPER AND BEGIN. I CAME BACK AN HOUR AND A HALF LATER— HE WAS GONE, AND THE PLANS AND ROUGH SKETCHES WERE FINISHED! I ASKED HIM HOW HE DID IT SO FAST. HE SAID IT WAS THE MODULE SYSTEM, WHICH IS LAID OUT FOR THE READER IN GREAT DETAIL IN THIS BOOK. NO DOUBT THE MODULE SYSTEM WAS PART OF IT—AND, IF SO, MORE ARCHITECTS AND DESIGNERS SHOULD USE IT. BUT THAT COULD NOT EXPLAIN THE BEAUTIFUL AND COMPLEX PLAN LYING BEFORE ME. WOODS (ONCE A HYPERACTIVE CHILD—WE WOULD SAY ADHD NOW) OBVIOUSLY COULD CREATE, VISUALIZE, PROBLEM SOLVE, AND DRAW WITH DAZZLING SPEED. CHARLIE'S INTENSITY AND EXTREME PASSION FOR DESIGN IS CATCHING AND CAN BE ALMOST SPIRITUALLY UPLIFTING IN PERSON. I BELIEVE HIS BOOK CAN BE EVEN A SPIRITUALLY STIMULATING EXPERIENCE, CARRYING HIS DRIVE AND TRULY EXPANDING THE SPHERE OF INFLUENCE OF THE AMERICAN SCHOOL OF ARCHITECTURE.

I AM VERY PLEASED TO SEE A FREER USE OF SYMMETRY AND ASYMMETRY IN WOODS' SEARCHING USE OF VARIOUS GEOMETRIES, WHICH CAN BE SO HIGHLY EXPRESSIVE AND SCULPTURAL AND DEMONSTRATES THAT THE MODULE CAN BE LIBERATING RATHER THAN CONSTRICTIVE. IN THIS BOOK, WOODS GUIDES US THROUGH ALL STAGES OF A PROJECT—A "SYSTEM" WE CAN LEARN FROM AND USE TO HELP US ALL COME CLOSER TO DOING THE SAME AS HE.

I WOULD LIKE TO END WITH BART PRINCE'S INSIGHTFUL SUMMARY OF WOODS' BOOK AS A TEACHING AID. PRINCE WRITES THAT "FOR SOMEONE WHO IS INTERESTED IN LEARNING ON HIS (OR HER) OWN, THE IDEAS PRESENTED WOULD CUT THROUGH MUCH OF THE USUAL FOG THAT ACCOMPANIES BOOKS OF THIS TYPE WHERE THERE SEEMS TO BE A DESIRE TO PROTECT THE 'MYSTERY' OF DESIGN RATHER THAN CLARIFY IT." AND HE GOES ON TO SAY THAT "EVERY PROJECT OFFERS LESSONS IN PLANNING, DESIGN, CONSTRUCTION, INTEGRITY OF CONCEPTION AND ILLUSTRATION, AND CLEAR PRESENTATION IN A WAY THAT THE STUDENT SELDOM ENCOUNTERS IN SCHOOL."

IT IS BECAUSE I AM PLEASED TO SEE NEW CREATIVE WORKS BEING DESIGNED IN THE ORGANIC-NATURAL TRADITION OF ARCHITECTURE AND BECAUSE I AGREE WITH BART PRINCE'S ASSESSMENT OF THE TEACHING POSSIBILITIES OF THIS BOOK, THAT I AM HAPPY TO EXPRESS MY ENTHUSIASM FOR THE FOLLOWING PAGES. <u>A NATURAL SYSTEM OF HOUSE DESIGN</u> SHOULD BECOME A CLASSIC WORK IN ITS FIELD.

I DID NOT INVENT MODULES OR MODULE SYSTEMS, BUT TO SOME EXTENT THE CONCEPT IS MINE, IN THAT IT TOOK ME SOME TWENTY YEARS OF WORK TO GET IT THIS SIMPLE. I THINK THIS SYSTEM IS EVEN SIMPLER THAN THAT OF MY ARCHITECTURAL GURU, FRANK LLOYD WRIGHT. AT TIMES, HE VARIED FROM HIS OWN MODULES. I AM NOT SAYING NEVER TO DO THAT, BUT I HAVE FOUND IN MY OWN WORK THAT YOU <u>NEED</u> NOT, NOR DO I THINK, FROM STUDYING HIS DESIGNS CAREFULLY, THAT FLW <u>HAD</u> TO.

REMOVING ALL THE "PHILOSOPHY," THE SYSTEM IS SO SIMPLE THAT IT MIGHT SEEM OBVIOUS—EVEN SIMPLISTIC—BUT ALL THE DESIGNS IN THIS BOOK WERE DONE WITH IT—AND SOME ARE HIGHLY COMPLEX.

THE SIMPLE RULES

1. <u>ALWAYS</u> DRAW ON FADE-OUT GRAPH PAPER WITH EIGHT SQUARES TO THE INCH. I USE 11" BY 17", 18" BY 24", AND 24" BY 36" PAPER. THERE IS LARGER AND SMALLER PAPER ALSO. AT ¼" SCALE, THAT MEANS EACH DARKER-BLUE-LINE SQUARE IS EQUIVALENT TO 4'0" BY 4'0", AND EACH SMALL SQUARE (LIGHTER BLUE LINE) IS 6" SQUARE. AT ⅛" SCALE, THE LARGER SQUARES NOW REPRESENT 8'0" BY 8'0" AND THE SMALLER SQUARES REPRESENT 1' BY 1'. AT 1/16" SCALE, THE BIG SQUARES ARE THEREFORE EQUIVALENT TO 16' AND THE SMALL SQUARES ARE EQUIVALENT TO 2'. AT ⅛" SCALE, I USUALLY CREATE DESIGN DRAWINGS ON 11" BY 17" OR 18" BY 24" PAPER (UNLESS IT IS A <u>LARGE</u> ONE-FLOOR DESIGN). CONSTRUCTION DRAWINGS ARE DONE ON 18" BY 24" PAPER AND, MORE OFTEN, ON 24" BY 36" PAPER. WITH THIS GRID PAPER, I VERY SELDOM HAVE TO "SCALE," AND THERE ARE LIGHT GUIDE LINES FOR LETTERING. SCALES OF ⅛", ¼", AND ⅜" WORK WELL, AND WHEN YOU PRINT, ALL THE LINES DISAPPEAR!

2. ALWAYS END A BUILDING DESIGN ON A MODULE—IN OTHER WORDS, A HOUSE WOULD BE 20', 24', 28', OR 32' WIDE, FOR INSTANCE, BY 60', 64', OR 68', <u>NOT</u> 23' BY 58'.

3. EXTERIOR WALLS CAN FALL <u>ON</u> THE MODULE CENTER OR <u>INSIDE</u> OR <u>OUTSIDE.</u> WITH A TRADITIONAL OR COLONIAL DESIGN WITH NO WINDOWS AT THE EDGE OF THE HOUSE, HAVING THE EXTERIOR WALLS FALL INSIDE THE MODULE IS FINE (SIMPLER FOR FOUNDATION EDGE TREATMENT). FOR

SMALL HOUSES (MY OWN EARTH-SHELTERED HOUSE IS ONLY 16′ BY 64′ ON MODULE), I PUT THE WALLS ON THE OUTSIDE OF THE MODULE LINES BECAUSE THE 16′ WAS TIGHT. BUT WHAT I DO NOW (AND SUGGEST THAT YOU DO) IS CENTER ALL WALLS ON MODULE LINES. IT IS BY FAR THE SIMPLEST APPROACH, AND WITH 8″ OR 12″ CONCRETE MASONRY UNITS (CMUS), IT IS UNBELIEVABLY SIMPLE—EVEN ON COMPLEX FOUNDATION PLANS.

4. FOR SHAPES MORE COMPLEX THAN RECTANGLES, PROCEED AS FOLLOWS. FOR ANGLED PLANS, CUT ACROSS THE SQUARE MODULE, FROM CORNER TO CORNER, CREATING 45° ANGLE MODULES (SEE THE COUNTRY RESIDENCE FOR MR. AND MRS. STAN FREEMAN, AND CRYSTAL, THE KANDEL BEACH HOUSE.) FOR IRREGULAR ANGLES, YOU CAN CONNECT THE CORNERS OF SQUARE MODULES WITH ANOTHER MODULE UP/DOWN OR LEFT/RIGHT OF THE FIRST ONE, CREATING ALL SORTS OF ANGLES (SEE CRAGGED ROCK). IF YOU WANT A CONSISTENT 30/60° (OR SOME OTHER DEGREE) ANGLE MODULE, YOU HAVE TO DRAW A MODULE GRID AND THEN TRACE OVER IT. BUT IT WILL NOT

WORK ON THE 4′ BY 4′ MODULE AND FADE-OUT GRID PAPER.

5. FOR CURVES, ALIGN RADIUS LINES WITH THE 4′ SQUARE MODULE. IN OTHER WORDS, THE RADII WOULD BE 24′, 28′, 32′, ETC. CURVING GLASS, OF COURSE, DOES NOT CONFORM WELL TO THE SQUARE GRID, SO I ADDED DEGREES-OF-ARC MODULES TO THE SQUARE ONE. I USUALLY USE 5, 7½, AND 10°. THE TWO SYSTEMS WORK SURPRISINGLY WELL TOGETHER. THE WINDOW COLUMNS ARE CENTERED ON THE ARC MODULES AND IF A 4′ BY 4′ FOOT MODULE (STRAIGHT WALL) DOESN'T ALIGN PERFECTLY WITH THE ARC MODULE, I SIMPLY "SPLAY" A WALL—I.E., ANGLE IT (SEE NAUTILUS).

6. THE REST IS REALLY SIMPLE! EVERYTHING IS ON THE MODULE—COLUMNS, DOORS, WINDOWS, CLOSETS, CHIMNEYS, SINKS, TUBS, ETC. ODD-SIZED THINGS—REFRIGERATORS AND TUBS, FOR INSTANCE—DON'T ALWAYS FIT PERFECTLY BETWEEN MODULES, SO I "CENTER" THEM. FOR EXAMPLE, IN AN 8′ O.C. (ON CENTER) BATHROOM, I HAVE ROUGHLY 7′6″ BETWEEN WALLS (WITH TWO-BY-SIXES). WITH A 5′0″ TUB ON THE FACE OF ONE WALL, I END UP WITH A 2′6″ SPACE—NOT

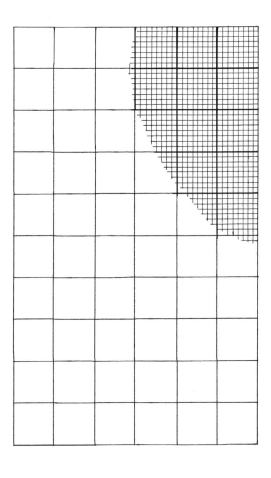

ON THE MODULE—WHICH I USUALLY USE BY ADDING A WALL AND MAKING A 2′ LINEN CLOSET. NOT TOO BAD, BUT MY EYE ALWAYS NOTES THAT IT ISN'T ON THE MODULE. NOW I JUST CENTER A 6′ OR 7′ TUB AND PUT THE LINEN CLOSET ON A HALF-MODULE ON ANOTHER WALL.

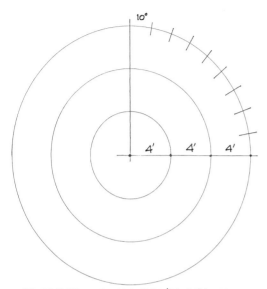

ON COMPLETE CIRCLES I USE A 'RADIAL' MODULE

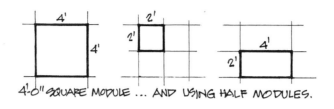

4'-0" SQUARE MODULE ... AND USING HALF MODULES.

45° ANGLE
MODULE

CURVE ON
MODULE

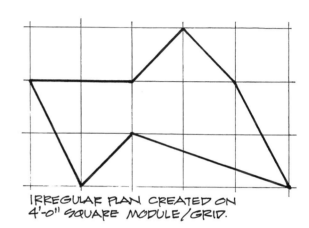

IRREGULAR PLAN CREATED ON
4'-0" SQUARE MODULE/GRID.

ANOTHER EXAMPLE: IN A 12' BY 12' BEDROOM WITH AN 8' CLOSET, I END UP WITH A 4' O.C. SPACE FOR A DOOR AND 3'6" (WITH TWO-BY-SIXES) BETWEEN WALLS. I USED A LOT OF 2-FOOT 6-INCH DOORS INSIDE, SO IF I STARTED WITH 2 TWO-BY-SIXES ON ONE SIDE OF A DOOR, OR 3", I WOULD HAVE 9" ON THE OTHER SIDE—NOT HORRIBLE MAYBE, BUT IT ALWAYS BOTHERED ME. THE NEW INCREASED AWARENESS OF THE DIFFERENTLY ABLED HAS SOLVED MY DOOR PROBLEM. I NOW CENTER 3'0" DOORS BETWEEN MODULES. IT WORKS PERFECTLY NOW WITH 3" ON

BOTH SIDES, LOOKS RIGHT, AND IS EASY TO ENTER FOR ALL OF US!

7. I CONTINUE USING THE MODULE AND HALF- OR QUARTER-MODULES FOR STRUCTURE. MOST OF MY JOISTS AND STUDS ARE 24" O.C. OR 12". NO DOUBT 16" IS MORE "NORMAL" AND IT IS STILL ON THE MODULE (3 × 16" = 48"), BUT IT IS HARDER TO SEE ON THE GRAPH PAPER. ALSO, WITH HIGHER R-VALUES IN WALLS, TWO-BY-SIXES AT 24" O.C. ARE FINE AND JUST AS STRONG AS TWO-BY-FOURS AT 16" O.C.

ALSO, TWO-BY-TWELVES AND PLYWOOD JOISTS CAN USUALLY (NOT ALWAYS) BE 24" O.C. INSTEAD OF 16". THIS ALSO ALLOWS MORE ROOM FOR HEATING DUCTS AND LIGHTING BETWEEN JOISTS.

8. ARE THERE THEN NO TRICKY SPOTS OR PROBLEMS? YES, LIGHTING—BUT THAT IS OFTEN TRUE FOR 16" O.C. AND OTHER SYSTEMS. IF ONE WANTS TO PUT CEILING LIGHTS IN THE CENTER OF A ROOM, IT USUALLY FALLS ON A 2" BY 12" JOIST. IF IT IS AN EXTERIOR

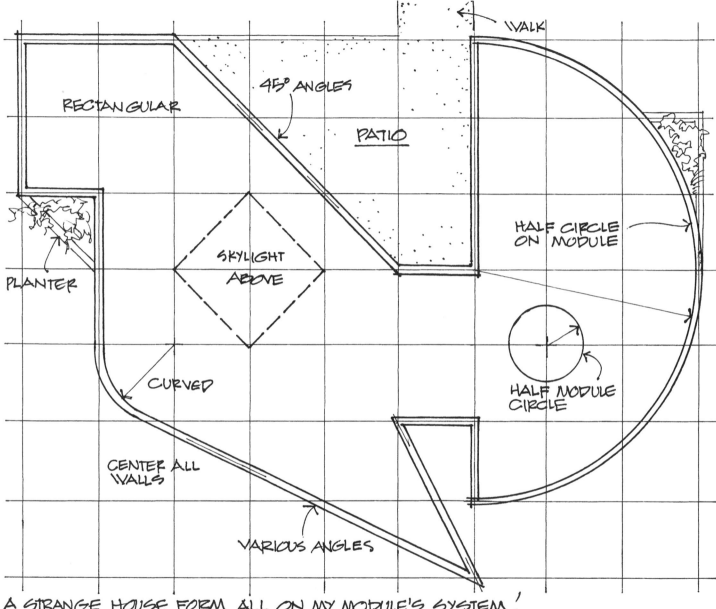

WALK

45° ANGLES

RECTANGULAR

PATIO

SKYLIGHT
ABOVE

PLANTER

HALF CIRCLE
ON MODULE

CURVED

HALF MODULE
CIRCLE

CENTER ALL
WALLS

VARIOUS ANGLES

A STRANGE HOUSE FORM ALL ON MY MODULE'S SYSTEM!

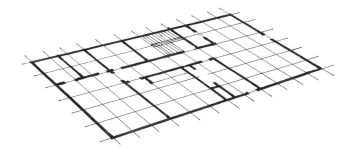

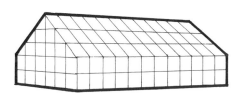

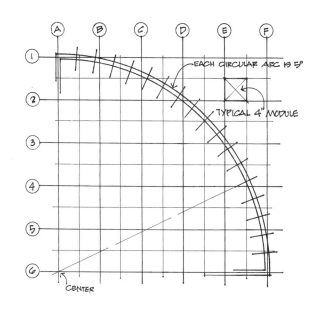

EACH CIRCULAR ARC IS 5°

TYPICAL 4" MODULE

CENTER

LIGHT, IT IS NOT MUCH OF A PROBLEM, BUT IF IT IS A RECESSED LIGHT, IT _IS_ A PROBLEM. MY SOLUTION IS TO USE TWO LIGHTS, ONE ON EACH SIDE OF THE CENTER MODULE. MY FRIEND AND A FINE ARCHITECT, JOHN BAKER, SUGGESTS DOUBLE-SPACING THE JOISTS ON THE CENTER MODULE AND STILL USING CAN LIGHTS—EITHER WORKS WELL.

THERE ARE A FEW MORE PROBLEMS OR TRICKY SPOTS, BUT I WOULD LIKE TO POINT OUT THAT _ALL_ DESIGN SYSTEMS HAVE SOME TRICKY PARTS— AND SINCE I HAVE A WAY AROUND THEM ALL, THE ADVANTAGES _FAR_ OUTNUMBER ANY PROBLEMS.

9. THE FINAL PROBLEMS, WITH SOLUTIONS:

WITH 6" COLUMNS AT 4'0" O.C., I GET 3'6" BETWEEN COLUMNS. THERE'S A TON OF WINDOWS THAT FIT EASILY INTO THAT SPACE. I OFTEN USE ANDERSEN ON MY LOW-COST HOUSES AND PELLA AND MARVIN ON MORE EXPENSIVE DESIGNS. AS A DESIGNER, I FIND SLIDING GLASS DOORS A PROBLEM. MY CLIENTS OFTEN LIKE THEM AND I DO, TOO, IN THEORY. TWO OF MY MODULES BETWEEN COLUMNS ARE 7'6", AND BETWEEN THREE MODULES IS 11'6". MOST SLIDERS ARE AROUND 8', 9', AND 12'. WHAT I DO IS CENTER A 9' SLIDER ON A 12' FOOT MODULE, AND IT WORKS! SO, WHAT'S THE PROBLEM? MY OWN DESIGNS ARE SO HIGHLY MODULAR—INCLUDING TRIM—THAT IT BOTHERS MY EYE. YOU ARE SEEING 4', 8', 12', AND 16' MODULES, THEN ALL OF A SUDDEN, A 3', 6', OR 9' SLIDER. WHAT I DO TO OFFSET THAT IS PUNCH OUT THE WALLS AND MAKE THEM "WING WALLS" ON BOTH SIDES OF THE 12' FOOT MODULE, TO HIGHLIGHT THOSE WALLS AND TRICK

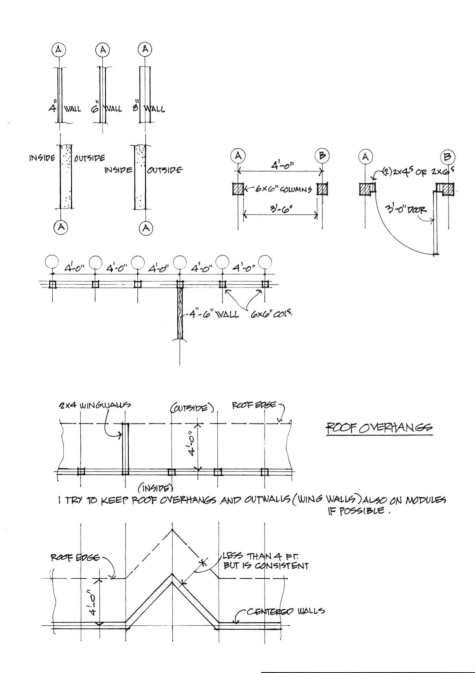

4" WALL   6" WALL   8" WALL

INSIDE OUTSIDE

INSIDE   OUTSIDE

4'-0"

6×6" COLUMNS

3'-6"

(2) 2x4s OR 2x6s

3'-0" DOOR

4'-0" 4'-0" 4'-0" 4'-0" 4'-0"

4"-6" WALL   6×6" COLS.

2x4 WINGWALLS   (OUTSIDE)   ROOF EDGE

ROOF OVERHANGS

4'-0"

(INSIDE)

I TRY TO KEEP ROOF OVERHANGS AND OUTWALLS (WING WALLS) ALSO ON MODULES IF POSSIBLE.

ROOF EDGE

LESS THAN 4 FT. BUT IS CONSISTENT

4'-0"

CENTERED WALLS

YOUR EYES. IT WORKS, BUT I PREFER NOT TO USE TRICKS, OR ELSE NO SLIDERS. ON AN EXPENSIVE HOUSE WITH MARVIN WINDOWS, I WOULD ORDER CUSTOM ONES.

ALSO, IF YOU HAVE A BOXED-OUT WINDOW—SAY, 8' BY 4'—AND HAVE WINDOWS RIGHT UP TO A BOXED SET, IT'S HARD TO FIT THE WINDOWS AND THE TRIM ON ONE 6" BY 6" COLUMN. BUILDERS DON'T LIKE IT. SOLUTION? YOU CAN EITHER CUT THE NAILING STRIPS ON THE WINDOW UNITS AND USE MINIMALIST TRIM TO MAKE IT WORK OR GO TO A HALF-MODULE ON WINDOWS THAT BUTT UP AGAINST THE BOXED WINDOWS.

CENTERING EXTERIOR WOOD WALLS ON A FOUNDATION WALL IS UNUSUAL AND CREATES A LITTLE SHELF. BUILDERS ARE NOT USED TO THIS. ALL THAT IS NEEDED IS A LITTLE SLOPING PIECE OF TRIM OR INSULATION AND FLASHING. IT'S EASY, BUT IT SHOULD BE DETAILED PROPERLY BY AN ARCHITECT. IF ONE USES MASONRY WALLS FOR THE ENDS—SAY, ON AN EARTH-SHELTERED OR COURTYARD HOUSE—THE END WINDOWS MUST BE CAREFULLY DETAILED OR MADE SMALLER—SAY, BY A HALF-MODULE.

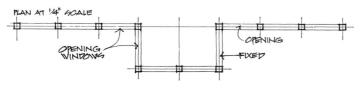

PLAN AT 1/4" SCALE

OPENING WINDOWS

OPENING

FIXED

TRICKY SPOTS IN DETAILING

SOME BUILDERS HAVE TOLD ME IN THE PAST THAT INSIDE CORNERS ARE A LITTLE TRICKY ON MY MODULE IF <u>TWO</u> OPENING WINDOWS ARE USED SIDE BY SIDE. IF ONLY ONE OPENING WINDOW IS USED IT'S SIMPLE.

ACTUALLY TWO OPENING WINDOWS <u>CAN</u> BE USED BUT THE METAL NAILING STRIP MUST BE CUT OR BENT, AND THE TRIM WORK IS PRETTY TIGHT. COMPARED TO REALLY 'DIFFICULT' DETAILING IT'S REALLY PRETTY SIMPLE.

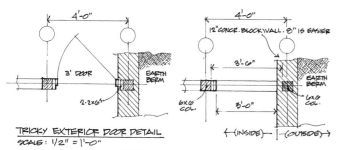

4'-0"
3' DOOR
EARTH BERM
2-2x6"

4'-0"
12" CONCR. BLOCK WALL. 8" IS EASIER
3'-6"
EARTH BERM
6x6 COL.
3'-0"
6x6 COL.
(INSIDE) (OUTSIDE)

TRICKY EXTERIOR DOOR DETAIL
SCALE: 1/2" = 1'-0"

IF ONE DOES AN EARTH-SHELTERED HOUSE AND KEEPS THE WALLS ON CENTER-LINES A 3'-0" DOOR IS REALLY TIGHT, SO I EITHER DON'T PUT A DOOR THERE AND PUT IN A CENTERED AND HALF MODULE GLASS WINDOW OR IF I <u>MUST</u> HAVE A DOOR AND A 3'-0" ONE (WHICH I RECOMMEND AND OFTEN IS CODE) I SET A 3"x6" INTO CUT OUT IN MASONRY

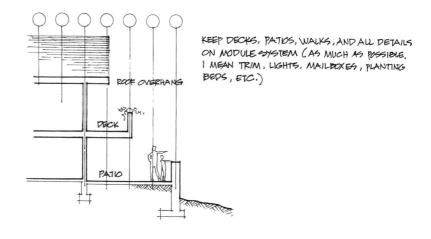

ROOF OVERHANG

DECK

PATIO

KEEP DECKS, PATIOS, WALKS, AND ALL DETAILS ON MODULE SYSTEM (AS MUCH AS POSSIBLE. I MEAN TRIM, LIGHTS, MAILBOXES, PLANTING BEDS, ETC.)

THESE FEW PROBLEMS <u>HAVE</u> SOLUTIONS, SO I DO NOT REALLY THINK THEY ARE "PROBLEMS" AT ALL—ESPECIALLY IF ONE GAINS THE SPEED OF DRAWING AND THE LOOK OF <u>INTELLIGIBILITY</u> IN ONE'S DESIGNS. I MENTION THEM SO THAT SOME NICE BUILDER WON'T HAVE PROBLEMS A YEAR FROM NOW AND CURSE ME AND ALL ARCHITECTS UNDER HIS BREATH: "SURE, A <u>SIMPLE, EASY</u>-TO-USE "MODULE" SYSTEM!" ALSO, MY FRIEND, NOTED ENVIRONMENTAL ARCHITECT DAVID WRIGHT, <u>STRONGLY</u> SUGGESTED I DEAL WITH THE PROBLEMS AS WELL AS THE ADVANTAGES OF THIS SYSTEM. BY CAREFULLY STUDYING MY DESIGN DRAWINGS, ONE WILL, I BELIEVE, SEE THAT THIS ATTENTION TO CONSISTENCY PAYS OFF IN HIGH-QUALITY DESIGNS.

FINALLY, I WOULD LIKE TO REEMPHASIZE A MAIN ADVANTAGE OF A MODULE SYSTEM: EASE OF COMMUNICATION. THE FACT THAT I HAVE NEVER MET (UNTIL RECENTLY) MY GREAT RENDERER, MALCOLM WELLS, SHOULD SAY A LOT. COMMUNICATION HELPS WITH CLIENTS (ESPECIALLY FOR CHANGES), DRAFTSMEN/WOMEN, AND BUILDERS, AND WOULD MAKE COMPUTER DESIGN STILL EASIER. TOTAL TIMESAVING IN DRAFTING, ETC., IS A MINIMUM 25 PERCENT. ARCHITECTS, PLEASE TRY IT. I'M ASKING YOU AS SCHINDLER ASKED FIFTY YEARS AGO—JUST TRY IT!

Staggered Cubes ...The yeager House   Charles G. Woods, AIA, Architect

"THE GREATEST AND FAIREST THINGS ARE MADE
BY NATURE AND THE LESSER BY ART."
—PLATO

A PLATONIC PHILOSOPHY
OF ARCHITECTURAL DESIGN

MY SYSTEM—TO THE EXTENT THAT IT IS MINE—IS NOT TOTALLY UNIQUE TO ME, OF COURSE. MODULES OR DESIGN GRIDS HAVE BEEN USED BY NUMEROUS ARCHITECTS THROUGHOUT HISTORY, AND FOR VARIOUS REASONS: DESIGN, STRUCTURE, OR MATERIAL.

LARGER BUILDINGS ALMOST ALWAYS ARE MODULAR IN THAT THEY USE REPETITIVE LARGE STRUCTURAL BAYS AND ARE OFTEN ON A SMALLER DESIGN MODULE OF 5'0" SQUARE. THIS IS BECAUSE OF THE SIZE OF OFFICE FURNITURE, WHICH IS 5'0" LONG BY 2½' WIDE. MODULES OF OTHER SIZES ARE, OF COURSE, ALSO USED IN LARGE BUILDING DESIGN.

THIS BOOK WILL TOUCH ON NONRESIDENTIAL DESIGN IN THE APPENDIX. FOR NOW, WE WILL CONCENTRATE ON HOUSE DESIGN, WHICH IS THE MAJOR THEME OF THIS BOOK.

FRANK LLOYD WRIGHT, ARGUABLY THE CENTURY'S GREATEST ARCHITECT (POSSIBLY THE GREATEST OF ALL TIME) AND CERTAINLY AMERICA'S GREATEST ARCHITECT, IS FAMOUS FOR HIS USE OF VARIOUS DESIGN MODULES: SQUARE, RECTILINEAR, POLYGONAL, ANGULAR, CURVED/ARC, AND CIRCULAR. ORIGINALLY, HIS DESIGN MODULES WERE BASED ON WINDOW MULLION SIZES. FOR INSTANCE, IN THE HENDERSON RESIDENCE (1901) IT WAS 41" O.C. AND WAS OFTEN, OF NECESSITY, DIFFERENT FOR VARIOUS WINDOW SIZES. I BELIEVE THAT WRIGHT'S WORK IN JAPAN WAS INFLUENCED BY THE LOCAL ARCHITECTURE, WHICH WAS DESIGNED ON A MODULE SYSTEM RELATED TO THE 3' BY 6' TATAMI FLOOR MATS USED IN JAPANESE HOMES. IN WRIGHT'S YAMAMURA RESIDENCE (1918, ASHIYA), WE FIND 3' BY 6' MODULES AND, POSSIBLY FOR THE FIRST TIME CONSCIOUSLY, THE 4'0" SQUARE MODULE. FROM THEN ON, THE 4'0" SQUARE UNIT BECAME WRIGHT'S MOST-USED MODULE. (SQUARE MODULES OF OTHER SIZES WERE ALSO USED.) THIS MODULE IS USED AT THE VERY END OF HIS PRAIRIE-STYLE HOUSES, ALMOST EXCLUSIVELY IN HIS CONCRETE ("TEXTILE") BLOCK HOUSES, AND IN ALMOST ALL HIS EARLY AND RIGHTLY FAMOUS USONIA HOUSE DESIGNS. SOMETIMES HE USED A 4' BY 2' MODULE. MANY OTHER

PROMINENT FOLLOWERS OF ORGANIC ARCHITECTURE HAVE ALSO USED MODULES—FOR INSTANCE, ARCHITECTS FAY JONES (THE 1990 A.I.A. GOLD MEDAL WINNER) AND JOHN HOWE ("THE HAND OF FRANK LLOYD WRIGHT").

RATHER THAN GO THROUGH A WHOLE LIST OF FAMOUS ARCHITECTS WHO HAVE USED MODULES (OFTEN THE 4' SQUARE MODULE) FOR VARIOUS REASONS, I WILL MENTION ONLY ONE MORE HISTORICAL ASIDE. RESEARCHERS OF GOTHIC CATHEDRALS HAVE DISCOVERED THAT MANY OF THESE DESIGNS WERE BASED ON A 4'0" SQUARE MODULE AND PROPORTIONS THEREOF. I FIND THIS PERSONALLY INTERESTING BECAUSE, OTHER THAN JAPANESE, GOTHIC IS THE ONLY ARCHITECTURE THAT WRIGHT ADMITTED TO APPRECIATING. FAY JONES' FAMOUS CHAPELS ARE ALSO GOTHIC IN INSPIRATION, BY HIS OWN ADMISSION. IN MY YOUTH, I THOUGHT THAT AS A GOOD MODERNIST OR EVEN ORGANICIST I SHOULD DISLIKE ALL HISTORICAL FORMS OF ARCHITECTURE, AND I GUILTILY WOULD THINK, WHEN LOOKING AT THE CATHEDRAL AT CHARTRES, "BUT IT _IS_ BEAUTIFUL!"

I GUESS BY NOW THE READER SUSPECTS THAT MY SYSTEM MUST BE BASED ON A 4'0" SQUARE MODULE? CORRECT! BUT IS THE FACT THAT WRIGHT AND THE GREAT CATHEDRAL BUILDERS USED IT A GOOD ENOUGH REASON TO PROMOTE THE IDEA IN A BOOK? I THINK SO, BUT IT IS NOT MY ONLY REASON.

BY ACCIDENT, COINCIDENCE, OR DIVINE PROVIDENCE, 4'0" IS THE BASIC DIMENSION OR MODULE OF MANY BUILDING MATERIALS—MOST NOTABLY PLYWOOD (4' BY 8'). CONCRETE BLOCK IS 8" BY 16" (16" GOES 3 TIMES INTO 4', AND 12" GOES 4 TIMES, OF COURSE). JOIST AND RAFTER SPACING IS 12", 16", AND 24" O.C. THUS, THIS MODULE IS WIDELY USED BOTH IN THE BUILDING INDUSTRY (PREFAB HOUSING) AND BY SOME ARCHITECTS. WHAT SURPRISES ME IS THAT IT IS _NOT_ USED MORE, OR MORE CONSISTENTLY, BY _MOST_ ARCHITECTS, NOR IS IT USED THROUGHOUT ALL STAGES OF THE ARCHITECT'S WORK—I MEAN THE WHOLE DESIGN PROCESS (INCLUDING COMMUNICATION WITH CLIENTS), CONSTRUCTION, AND SUPERVISION.

I WOULD LIKE TO QUOTE FROM A BOOK BY AN ARCHITECT WHOSE WORK I ADMIRE. HIS WORK IS INTERESTING AND BEAUTIFUL, IT IS BUILT WITH TYPICAL CONSTRUCTION TECHNIQUES, AND IT IS OFTEN VERY REASONABLY PRICED. I AM SPEAKING OF ALFREDO DE VIDO, F.A.I.A., AND HIS BOOK, _DESIGNING YOUR CLIENT'S HOUSE_ (NEW YORK: WHITNEY LIBRARY OF DESIGN, 1983). THEREIN HE STATES:

USING GRIDS AND MODULES CAN SAVE MONEY BY AVOIDING WASTE OF MATERIALS. OF EQUAL IMPORTANCE, HOWEVER, IS THEIR VALUE IN _FACILITATING COMMUNICATIONS_—IN THE OFFICE, A PLANNING GRID CAN MAKE A ROUGH SKETCH EASILY UNDERSTOOD, AND IT CAN EASILY BE TRANSLATED INTO WORKING DRAWINGS QUICKLY. ONCE CLIENTS UNDERSTAND THE SYSTEM, THEY REALIZE THAT SMALL DIMENSIONAL CHANGES ARE DIFFICULT, WHICH WILL MAKE YOUR WORK EASIER; CLIENTS WILL ALSO APPRECIATE THAT SIMPLIFYING CONSTRUCTION WITH A MODULE WILL SAVE THEM MONEY. FOR A BUILDER, THE GRID OR MODULE IS A QUICK CHECK ON DIMENSIONS. CONTRACTORS CAN PICK UP POTENTIAL ERRORS IN DRAWINGS BEFORE THEY ARE BUILT. IN SHORT, GRIDS AND MODULES ARE HELPFUL TO ALL INVOLVED. ". . . USE A GRID OR MODULE THAT MAKES GOOD PRACTICAL SENSE. A FAIRLY COMMON SIZE IS 4 FEET. . . . * [EMPHASIS MINE.]

REMEMBER THAT WE ARE DISCUSSING A _HORIZONTAL_ OR _PLAN_ MODULE NOW. LATER, WE WILL TOUCH UPON THE MORE

* PAGES 15–16.

DIFFICULT <u>VERTICAL</u> BUILDING MODULE. BEFORE ADDRESSING THE SIMPLICITY OF THE SYSTEM IN DETAIL WITH EXAMPLES FROM DESIGN AND CONSTRUCTION, I WOULD LIKE TO ASK SOME FURTHER PHILOSOPHICAL QUESTIONS.

IS THERE AN ARTISTIC OR EVEN A PHILOSOPHICAL REASON FOR USING A MODULE SYSTEM? ARTISTICALLY, IT IS HARD TO DO A REALLY UGLY BUILDING ON A CONSISTENTLY MODULAR DESIGN BASIS, FOR THERE IS A CONSISTENCY TO THESE BUILDINGS THAT SPEAKS OF AN ORDERING MIND. IT IS MORE LIKELY (NEGATIVELY) THAT A MODULAR HOUSE IS BORING RATHER THAN UGLY—BUT IT NEED NOT BE, AS I HOPE MY DESIGNS IN THIS BOOK WILL SHOW.

WHAT ABOUT PHILOSOPHICALLY? WAIT— WHY PHILOSOPHY AT ALL? FOR ONE REASON, I AM A DOCTORAL CANDIDATE IN PHILOSOPHY; FOR TWO, PHILOSOPHY HAS INFLUENCED MANY GREAT ARCHITECTS. FOR INSTANCE, THE ABBOT OF SUGER BUILT THE FIRST GOTHIC CATHEDRAL, ST. DENIS. THIS WAS POSSIBLY THE FIRST CATHEDRAL TO USE STAINED GLASS. ABBOT SUGER WAS A STUDENT OF THE WRITINGS OF ST. DIONYSIUS THE AREOPAGITE (CALLED "PSEUDO," AS HE WAS THOUGHT TO BE THE

DIRECT DISCIPLE OF ST. PAUL AND, IN FACT, WAS A FIFTH-CENTURY AUTHOR). DIONYSIUS USED LIGHT AS A SYMBOL OR METAPHOR FOR GOD. "GOD AS LIGHT" ANALOGOUSLY ILLUMINES OUR SOUL, MIND, AND NATURE, AND THE ABBOT BUILT A CHURCH OF TRANSLUCENT WALLS THAT SEEMED TO ALMOST DISAPPEAR INTO A MYRIAD AND COLORED LIGHT—THE "LIGHT OF GOD."

HERE IS ANOTHER EXAMPLE OF PHILOSOPHY (OR RELIGION) INFLUENCING ARCHITECTS. FRANK LLOYD WRIGHT WAS AN ADMITTED LOVER OF THOREAU (AS IS OUR ILLUSTRATOR, ARCHITECT MALCOLM WELLS) AND EMERSON, BUT HE DID NOT OPENLY ADMIT HIS OTHER READINGS OF CARLYLE AND COLERIDGE, FOR THEY WERE ENGLISH AND NOT AMERICAN. BOTH OF THESE ENGLISH PHILOSOPHERS INFLUENCED THOREAU AND EMERSON, BUT WORSE (TO WRIGHT), THEY WERE STUDENTS OF THE GREAT GERMAN PHILOSOPHER, HEGEL, WHO SAW NATURE AS AN ASPECT OR MODE OF GOD. HEGEL SPOKE OF A MORE "ORGANIC" PHILOSOPHY. (REMEMBER THAT WRIGHT CALLED HIS ARCHITECTURE "ORGANIC" ARCHITECTURE.) WRIGHT ALSO SPOKE, AS DID HEGEL (IN VARIOUS WAYS), OF "NATURE AS THE BODY OF GOD". WHETHER NATURE TRULY IS THE BODY OF GOD, OR EVEN

PANTHEISM (THE DOCTRINE THAT GOD IS EVERYTHING), IS NOT MY POINT HERE. (WRIGHT PROBABLY DID NOT INTEND PANTHEISM.*) WRIGHT ALSO WAS A LONG-TIME STUDENT OF THE WRITINGS OF THE CHINESE SAGE LAO-TZU. EVEN AN ORTHODOX CATHOLIC THEOLOGIAN LIKE ST. BONAVENTURE (THIRTEENTH CENTURY) SPOKE OF CHRIST AS THE "WORD" OF GOD, MAN AS THE "IMAGE" OF GOD, AND NATURE AS THE "SHADOW" OF GOD. ALL OF NATURE WAS TO BE SEEN AS VESTIGES OR SYMBOLS OF GOD.

MY POINT HERE IS THAT PHILOSOPHY INFLUENCES ARCHITECTURE (AND EVERYTHING ELSE, FOR THAT MATTER!) AND THAT IT INFLUENCED WRIGHT'S ARCHITECTURE PROFOUNDLY.

---

* ONLY AFTER WRITING THIS DID I COME ACROSS THIS QUOTATION FROM FRANK LLOYD WRIGHT: "THE PRINCIPLES THAT BUILD THE TREE WILL BUILD THE MAN—THAT'S WHY I THINK NATURE SHOULD BE SPELLED WITH A CAPITAL N—<u>NOT</u> BECAUSE NATURE IS GOD BUT BECAUSE ALL THAT WE CAN LEARN OF GOD WE WILL LEARN FROM THE BODY OF GOD, WHICH WE CALL NATURE." [EMPHASIS MINE.] QUOTED BY NANCY FRAZIER IN <u>THE EARLY WORK OF FRANK LLOYD WRIGHT,</u> (ED.) H. TH. WIJDEVELD, NEW YORK: GRAMERCY BOOKS, 1994.

OTHER QUICK EXAMPLES I KNOW OF INCLUDE MIES VAN DER ROHE, WHO STUDIED THE GERMAN MYSTIC MEISTER ECKHART AND THOMAS AQUINAS, AND PHILIP JOHNSON, WHO STUDIED THE GERMAN PHILOSOPHER NIETZSCHE. ARCHITECT FAY JONES SAID THAT IN ARCHITECTURE SCHOOL, HIS PHILOSOPHY CLASSES WERE PROBABLY MOST INFLUENTIAL.

REVERSING INFLUENCES IS ALSO INSTRUCTIVE. MANY NOTED PHILOSOPHERS HAVE SAID THEY ARE VERY INTERESTED IN ARCHITECTURE, AND SOME HAVE SAID THEY CONSIDERED ARCHITECTURE AS A POSSIBLE CAREER IN THEIR YOUTH.

SOME PHILOSOPHICAL SYSTEMS ARE EVEN CHARACTERIZED BY ARCHITECTURAL TERMS. FOR INSTANCE, THE VAST THEOLOGICAL SYSTEMATIC OF THE GREAT ST. THOMAS AQUINAS IS OFTEN DESCRIBED AS "ARCHITECTONIC."

ROBERT BRUMBAUGH, NOTED PLATONIST AND YALE PROFESSOR, WROTE TO ME IN 1984 THAT "ARCHITECTURE AND PHILOSOPHY, PARTICULARLY IN THE PLATONIC TRADITION, GO TOGETHER WELL. (ONE SIGN OF THIS, OF COURSE, IS ARMSTRONG'S CHOICE OF A TITLE FOR HIS WORK THE ARCHITECTURE OF THE INTELLIGIBLE WORLD IN THE PHILOSOPHY OF PLOTINUS.)"

BEFORE I EXPLAIN WHY, I WOULD LIKE TO MENTION THE RELATIONSHIP BETWEEN RELIGION AND ARCHITECTURE. ALL THE GREAT CIVILIZATIONS AROSE AROUND THE GREAT RELIGIOUS REVELATIONS. AND (AS THE PSYCHOLOGIST OTTO RANK POINTED OUT) THE GREAT ARCHITECTURE OF THE WORLD HAS PRIMARILY BEEN RELIGIOUS: THE THREE HOUSES, WHICH ARE THE HOUSE OF GOD (CHURCHES, TEMPLES, ETC.), THE HOUSE OF THE LIVING (OUR HOMES), AND THE HOUSE OF THE DEAD (TOMBS, THE PYRAMIDS, ETC.). IT IS INDISPUTABLE THAT RELIGION AND ARCHITECTURE ARE CLOSELY ASSOCIATED. WITHOUT GOD OR RELIGION OF SOME SORT (EVEN A NATURE RELIGION), ARCHITECTURE DECAYS FROM CATHEDRALS TO CORPORATE OFFICE BUILDINGS. CORPORATE OFFICES, NO DOUBT, HAVE THEIR PLACE, BUT THERE WAS SOMETHING BEAUTIFUL ABOUT THE TALLEST BUILDINGS IN A CITY BEING CATHEDRALS. EVEN PHILIP JOHNSON, AN ADMITTED ATHEIST AND A GOOD ARCHITECT, SAYS HIS FAVORITE BUILDINGS ARE CATHEDRALS.

THERE ARE A THOUSAND PHILOSOPHERS AND PHILOSOPHIES, BUT, TO KEEP IT SIMPLE, LET'S GO BACK TO THE BEGINNING (AT LEAST IN THE WEST). WE WILL DISCUSS THE PROFOUND GREEK PHILOSOPHERS, PLATO AND ARISTOTLE, WHOM THE GREAT GERMAN PHILOSOPHER HEGEL CALLED "THE TEACHERS OF MANKIND."

IN ANTIQUITY AND UNTIL MODERN TIMES, PLATO WAS CALLED "THE DIVINE" AND ARISTOTLE "THE MASTER OF THOSE WHO KNOW." BOTH PLATO AND ARISTOTLE SAW THE WORLD AS MADE UP OF TWO ASPECTS: (IN ENGLISH) FORM AND MATTER. LET'S TAKE OUR 4' SQUARE MODULE AND MAKE IT FOUR-DIMENSIONAL AND SOLID—LET'S SAY A 4' CUBE OF STONE. PLATO WOULD SAY THAT THERE IS A PERFECT AND TIMELESS EUCLIDIAN 4' CUBE IN THE WORLD OF IDEAS, OR FORMS (EIDOS IN GREEK). THIS CUBE IS A PURE AND MATTERLESS FORM. OUR STONE CUBE PARTICIPATES OR SHARES IN THE PERFECT FORM OF THE CUBE. A HUNDRED SUCH STONE CUBES ALL SHARE IN THIS SAME AND SINGLE FORM OF THE PLATONIC CUBE.

ARISTOTLE WOULD ALSO EMPHASIZE THE FORM OF THE STONE CUBE, BUT HE WOULD INSIST THAT THE FORM EXISTS ONLY IN AN ACTUAL STONE CUBE AND THAT IT IS OUR MINDS THAT ABSTRACT OR TAKE OUT THE FORM. IN OTHER WORDS, TO ARISTOTLE THE FORM EXISTS FIRST AND ORIGINALLY IN THE

THE SISSON HOUSE - SCHEME B   CHARLES G. WOODS, AIA, ARCHITECT

ACTUAL STONE CUBE AND ONLY SECONDLY IN OUR MINDS, BUT <u>NOT EVER</u> IN A TIMELESS WORLD OF FORMS OR IDEAS—THE FAMOUS PLATONIC IDEAS, FROM WHICH WE ALSO GET OUR EVERYDAY WORD "IDEA."

PLATO AND ARISTOTLE BOTH AGREE, HOWEVER, THAT <u>ALL</u> THAT EXISTS IN SPACE AND TIME CONSISTS OF FORM AND MATTER. BUT TO PLATO, FORM AND MATTER ARE, OR CAN BE, ULTIMATELY DISTINCT: A TIMELESS FORM OR BEING IS DIFFERENTIATED FROM MATTER, WHICH CAN CHANGE OR BECOME (<u>POTENTIA</u> IN LATIN—A POTENTIAL FOR BECOMING). ARISTOTLE THOUGHT, ON THE CONTRARY, THAT FORM AND MATTER COULD BE DISTINGUISHED BY THE MIND BUT ARE REALLY INDISTINGUISHABLE IN <u>REALITY.</u>

EIGHTEEN CENTURIES LATER, ST. THOMAS AQUINAS, THE CATHOLIC THEOLOGIAN/ PHILOSOPHER (THIRTEENTH CENTURY) SYNTHESIZED NOT ONLY GENERALLY BIBLICAL AND PHILOSOPHICAL/GREEK THOUGHT, BUT ALSO, MANY SAY, PLATO AND ARISTOTLE, IN HIS FAMOUS <u>THOMIST SYNTHESIS.</u> AQUINAS THOUGHT THAT <u>BOTH</u> PLATO AND ARISTOTLE WERE IN PART RIGHT BUT THAT THE BIBLICAL VIEW OF A "CREATOR GOD" ADDED MORE TO THE SOLUTION. EVEN IF YOU DON'T SEE WHAT AN ARCHITECTURAL

MODULE HAS TO DO WITH ALL THIS, PLEASE TAKE MY WORD FOR THIS MUCH: THE PROBLEM OF FORM AND MATTER IS IMPORTANT TO US ALL—TO ALL THOUGHT, EVEN NOW.

AQUINAS THOUGHT THAT THE FORMS OR IDEAS EXISTED FIRST AND TIMELESSLY (PLATO) IN "GOD'S MIND", SECOND, IN THE "CREATED" WORLD OF SPACE AND TIME—OUR 4' STONE CUBE (ARISTOTLE), AND LAST, IN OUR MINDS THROUGH ABSTRACTION (ARISTOTLE AGAIN!). ARISTOTLE WAS TWO-THIRDS RIGHT, BUT PLATO'S ONE-THIRD WAS ULTIMATELY MORE IMPORTANT THEOLOGICALLY.

AGAIN, ONE MIGHT WONDER IF I'M POSSIBLY <u>OVER</u>EMPHASIZING THE IMPORTANCE OF PHILOSOPHY OR RELIGION OR ST. THOMAS AQUINAS FOR ARCHITECTURE? I MYSELF BEGAN TO WONDER THIS, SO I WAS VERY HAPPY TO DISCOVER (<u>AFTER</u> WRITING THE ROUGH DRAFT OF THIS SECTION) JOHN PETER'S HELPFUL BOOK, <u>THE ORAL TRADITION OF MODERN ARCHITECTURE</u> (NEW YORK: ABRAMS, 1994), WHICH IS A COLLECTION OF INTERVIEWS WITH FAMED ARCHITECTS, WHEREIN MIES VAN DER ROHE (WHOM THE ARCHITECT/SCHOLAR PETER BLAKE CALLED ONE OF THE THREE "MASTER BUILDERS" OF

THE TWENTIETH CENTURY, ALONG WITH WRIGHT AND LE CORBUSIER) SAYS, "MY <u>ARCHITECTURAL</u> PHILOSOPHY CAME OUT OF READING <u>PHILOSOPHICAL</u> BOOKS"* [EMPHASIS MINE] AND ALSO, "I WAS INTERESTED IN THE PHILOSOPHY OF VALUES AND PROBLEMS OF THE SPIRIT. . . . I ASKED MYSELF THE QUESTION, 'WHAT IS THE TRUTH?' UNTIL I STOPPED AT <u>THOMAS AQUINAS,</u> YOU KNOW. I FOUND THE ANSWER FOR THAT."[†] [EMPHASIS MINE.] HE ALSO MENTIONS AQUINAS A <u>SECOND</u> TIME IN THE SAME INTERVIEW ON HIS ARCHITECTURE. TO MY KNOWLEDGE, MIES WAS NEITHER A PRACTICING CATHOLIC NOR OVERTLY RELIGIOUS, SO THIS IS ESPECIALLY INTERESTING.

LET'S LOOK AT THE ETYMOLOGY FOR THESE TWO WORDS, "FORM" AND "MATTER." THE ROMAN PHILOSOPHER BOETHIUS BRILLIANTLY COINED MANY OF THESE LATIN WORDS FROM THE GREEK ROOTS AT ABOUT THE TIME OF THE FALL OF ROME. "FORM," OR <u>FORMA</u> IN LATIN, CAN MEAN "FORM," "CONTOUR," "FIGURE," "SHAPE," "APPEARANCE," "LOOKS," "NATURE," "MANNER," "KIND,"

---

* PAGE 159.
[†] PAGE 158.

"CONDITION," "OUTLINE," "PLAN," "SKETCH," AND "DESIGN." QUITE A FEW WORDS USED IN ARCHITECTURE, NO?

CONSIDER "MATTER," OR MATERIA: "STUFF," "MATTER," "TIMBER" [OR WOOD], "SUBSTANCE," "CAUSE," "OCCASION," "SOURCE," "OPPORTUNITY," "NATURAL ABILITIES," "CAPACITY," OR "DISPOSITION" (AND THE SOURCE OF THAT WORD IS MATER OR MA: MOTHER). AGAIN, MANY ARCHITECTURAL TERMS.

I THINK IT WAS COLERIDGE WHO SAID THAT ALL MEN ARE BY NATURE EITHER PLATONISTS OR ARISTOTELIANS, MEANING THAT WE ALL, TO SOME EXTENT, EMPHASIZE FORM (TIMELESS BEING) OR MATTER (BECOMING OR POTENTIALITY). WHETHER COLERIDGE WAS RIGHT IS NOT IMPORTANT HERE. WHAT IS IMPORTANT IS THAT (THE PLATO VS. ARISTOTLE DEBATE NOTWITHSTANDING) ARCHITECTURE AS THE ART OF BUILT STRUCTURE DOES, OF NECESSITY, EXIST IN SPACE AND TIME. A STONE CUBE IS A CUBE AND STONE, OR INFORMED MATTER. IT IS INTERESTING THAT GOD IS OFTEN CALLED AN "ARCHITECT" IN RELIGION AND PHILOSOPHY—IN FACT, THE ARCHITECT. JESUS WAS CALLED A CARPENTER, A SHAPER OF WOOD (FORM AND MATTER). AT THE TIME OF JESUS IN ISRAEL,

"CARPENTER" MEANT "ARCHITECT" IN THAT CARPENTERS DESIGNED AND BUILT BUILDINGS, JUST AS THE ALMOST ANONYMOUS MEDIEVAL CATHEDRAL BUILDERS DID.

IT IS ALSO INTERESTING THAT, IN THE BIBLE AND OTHER MYSTICAL WRITINGS, THE WORD "HOUSE" IS A METAPHOR FOR THE SOUL; REMEMBER THAT JESUS SAID, "YOU ARE A TEMPLE OF THE LIVING GOD." THE READER MAY BE WONDERING NOW WHETHER THIS IS A REALLY TRICKY FORM OF CHRISTIAN APOLOGETICS. AM I TRYING TO CONVERT YOU TO CHRISTIANITY OR EVEN TO PLATONISM? NO—THOUGH I AM, IN FACT, A CHRISTIAN PHILOSOPHER, I HAVEN'T ALWAYS BEEN, AND THAT IS NOT MY INTENT. THIS PROBLEM OF FORM AND MATTER REALLY IS IMPORTANT TO ALL THOUGHT AND, THEREFORE, TO ALL ARCHITECTS, CONTRACTORS, AND EVEN POTENTIAL HOME BUILDERS AND BUYERS. I ALSO HAVE A GREAT ADMIRATION FOR OTHER RELIGIONS, INCLUDING EASTERN ONES (THE PROBLEM EXISTS IN THE EAST, TOO), AND ALSO FOR THEIR ARCHITECTS. WHEN ASKED WHAT HE READ THAT INFLUENCED HIS DESIGN THINKING, THE GREAT ARCHITECT I. M. PEI SAID, "I READ LAO-TZU A VERY GREAT DEAL . . . AND I THINK THAT HIS WRITING HAS PROBABLY MORE EFFECT ON

MY ARCHITECTURAL THINKING THAN ANYTHING ELSE."* [EMPHASIS MINE.]

FOR INSTANCE, IN THE VEDANTA (THE SO-CALLED HINDU PHILOSOPHY) APPEAR THE SANSKRIT WORDS NAMA-RUPA, WHICH ARE TRANSLATED AS "NAME AND FORM" BUT, UNFORTUNATELY (FOR OUR DISCUSSION), MEAN THE OPPOSITE OF WHAT THEY DO IN THE WEST. THERE IS STILL THE IDEA OF FORM AND MATTER, BUT, STRANGELY, NAMA MEANS "NAME" AND RUPA, OR "FORM," MEANS "MATTER"!

WHAT DO WE DO IN THE ART OF ARCHITECTURE? LET US ASK A PRELIMINARY QUESTION. HOW DOES ARCHITECTURE RELATE TO AND DIFFER FROM THE OTHER ARTS?

ONE WAY TO UNDERSTAND AND RATE THE ARTS IS TO ASK WHICH IS PURER—WHICH INVOLVES THE MOST FORM AND THE LEAST MATTER? TO PUT IT IN A DIFFERENT WAY, WHICH IS MORE MENTAL AND CONTEMPLATIVE, AND WHICH IS MORE PHYSICAL AND PRACTICAL (ARISTOTLE AGAIN)? THIS HAS BEEN DONE IN WESTERN INTELLECTUAL HISTORY.

---

* PAGE 262, JOHN PETER INTERVIEW.

WITHOUT DRAWING ALL THIS OUT AGAIN UNDULY, WITHIN THIS UNDERSTANDING, MANY WOULD RATE MUSIC AS A POSSIBLE HIGHEST ART—OR POETRY OR EVEN PHILOSOPHY. THESE ARE UNDERSTOOD AS ARTS BECAUSE THEY ARE ALL ALMOST FREE OF MATTER. THE MATTER OF MUSIC IS SOUND (AND THE PRINTED NOTES, IF WRITTEN). POETRY AND PHILOSOPHY ARE BOTH MENTAL BUT CAN BE WRITTEN. EVEN THERE, ANTIQUITY INFORMS US INTERESTINGLY.

BOTH THE GREEK ILIAD AND THE VENDANTIC SCRIPTURES (UPANISHADS) WERE PURPOSELY NOT WRITTEN DOWN FOR HUNDREDS OF YEARS (AFTER THE INVENTION/REVELATION OF WRITING). SOCRATES, THE TEACHER OF PLATO, ALSO WOULD NOT WRITE AT ALL, AND EVEN PLATO HIMSELF WOULD NOT DIRECTLY WRITE OF GOD. (SEE PLATO'S SEVENTH LETTER, AND BOOK VII OF THE REPUBLIC.)

I THINK THAT THESE ARE ALL EXAMPLES OF TRYING TO SEPARATE FORM FROM MATTER OR TRYING TO BE PURE FORM. PATAÑJALI, THE CODIFIER OF YOGA, SAYS WE SHOULD TRY TO SEPARATE THE PRAKRITTI (MATTER) FROM THE PURUSHA, (THE SELF, OR PURE FORM).

THE INDIVIDUAL ARTS CAN BE EVEN FURTHER RATED IN A HIERARCHY OF PURITY. MOZART AND BACH HAVE OFTEN BEEN SEEN AS PURER OR SUPERIOR TO BEETHOVEN BECAUSE THEIR MUSIC CAN BE SEEN AS MORE PURELY INTELLECTUAL OR LESS PASSIONATE. THE SAME IS SAID ABOUT BEETHOVEN COMPARED TO HARD ROCK, AND SO ON. ON THE OTHER END ARE THE EXTREMELY PRACTICAL ARTS. THE MOST PRACTICAL OF OBJECTS HAVE BOTH FORM AND MATTER, BUT MOST WOULD AGREE THAT A BEAUTIFUL VASE IS MORE BEAUTIFUL THAN A (POSSIBLY) EQUALLY BEAUTIFUL TOILET DESIGN, FOR INSTANCE. RIGHTLY OR WRONGLY, WE INSTINCTIVELY DO NOT EVEN WANT THE TOILET TO BE AS BEAUTIFUL AS THE VASE.

THERE HAVE BEEN NUMEROUS AESTHETICS, OR PHILOSOPHIES OF BEAUTY, AND, NO DOUBT, THERE HAS BEEN AT TIMES TOO MUCH DUALISM AND EVEN AN ANTIMATTER ATTITUDE, NOT ONLY IN ART, BUT IN RELIGION. FOR INSTANCE, IN CHRISTIANITY (AND JUDAISM AND ISLAM), THE WORLD IS "FALLEN," ALTHOUGH IT WAS CREATED AS GOOD AND STILL IS LARGELY GOOD. (MANY PEOPLE FORGET THIS IMPORTANT LAST PART.)

SOCRATES SAW PHILOSOPHY AS "THE ART OF LEARNING TO DIE"—TO SEPARATE THE IMMORTAL SOUL FROM THE BODY (TOMB).

ST. AUGUSTINE THOUGHT SIMILARLY (UNDER THE INDIRECT INFLUENCE OF PLATO AGAIN). AUGUSTINE SAW THE PERSON AS AN IMMORTAL SOUL IN A BODY—THE BODY WAS NOT SEEN AS PART OF THE ESSENCE OF A PERSON. THIS WILL CONNECT DIRECTLY WITH ARCHITECTURE AGAIN SOON. IT IS ONLY AGAIN WITH AQUINAS THAT THE PERSON IS UNDERSTOOD AS A SOUL AND A BODY COMBINED: THE SOUL IS THE FORM OF THE BODY (ARISTOTLE AGAIN).

NOW ARCHITECTS AND ARCHITECTURE ARE OFTEN JUDGED BY THESE MORE PLATONIC AND ARISTOTELIAN STANDARDS. FOR INSTANCE, IN MY OWN JUDGMENT, ARCHITECTS SUCH AS MIES VAN DER ROHE, LE CORBUSIER, OR, MORE RECENTLY, RICHARD MEIERS, ARE PRETTY OBVIOUSLY ALMOST PURE PLATONISTS BY INTENTION. ALL THREE USED PURE EUCLIDIAN FORMS— WITH ALMOST NO COLORS, OR AT MOST, ONLY PRIMARY OR PURE COLORS. THERE IS LITTLE OR NO OBVIOUS RELATION TO NATURE, AND THEY USED NON-NATURAL (OR APPARENTLY SO) MATERIALS. THIS IS EMPHASIZED EVEN BY LIFTING THE BUILDINGS OFF THE GROUND AS IN CORBU'S FAMOUS VILLA SAVOYE, MIES' FARNSWORTH HOUSE, AND MANY OF MEIERS' EARLY WORKS. (I AM

SISSON SCHEME III
SOLAR CURVE

CHARLES G. WOODS, AIA, ARCHITECT

THE JAMES AND LYNETTE FOSTER HOUSE – HOT SPRINGS, NORTH CAROLINA
"CRYSTAL CAVE" – ECONOMY – EARTH SHELTERED – PASSIVE SOLAR – SUPERINSULATED

CHARLES G. WOODS, AIA, ARCHITECT

GENERALIZING—THERE ARE, OF COURSE, EXCEPTIONS.)

IF YOU LOOK, I THINK YOU WILL SEE IN THEIR WORK MAINLY FORM, NOT MATTER; BEING, NOT BECOMING; IDEA, NOT NATURE. THE LATER WORK OF BOTH LE CORBUSIER AND MEIERS BECAME MUCH MORE INTEGRAL (CORBU'S CHAPEL AND MEIERS' CALIFORNIA ART COMPLEX, FOR EXAMPLE).

LET'S TAKE THE OTHER EXTREME OF MATTER AND BECOMING, WHICH I THINK WE ALSO SEE IN ARCHITECTS SUCH AS BRUCE GOFF (FROM HIS MIDDLE PERIOD ON) OR IN BART PRINCE, KELLOG, OR SOME OF THE LATE GREAT JOHN LAUTNER'S WORK. HERE WE NO DOUBT STILL SEE FORM—NOT AN EASILY UNDERSTOOD EUCLIDIAN FORM, BUT AN ALMOST CHAOTIC FORM, AND VERY NATURAL, WITH EVEN CRUDE MATERIALS USED AT TIMES. THE BUILDINGS ALMOST MOVE—THEY APPEAR AS ALMOST PURE BECOMING.

ANOTHER WAY TO DISCUSS THIS IS IN TERMS OF ORDER AND CHAOS OR THE GREEK APOLLONIAN AND DIONYSIAN TERMS, WHICH DERIVED FROM THE GREEK GODS APOLLO (SUN/LIGHT) AND DIONYSIUS (WINE/DANCE). FOR AN EXAMPLE OF THE EXTREMES, THE EARLY LE CORBUSIER IS ALMOST PURELY APOLLONIAN AND BRUCE GOFF'S LATER WORK IS ALMOST PURELY DIONYSIAN.

YET ANOTHER WAY TO LOOK AT THIS IS IN TERMS OF IDENTITY AND DIFFERENCE (ANOTHER ASPECT OF FORM AND MATTER, BECAUSE FORM KEEPS ITS IDENTITY AND MATTER IS DIVERSE AND CHANGEABLE). REMEMBER, WE ARE SPEAKING OF TENDENCIES—NO ONE IS PURELY ONE WAY OR THE OTHER. MIES IS NOT COMPLETELY A PLATONIST (HIS BUILDINGS RUST AND NEED REPAIRS). GOFF IS NOT COMPLETELY AN ARISTOTELIAN (OR, RATHER, WITH GOFF, A DIONYSIAN). FOR WITH ALL THEIR NATURAL AND EVEN, AT TIMES, BIZARRE SHAPES, THEY CAN STILL (WITH WORK) BE BROKEN DOWN INTO SIMPLE AND PLATONICALLY PURE EUCLIDEAN SHAPES.

TO SUMMARIZE, ARCHITECTURE IS (LIKE EVERYTHING) A SYNTHESIS OF FORM AND MATTER, BEING AND BECOMING, ORDER AND CHAOS, IDENTITY AND DIFFERENCE. AND ARCHITECTURE IS ALWAYS RELATED TO PHILOSOPHY, CONSCIOUSLY OR UNCONSCIOUSLY. THE POSTMODERNISM OF THE 1970S AND '80S WAS A PHILOSOPHICAL RESPONSE TO THE MODERNISM OF THE EARLIER DECADES, AS ARE THE DECONSTRUCTIONISTS, SUCH AS THE GREAT FRANK GEHRY, INFLUENCED BY BRILLIANT PHILOSOPHERS SUCH AS THE FRENCH JACQUES DERRIDA (WHO, IN MY OPINION, IS, UNFORTUNATELY, A BORDERLINE NIHILIST). I FIND IT PERSONALLY INSTRUCTIVE THAT GEHRY'S INTERESTING WORK IS BECOMING MORE BEAUTIFUL AND LESS CHAOTIC AS HE BECOMES MORE NOTED.

THE REASON I'VE LOVED WRIGHT'S WORK SO MUCH IS THAT I SEE IT AS A GOOD BALANCE OF FORM AND MATTER, BEING AND BECOMING, IDENTITY AND DIFFERENCE (OR BETTER, IDENTITY IN DIFFERENCE). ARCHITECTURE IS NOT, AND SHOULD NOT STRIVE TO BE PURELY PLATONIC OR ARISTOTELIAN, BUT A MIXTURE—POSSIBLY SOMEWHAT THOMIST.

WE ARE NOW READY TO MOVE BEYOND ALL THIS PHILOSOPHIC AND RELIGIOUS HISTORY. I HOPE YOU FOUND IT EVEN HALF AS INTERESTING AS I DO! NOW AT LAST WE WILL PROCEED TO THE DESIGN PROCESS AND THE ACTUAL PHILOSOPHY OF ARCHITECTURAL DESIGN, THOUGH STILL IN AN ABSTRACT WAY.

LET'S RETURN NOW (HOPEFULLY, ENRICHED) TO THE DESIGN PROCESS ITSELF. WHAT IS IT THAT AN ARCHITECT DOES IN THE DESIGN PROCESS? IT IS DIFFICULT TO SPEAK FOR ALL ARCHITECTS, SO I WILL DESCRIBE MY

OWN DESIGN THINKING AS A PHENOMENON, AS I OBSERVE IT— PHENOMENOLOGICALLY. I DO BELIEVE THAT SOMETHING LIKE THIS IS DONE BY ALL ARCHITECTS—CONSCIOUSLY OR UNCONSCIOUSLY, AS THE CASE MAY BE. MY SIMPLE SYSTEM, HOWEVER, DOES NOT PRACTICALLY REST ON MY PHILOSOPHICAL DESCRIPTION. BUT SINCE MOST—EVEN FAMOUS—ARCHITECTS HAVE BEEN QUITE MUTE ON THE PROCESS—EITHER THROUGH LACK OF INTEREST, VERBAL ABILITY, OR INCLINATION—I HOPE THIS ATTEMPT WILL PROVE USEFUL.

EVEN WRIGHT, FOR ALL HIS ROMANTIC VERBOSITY, WAS NOT THAT HELPFUL, I BELIEVE, IN ACTUALLY DESCRIBING HIS OWN PERSONAL DESIGN EXPERIENCE, FOR INSTANCE. AND WHEN ASKED HOW HE DID HIS DESIGNS, THE TRULY GREAT (MY FAVORITE) ALVAR AALTO SAID (AS I REMEMBER), "I DON'T KNOW!" I THINK HE WAS BEING HONEST, AND IN A SENSE I COULD SAY THE SAME, IN THAT A DESCRIPTION OF TECHNIQUE CANNOT EXPLAIN ART. STILL, I THINK SOMETHING MORE CAN BE ATTEMPTED.

IN MY OWN WORK, I BELIEVE I AM ATTEMPTING TO INCARNATE PURE FORM OR INSTANTIATE FORM INTO MATTER.

ANOTHER WAY OF DESCRIBING THIS WOULD BE TO SAY THAT I WANT TO IMPREGNATE MATTER WITH FORM. BY THE WAY, TRADITIONALLY, FORM WAS SEEN AS MALE AND MATTER AS FEMALE (REMEMBER "MOTHER"). THIS SHOULD NOT BE REGARDED AS A CRITICISM OF WOMEN ARCHITECTS, FOR IT IS NOT; IT'S JUST THE LATIN LANGUAGE.

WHETHER PLATO OR ARISTOTLE IS RIGHT, I HAVE AN IDEA OF A PERFECT EUCLIDIAN CIRCLE, FOR INSTANCE. LET'S SAY I WANT TO DESIGN A CIRCULAR HOUSE, SUCH AS MY RADIANT HOUSE.* THOUGH IT IS CLEAR TO ME THAT THIS CIRCLE MUST BE MADE OF SOMETHING IN THIS WORLD, I STILL BELIEVE I PERCEIVE IN MY MIND'S EYE THE IDEA OF A "PERFECT" CIRCLE. WHAT IS A PERFECT CIRCLE? THERE ARE MANY WAYS TO DEFINE IT. FOR ONE, IT IS A FORM SUCH THAT ANY (OF AN INFINITE NUMBER) OF POINTS ON THE FORM ARE EQUIDISTANT FROM THE CENTER. AS A SECOND DEFINITION, YOU COULD SAY THAT IT IS A FORM MADE OF AN INFINITE NUMBER OF EQUAL LINES ALL MEETING ON ONLY ONE END. WHY AN INFINITE NUMBER? IS THIS JUST MORE

* PAGE 213 IN MY PREVIOUS BOOK WITH MAC, DESIGNING YOUR NATURAL HOUSE, (NEW YORK: VNR, 1992).

PLATONIC NUMBER MYSTICISM? ACTUALLY, NO—IF THE NUMBER WERE NOT INFINITE, YOU MIGHT HAVE ONLY AN ARC, OR PARTIAL CIRCLE.

MY KNOWLEDGE OF HIGHER MATHEMATICS IS NOT IMPRESSIVE AND I AM WRITING THIS PURPOSELY WITHOUT REFERRING TO EUCLID'S ELEMENTS. WHY? TO PROVE PLATO'S POINT IN HIS MENO DIALOGUE THAT WE EACH HAVE AN IMPLICIT KNOWLEDGE OF AT LEAST SIMPLE MATHEMATICS AND GEOMETRY. FOR INSTANCE, IT IS VERY CLEAR TO ME THAT, EVEN THOUGH I CANNOT IMAGINE IT, I DO UNDERSTAND WHAT A CIRCLE IS. FOR INSTANCE, NEITHER YOU NOR I CAN EVER SEE A PURE CIRCLE AS SUCH. FORGET FOR A MOMENT THAT A LINE, CURVED OR OTHERWISE, IS MADE UP OF INFINITE (OR INDEFINITE) POINTS—STILL, ONE MUST, OF NECESSITY, VIEW IT IN PERSPECTIVE—EVEN IN PLAN.

I HAVE CONFUSED MANY CLIENTS— INCLUDING A SMART AND EXCELLENT PHOTOGRAPHER—AND SOMETIMES EVEN MYSELF BY TRYING TO EXPLAIN THAT AN ELEVATION IS NOT JUST A SIDE VIEW AND THAT A PERSPECTIVE IS NOT JUST AN ANGLE VIEW. YOU COULD, OF COURSE, DO A PERSPECTIVE OF A SIDE OF A HOUSE AND AN ELEVATION OF AN ANGLE—ANY ANGLE—

BECAUSE AN ELEVATION IS A TWO-DIMENSIONAL DRAWING SUCH THAT YOUR EYE IS "EVERYWHERE" EQUALLY. AN ELEVATION IS AN ATTEMPT TO DRAW A PLATONIC, EUCLIDIAN PERFECT SHAPE IN THE IMPERFECT WORLD OF SPACE/TIME.

I DO NOT MEAN TO SOUND OVERLY PROFOUND ABOUT SOMETHING ALL ARCHITECTS KNOW, BUT STRICTLY SPEAKING, IT IS A PARADOX, FOR NOT ONLY DO OUR LEAD OR EVEN "SIX-O" (VERY THIN LINE) PENS HAVE SOME THICKNESS AND IMPERFECTION, BUT OUR EYES ARE NOT ABLE TO LOOK EVERYWHERE AT ONCE, SO WE OF NECESSITY SEE IN PERSPECTIVE WHAT WE ARE TRYING TO DRAW IN A PERSPECTIVELESS WAY—A GOD'S-VIEW WAY.

ALTHOUGH I AM NOT A MASTER OF HIGHER MATHEMATICS, I AM INTERESTED IN THE PHILOSOPHY OF MATHEMATICS. IN MY YOUTH, I ATTENDED ST. JOHN'S COLLEGE (THE "GREAT BOOKS" SCHOOL) IN ANNAPOLIS, MARYLAND. THE SCHOOL WAS SET UP SUCH THAT TEACHERS WERE SEEN AS GUIDES AND YOU COULD QUESTION ENDLESSLY WITH NO NEGATIVE FALLOUT. EUCLID'S FIRST DEFINITION IS THAT A POINT HAS NO BREADTH OR DIMENSION. STUDENTS OFTEN QUESTION THIS FOR A TIME. ONE STUDENT AT ST. JOHN'S HAD PURSUED IT

FOR THREE WEEKS. MY TEACHER, MR. GOLDING, KINDLY BEGGED ME TO ALLOW THE CLASS TO MOVE ON PAST DEFINITION ONE AFTER A NEW RECORD OF SIX WEEKS. I LET THEM MOVE ON AND QUIT THE SCHOOL (TO MY LOSS) SHORTLY THEREAFTER. I THEREFORE BELIEVE (OR AM DECEIVED) THAT I UNDERSTAND A "MATTERLESS" AND "PERFECT" CIRCLE, EITHER BY PLATONIC PARTICIPATION OR BY ARISTOTELIAN ABSTRACTION.

I BELIEVE THAT THERE IS A CERTAIN ACT OF DECISION AND EVEN WILLFULNESS IN DESIGN. IF I DECIDE TO MAKE A HOUSE WITH A CIRCULAR PLAN, I EXCLUDE AN INDEFINITE AMOUNT OF OTHER REGULAR AND COMPLEX SHAPES. I IMMEDIATELY GO FROM AN ABSTRACT INFINITY OF POSSIBILITIES TO FINITE ONES, AND, IN PLAN, ONLY ONE—A CIRCLE.

A DIALECTICAL SERIES OF QUESTIONS SOON FOLLOWS. SO I WILL USE A CIRCLE PLAN FOR THIS HOUSE. HOW LARGE OF A CIRCLE WILL I NEED? AT FIRST, I GUESSTIMATE, AND THIS IS REVISED BACK AND FORTH IN THE ACTUAL DESIGN PROCESS.

I WOULD LIKE TO ADDRESS TWO INTERESTING AND FAMOUS EXAMPLES OF CREATIVE GENIUS: MOZART AND FRANK LLOYD WRIGHT. MOZART WAS SAID TO KNOW EVERY NOTE BEFORE WRITING AND WRIGHT WAS SAID TO HAVE HAD THE WHOLE BUILDING IN HIS MIND BEFORE PUTTING PEN TO PAPER. ALTHOUGH I HAVE NO DOUBT OF EITHER ONE'S GENIUS OR GIFTS PROBABLY SUPERIOR TO MY OWN, I DOUBT BOTH THESE STORIES. THERE WOULD BE NO REASON FOR WRIGHT TO HAVE SPENT OVER TEN YEARS REDESIGNING THE GUGGENHEIM MUSEUM OR FOR MOZART'S LONG AND DIFFICULT WORK ON HIS BRILLIANT REQUIEM IF THESE STORIES WERE TRUE. I DO BELIEVE THAT THE BASIC, DEEP STRUCTURES OR FORMS ARE OFTEN KNOWN QUITE CLEARLY BY GENIUSES—BUT NOT EVERY MINOR POINT. I KNOW THE STORY OF WRIGHT'S DRAWING UP FALLING WATER IN THREE HOURS WHILE THE KAUFMANNS WERE DRIVING TO THE SITE, AND I BELIEVE IT. I DO NOT BELIEVE, HOWEVER, THAT HE HAD AN EXACT KNOWLEDGE OF EVERY TOILET, HEATING DUCT, OR LIGHT BULB—NOR NEED HE HAVE. I ALSO DOUBT THAT MOZART HEARD EVERY MINOR NOTE OF HIS GREAT JUPITER SYMPHONY—NOR NEED HE HAVE. FOR ONE THING, IT'S SOMEHOW PAINFUL TO LIVE WITH A COMPLEX FORM IN YOUR MIND. YOU WANT TO GET IT DOWN ON PAPER AND OUT OF YOU—GIVE IT 'BIRTH, USUALLY IN A SCRIBBLED SKETCH ON A NAPKIN OR PLACEMAT IN A

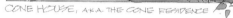

CONE HOUSE, A.K.A. THE CONE RESIDENCE

CHARLES G. WOODS, AIA, ARCHITECT

SEASHELL
CHARLES G WOODS, AIA, ARCHITECT

RESTAURANT, OR ON AN ENVELOPE AT 3 A.M. THAT SCRIBBLED SKETCH OR "PARTI" IS REALLY THE WHOLE SEED OF THE DESIGN IN INVOLUTED FORM, WHICH CAN NOW, AFTER THE BIRTH PROCESS, EVOLVE.

ONE OF MY FAVORITE MODERN ARCHITECTS, ERICH MENDELSOHN (DESIGNER OF THE EINSTEIN TOWER), DID SOME OF THE MOST BEAUTIFULLY VAGUE SKETCHES IN BLACK AND WHITE WITH THE TOUCH OF A ZEN MASTER. WHEN HIS DISCIPLES LATER ASKED HIM TECHNICAL QUESTIONS, HE WOULD OFTEN TELL THEM, "GO BACK TO THE SKETCH—IT'S ALL IN THE SKETCH." NO DOUBT, THAT'S TRUE, BUT I ALWAYS HAD SYMPATHY FOR HIS STUDENTS TRYING TO WORK OUT THE HVAC ON HIS FREE-FORM ORGANIC BUILDINGS!

IT WAS ALSO OFTEN SAID THAT WRIGHT, UNLIKE OTHER ARCHITECTS, DESIGNED FROM THE INSIDE OUT, NOT THE OUTSIDE IN. ONE OF HIS DISCIPLES WITH WHOM I WORKED TOLD ME I WAS DESIGNING THE OPPOSITE WAY. THAT HURT ME AT THE TIME AND I THINK I HAVE DISCOVERED WHY. IF YOU ARE WORKING WITH PURE FORMS— SQUARES, TRIANGLES, CIRCLES, ETC.—YOU MUST DESIGN SOMEWHAT FROM THE OUTSIDE IN. I HAVE NO DOUBT THAT ON THE GUGGENHEIM OR UNITY TEMPLE

WRIGHT ALSO DESIGNED THAT WAY MORE THAN ON HIS COMPLEX AND ASYMMETRICAL USONIA HOUSES. AT THE TIME I WAS TOLD THIS, I WAS DOING ONE- AND TWO-STORY RECTILINEAR EARTH-SHELTERED HOUSES. TO KEEP COSTS DOWN AND SINCE MUCH WAS UNDERGROUND, I DID STAY WITH SIMPLE SHAPES AND THEREFORE HAD TO WORK SOMEWHAT OUT TO IN. I DO NOT THINK THAT WAS TRUE OF MY PATIOS, DECKS, ETC., THOUGH LATER I DID THE HIGHLY ASYMMETRICAL SENALIK HOUSE.* IN THIS HOUSE, I DESIGNED VERY DEFINITELY FROM THE INSIDE OUT— CENTRIFUGALLY, LIKE A MINI BIG BANG!

I THOUGHT THE PRECEDING DISCUSSION WOULD BE HELPFUL BEFORE GOING BACK TO OUR CIRCLE HOUSE DESIGN. SO NOW WE HAVE A HOUSE WITH A CIRCULAR PLAN. WILL IT BE ONE OR TWO STORIES? MANY TIMES, PRACTICAL, REAL-WORLD RESTRAINTS WILL HELP ANSWER THIS QUESTION. WHAT TYPE OF ROOF WILL I USE—FLAT, SHED, GABLE, DOME, HIP, ETC.? I DECIDED IN MY OWN DESIGN TO GO WITH ONE STORY (WITH WALKOUT LOWER LEVEL) AND A HIP ROOF. I DECIDED TO EARTH-BERM THE NORTH SIDE IN

* SEE PAGES 222–226 IN MY PREVIOUS BOOK, DESIGNING YOUR NATURAL HOUSE.

ADDITION TO THE BASEMENT LEVEL. FOR PRACTICAL PURPOSES, I DECIDED ON FLAT, RATHER THAN CURVED, GLASS. I WANTED CONSISTENT WINDOW COLUMNS, SO I DECIDED ON AN ARC MODULE OF 10° AND A RADIAL MODULE OF 4' O.C. (I HAD TO KEEP THE 4' IN SOMEHOW!) I KNEW AT THIS POINT THAT, IN ITS ABSTRACT FORM, I HAD CREATED A HOUSE THAT COULD EASILY LOOK MORE LIKE A CAROUSEL OR A FLYING SAUCER THAN I WANTED. IF THE HOUSE WAS UP ON COLUMNS AND YOU ENTERED FROM BELOW, IT MIGHT LOOK AS IF IT COULD TAKE OFF—MUCH LIKE THE LATE, GREAT JOHN LAUTNER'S NIFTY CIRCLE HOUSE OR MY RECENT LOOKOUT DESIGN.

LAYING OUT THE ROOMS WAS SOMEWHAT OF A TRIAL-AND-ERROR PROCESS, THOUGH I DECIDED EARLY ON FOR A (COVERED) CENTRAL GARDEN ATRIUM. I WANTED TO USE REALLY NATURAL MATERIALS TO FURTHER INCARNATE THIS PURE PLATONIC FORM, SO I USED CEDAR SHINGLES ON THE ROOF, WOOD COLUMNS, CEDAR SIDING, AND STONE PATIOS AND RETAINING WALLS. THE EARTH-BERM GROUNDS THE HOUSE AND THE CANTILEVERED DECK AND EXTERIOR STAIR GIVE JUST A TOUCH OF ASYMMETRY. THIS IS A SOMEWHAT PROSAIC DESCRIPTION, ALTHOUGH IT IS QUITE FACTUAL ABOUT, I THINK, A QUITE BEAUTIFUL HOUSE.

I MULL OVER SOME DESIGN PROBLEMS FOR DAYS AS IF THEY WERE ZEN KOANS, AND I SOLVE THEM WITH A SHOUT OF "EUREKA!" I HAVE ALSO OFTEN DREAMED OF DOZENS OF ALMOST TRANSCENDENTALLY BEAUTIFUL BUILDINGS. I HAVE GONE DOWN TO MY OFFICE IN TOWN AT 9 OR 10 P.M. TO START DRAWING. ONCE, WHEN A ROOF PROBLEM TO A SPIRAL CHAPEL PLAN WAS SOLVED IN A FITFUL SLEEP, I JUMPED OUT OF BED AND DREW FROM 3 TO 7 A.M.

SO, IN MY OWN EXPERIENCE, THE DESIGN PROCESS IS A GRAB BAG OF INSPIRATION, MEMORY, ALMOST COMPUTER-LIKE COMPARISONS, AND, IMPORTANTLY, INSIGHTS FROM AREAS OTHER THAN ARCHITECTURE—A PHILOSOPHY OR AN ASPECT OF NATURE—A FLOWER, FOR INSTANCE, OR A GEOMETRICAL SHAPE NOTICED AT RANDOM.

EACH BUILDING IS NOT A COMPLETELY NEW IDEA. I THINK IT WAS HEGEL WHO SAID THAT EVERY PHILOSOPHER IS TRYING TO WORK OUT ONE GREAT IDEA. THE SECRET IS TO HAVE AT LEAST ONE! FOR INSTANCE, WRIGHT'S USONIA HOUSES WERE ALMOST ALL DERIVATIONS FROM ONLY ONE GREAT IDEA SYSTEM AND A FEW LESSER IDEAS— BASICALLY DIFFERENT MODULES. HIS DETAILS REMAINED REMARKABLY

CONSISTENT AND EVOLVED ONLY SLOWLY, OVER DECADES.

ANY CREATIVE ARCHITECT (OR ARTIST OF ANY SORT) WILL TELL YOU HE OR SHE HAS BEEN UNPACKING ONE IDEA FOR YEARS— TAKE MONDRIAN'S PAINTINGS, FOR INSTANCE. UNFORTUNATELY, ARCHITECTS' CLIENTS USUALLY LIKE OUR OLDER DESIGNS. FOR NOW, I AM BURNT OUT ON RECTANGLES AND SOMEWHAT BURNT OUT ON ANGLES, EVEN CURVES. WHAT'S LEFT? A MIXTURE OF THEM. A FAMOUS ARCHITECT SAID, "ALL WE HAVE IS THE FIVE PLATONIC SOLIDS. THAT'S IT, NO MORE SHAPES TO WORK WITH!"

I WOULD ALSO LIKE TO ADDRESS WHAT IS, FOR ME, A SPIRITUAL ASPECT OF DESIGN. A PLAN, TO ME, IS LIKE A MANDALA—A VISUAL FORM OF THE SOUL. WRIGHT POINTED OUT THAT A GOOD PLAN SHOULD BE A WORK OF ART ON ITS OWN. IT MUST HAVE BALANCE, BUT A COMPLEX BALANCE. WHEN I DESIGN A COMPLEX BUT BEAUTIFULLY BALANCED PLAN, I FEEL THAT, NOT ONLY AM I ADDING HARMONY AND BEAUTY TO THE WORLD, BUT I AM ALSO BALANCING MY OWN SOUL (OR PSYCHE, IF YOU WILL).

THIS HARMONY FADES OUT BOTH IN TIME AND SPACE. IN TIME, IT INFLUENCES ME

MOST POWERFULLY WHILE DESIGNING AND IMMEDIATELY AFTER, AND THEN TO A LESSER EXTENT ONLY YEARS LATER. EVEN A CONSTRUCTED BUILDING LOOKS AND FEELS MORE HARMONIOUS BEFORE THE STAIN FADES TOO MUCH, OR WITH A GARBAGE TRUCK IN THE DRIVEWAY, OR DURING A FAMILY ARGUMENT, OR WITH SOME HEAVY METAL MUSIC ON IN THE BACKGROUND. THE HARMONY INCREASES AND DECREASES AND FADES OUT AS IT MERGES WITH THE NEIGHBOR'S YARD, THE SUBDIVISION, AND SO ON. AND WHAT IS THE HOUSE? THE BOARDS, THE BRICKS, THE SHAPE?

THE BUDDHIST KING, MILINDA, ASKED SOME FAMOUS QUESTIONS REGARDING THE "SELF." THE EARLY BUDDHISTS DID NOT APPARENTLY BELIEVE IN A SELF. THE HINDU PHILOSOPHERS SPOKE OF ATMAN OR "THE SELF," AND THE BUDDHISTS OF ANATMAN OR "NO-SELF." BY ANALOGY, KING MILINDA ASKED OF A CART WHEEL, IS THE WHEEL THE SPOKES, THE RIM, OR THE CENTER HOLE? HOW MANY SPOKES COULD YOU TAKE AWAY AND STILL HAVE A WHEEL?

THE SCOTTISH SKEPTICAL PHILOSOPHER, DAVID HUME, SIMILARLY ASKED, "WHERE IS THE SELF?" THE MORE HE LOOKED FOR IT, THE LESS HE COULD FIND IT. A POSSIBLE

ANSWER TO BOTH MILINDA AND HUME IS THAT THE SELF IS THE "SEER"—THE SUBJECT, NOT A POSSIBLE OBJECT; THE FORM, NOT THE MATTER.

I BRING THIS UP BECAUSE I READ SOMEWHERE THAT A FEW OF WRIGHT'S EARLY USONIAS HAVE BEEN RESTORED TO THE EXTENT THAT ALMOST NOTHING IS LEFT OF THE ORIGINAL BUILDING MATERIALS, OR THE MATTER. IS IT THE SAME HOUSE OR NOT? I WOULD ANSWER YES AND NO—A SAGE ANSWER, NO DOUBT, BUT AN ASYMMETRICAL ONE. IN ONE SENSE, IT IS NOT THE SAME HOUSE, BUT TO A LESSER EXTENT, IT WAS NOT THE SAME HOUSE FROM YEAR TO YEAR OR HOUR TO HOUR. OF COURSE, WE'RE ALL FAMILIAR WITH THE IDEA THAT EVERY SEVEN YEARS, WE HAVE NEW ATOMS IN OUR BODIES; TO SOME (ANALOGOUS) EXTENT, SO DO OUR BUILDINGS.

SO IN ONE SENSE, BUILDINGS CHANGE, BUT IN ANOTHER SENSE, I WILL SIDE WITH PLATO AND SAY THAT IN SOME WAY THE FORM OF THE HOUSE IS ETERNAL. WRIGHT'S ROBIE HOUSE IS AS ETERNAL AS HIS UNBUILT DESIGNS IN SOME SENSE—BUT NOT IN A COMPLETE SENSE. ARCHITECTURE IS NOT JUST THE PURE FORM, IT IS THE MATTER ALSO—THE ROTTING WOOD AND GROUT, THE

THE **NEW VENETIAN**
A MODULAR DESIGN.....
SPECULATIVE OFFICE/APARTMENT BUILDING
FT. LAUDERDALE, FLORIDA
CHARLES G. WOODS, A.I.A., ARCHITECT

v.e. van de venter delineator

RENDERING BY VINCE VAN DE VENTER

LEAKING TOILETS, AND SO ON. IT IS A PERFECT MEETING OF FORM AND MATTER, HEAVEN AND EARTH. IT HAS THE ABSTRACT FORM LIKE THAT OF MUSIC (GOETHE CALLED ARCHITECTURE BRILLIANTLY "FROZEN MUSIC") AND, ON THE OTHER END, IT HAS THE MATTER LIKE THAT OF THE PRACTICAL ART OF POTTERY. THE GREEKS CALLED IT "THE MOTHER ART."

I BELIEVE THAT MY MODULE SYSTEM PROVIDES AN EASY WAY TO LEND INTELLIGIBILITY (IF NOT, OF NECESSITY, ART) TO A STRUCTURE. THE MODULE IS THE IDENTITY, FORM, ESSENCE, AND BEING OF THE DESIGN IN CONTRAST TO THE BECOMING OF MATTER OF THE BUILT STRUCTURE. WHERE DOES THE FORM AND MATTER COME FROM THAT ARCHITECTS USE HUMBLY OR AS MAD MAGICIANS? PERSONALLY, AND WITHOUT SPENDING ANOTHER TWENTY PAGES ARGUING FOR IT, I BELIEVE, ALONG WITH THE CATHEDRAL BUILDERS, MOZART, BRAHMS, AND WRIGHT, THAT IT IS FROM GOD, OR AT LEAST GOD AS NATURE (WITH A CAPITAL "N"), BUT NOT JUST FROM MY PUNY SELF. I DO NOT SEEM TO CREATE EITHER THE NUMBER FOUR, THE TRIANGLE, OR THE LAW OF CONTRADICTION IN LOGIC. I SEEM TO DISCOVER IT. IN THE SAME WAY, MY ARCHITECTURAL CREATION IS ALSO IN PART A DISCOVERY, AS WELL AS A SEARCH—A SEARCH FOR THE BEAUTY OF INTELLECT.

SUMMER HOUSE FOR THE JAMILS AND THE MAHMOODS

MODULE HOUSE DESIGNS

THIS HOUSE WAS DESIGNED FOR <u>TWO</u> FAMILIES TO SHARE ON WEEKENDS, DURING SUMMERS AND VACATIONS, AND POSSIBLY LATER IN RETIREMENT. THE CLIENTS WERE MUSLIM BY RELIGION, THEY WERE PROFESSIONALS, AND THEY WERE ON A TIGHT BUDGET BECAUSE THEY HAD CHILDREN TO PUT THROUGH COLLEGE. THE HOUSE WAS ALSO TO HAVE A DETACHED BUT MATCHING TWO-AND-A-HALF CAR GARAGE (NOT SHOWN).

THE CLIENTS ORIGINALLY SUGGESTED A TWO-STORY DESIGN, THINKING EACH FAMILY COULD LIVE ON ONE FLOOR. I DID NOT THINK THAT A GOOD IDEA, FOR IT WOULD REQUIRE <u>TWO</u> LIVING/KITCHEN/DINING AREAS—AND THE BUDGET FOR THE HOUSE WAS LESS THAN $150,000. IN ADDITION, THE FAMILY UPSTAIRS WOULD HAVE A NICER ENVIRONMENT BECAUSE OF THE HIGHER CEILINGS THAT I PLANNED, AS WELL AS A BETTER VIEW.

THE TWO FAMILIES WERE CLOSE AND COMFORTABLE TOGETHER, SO I SUGGESTED A ONE-FLOOR RANCH HOUSE WITH EARTH BERMS. THE HOUSE IS 2000 SQUARE FEET PLUS GARAGE AND STORAGE. AT THE LAST MINUTE, THE CLIENT INSISTED THAT THE TWO LARGE, COMPARTMENTALIZED BATHS BE MADE INTO FOUR. I THOUGHT—AND STILL THINK—THIS WAS EXCESSIVE. IF REDESIGNING, I WOULD ALSO FIND A WAY TO ENLARGE THE KITCHEN. A TWO-STORY HOUSE WOULD HAVE BEEN CONSIDERABLY LESS EXPENSIVE—EXCEPT THAT WITH THE 3' EARTH BERM, THE FOOTINGS WERE PLACED JUST BELOW THE CONCRETE SLAB, WHICH SAVED MONEY ON FROST FOOTINGS.

* CONSTRUCTION PLANS AVAILABLE.

THE JAMIL/MAHMOOD
SUMMER HOUSE
1

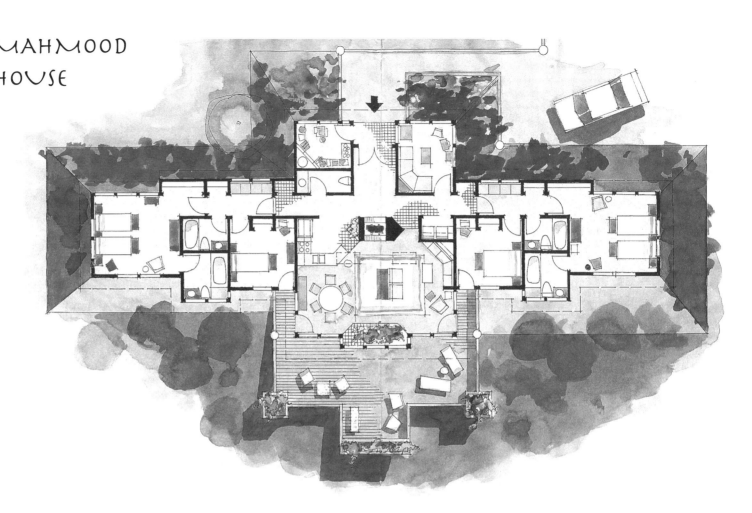

ALTHOUGH SUFFICIENTLY GLAZED, I USED LESS GLASS THAN IS USUAL FOR ME. THE 4′
SQUARE MODULE, WHICH WAS TO BE SCORED INTO THE DYED CONCRETE FLOOR, IS CLEARLY
SEEN IN THIS PLAN. UNFORTUNATELY, ON THE EVE OF CONSTRUCTION, THE CLIENTS DECIDED
TO PUT OFF BUILDING FOR THREE YEARS.

A NOTE ON THE PERSPECTIVE RENDERING: I ESPECIALLY LIKE THE TREE THAT MAC DREW IN
THE FOREGROUND, WHICH BREAKS THE FRAME AS IN A JAPANESE PRINT OR A WESTERN
MEDIEVAL THREE-PART DRAWING.

GREAT ROOM SECTION
■ THE JAMIL/MAHMOOD HOUSE

BROWN RESIDENCE ELK LAKE, PA

NATURAL ARCHITECTURE / C.G. WOODS

THIS HOUSE WAS DESIGNED FOR SHAWN BROWN, THE BROTHER-IN-LAW OF ONE OF MY BEST FRIENDS, ARTIE BRYANT. HE ORIGINALLY CAME TO ME FOR AN ADDITION/REMODELING TO A SMALL HOUSE OR CABIN, BUT I SUGGESTED SELLING HIS OLD CABIN, BUYING THE LOT NEXT DOOR, AND LOOKING AT MY SKETCHES FOR A COMPLETELY NEW HOUSE. HE SAID, "CHARLES, YOU BASTARD! IT'S GREAT! HOW CAN I STAY WITH MY OLD HOUSE NOW?"

UNFORTUNATELY, AFTER THE FINAL DESIGN DRAWINGS, MR. BROWN'S JOB WAS TRANSFERRED AND HE HAD TO BUY ANOTHER HOUSE QUICKLY. HE STILL HOPES TO BUILD THE HOUSE IN THE FUTURE.

LUCKILY, EDITOR LARRY ERICKSON INCLUDED THREE OF MY HOUSES IN AN ARTICLE IN BETTER HOMES AND GARDENS BUILDING IDEAS MAGAZINE (SPRING 1994) AND WE SOLD STOCK PLANS FOR IT. A MRS. COOPER BOUGHT THE PLANS AND HIRED A GOOD LOCAL ARCHITECT TO MAKE MINOR CHANGES IN ACCORDANCE WITH HER LOT AND PROGRAM AND BUILT IT FOR APPROXIMATELY $75 PER SQUARE FOOT. (SEE PHOTOS IN "CONSTRUCTION" SECTION LATER IN THIS BOOK.)

ALTHOUGH NOT OBVIOUSLY DERIVATIVE, I WAS INSPIRED BY TWO OF FRANK LLOYD WRIGHT'S HOUSES: THE STURGES HOUSE (SEE THE PERSPECTIVE WITH LARGE CANTILEVERED DECKS) AND FALLING WATER (SEE SIDE ELEVATION). THE HOUSE IS 4500 GROSS SQUARE FEET (PLUS DECKS). THE 4' SQUARE MODULE IS ESPECIALLY AND CLEARLY UNDERSTANDABLE IN THIS GOOD-SIZED, RECTILINEAR PLAN. (THE LOWER LEVEL PLAN IS NOT SHOWN.)

* CONSTRUCTION PLANS AVAILABLE.

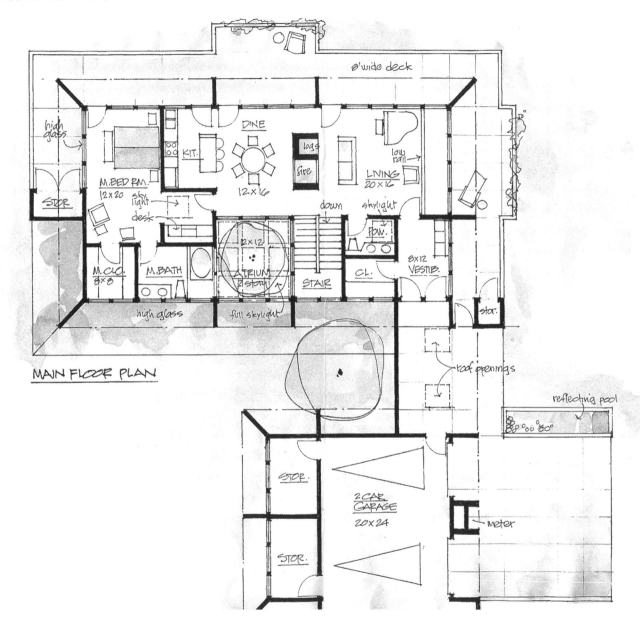

high glass

DINE

KIT.

log$

low rail

M.BED RM.
12 x 20

LIVING
20 x 16

12 x 16

sky light

desk

down

skylight

STOR

pow.

8 x 12
VESTIB.

M.CLO.
8 x 8

M.BATH

12 x 12

ATRIUM
2 story

CL.

STAIR

high glass

full skylight

stor.

MAIN FLOOR PLAN

roof openings

reflecting pool

STOR.

2 CAR
GARAGE
20 x 24

meter

STOR.

SOUTH ELEVATION

WEST-EAST SECTION

Lake

NATURAL ARCHITECTURE / C.G. WOODS DESIGN ●

BROWN RESIDENCE · ELK LAKE, PA

LIVING ROOM PERSPECTIVE LOOKING NORTH

BROWN RESIDENCE   ELK LAKE, PA   NATURAL ARCHITECTURE / CGWOODS

BRIAN COBB IS A YOUNG FRIEND OF MINE. WHEN HE WAS SIXTEEN YEARS OLD, I HAD AN
OFFICE DOWN THE HALL FROM HIS PARENTS' PRINTING BUSINESS. HE OFTEN SAID TO ME,
"WHEN I GROW UP, I AM GOING TO HAVE YOU DESIGN MY HOUSE!" MANY PEOPLE MAKE
SIMILAR PROMISES—FEW MAKE GOOD ON THEM! THE YEARS WENT BY, WE NODDED TO ONE
ANOTHER ON THE STREET, AND THEN FOUR YEARS AGO, I HEARD A KNOCK AT MY DOOR AND
THERE WAS BRIAN (NOW TWENTY-SIX) WITH A FRIEND.

HE ASKED ME STRAIGHT OUT, "CAN YOU BUILD ME A HOUSE FOR $100,000?" I REPLIED,
"MAYBE." HE PERSISTED, "A REAL STRIKING ONE?" "WELL . . . ," I SAID. THERE WAS NOT
MUCH LEFT FOR A FEE, SO I DID IT FOR ONE-QUARTER OF MY REGULAR FEE. AT LEAST, IT WAS
LOCAL AND HE WOULD LET ME DO SOMETHING STRIKING.

THE ROOF RUNS DIAGONALLY FROM CORNER TO CORNER OF THE SQUARE PLAN. IT CREATES A
UNIQUE GEOMETRICAL SHAPE ON A SIMPLE SQUARE PLAN. WRIGHT USED A SIMILAR ROOF IN
THE 1950S, AND EXPO '67 HAD A HOUSING EXHIBIT WITH THIS STYLE OF ROOF. I DISCOVERED
THE ROOF MYSELF FROM ARCHITECT DENNIS BLAIR, WHO WAS A STUDENT OF FRANK LLOYD
WRIGHT. DENNIS IS A GREAT ARCHITECT AND I WAS LUCKY TO DO MUCH OF MY APPRENTICE
WORK UNDER HIM ON AND OFF FOR OVER TEN YEARS. IN HIS OWN WORK, HE HAS CREATED
EVEN MORE INCREDIBLE AND COMPLEX DESIGNS WITH THIS ROOF IDEA. I LATER FOUND A
SIMILAR ROOF ON A TWELFTH-CENTURY GOTHIC CATHEDRAL!

* CONSTRUCTION DRAWINGS AVAILABLE.

THE BRIAN COBB HOUSE
3

THE HOUSE, AS RENDERED WITH SEPARATE GARAGE, PROVED TO BE TOO EXPENSIVE, SO WE PUT THE GARAGE IN THE BASEMENT. I ALSO STEEPENED THE ROOF TO INCREASE THE LOFT SPACE AND ADDED A U-SHAPED STAIRCASE. THE HOUSE WAS BUILT IN 1993 AND WILL BE LANDSCAPED AND FURNISHED IN SUBSEQUENT YEARS, AS FINANCES PERMIT. (SEE CONSTRUCTION PHOTO.) THE RENDERINGS APPEARED IN <u>BETTER HOMES AND GARDENS BUILDING IDEAS</u> (SPRING 1994).

THE HOUSE IS BUILT WITHIN A SMALL AIRPORT SUBDIVISION. MANY VISITING PILOTS SEE IT UPON LANDING AND WALK OVER TO VISIT. IT DOES LOOK SORT OF LIKE A LARGE SPACE BIRD WITH FOLDED WINGS.

WE COULDN'T, HOWEVER, MAKE THE $100,000 FIGURE, BUT BRIAN AGREED TO $125,000 AND WE JUST BARELY MADE THAT. (I THINK IT WOULD COST AT LEAST $150,000 TO DO NOW, HOWEVER.) THE HOUSE IS 2500 GROSS SQUARE FEET (PLUS DECKS). I NEVER WORKED SO HARD FOR SUCH A SMALL FEE—OR ENJOYED IT SO MUCH!

DESIGN: CHARLES G. WILLIS
RENDERING BY MALCOLM WELLS

THE BRIAN COBB HOUSE

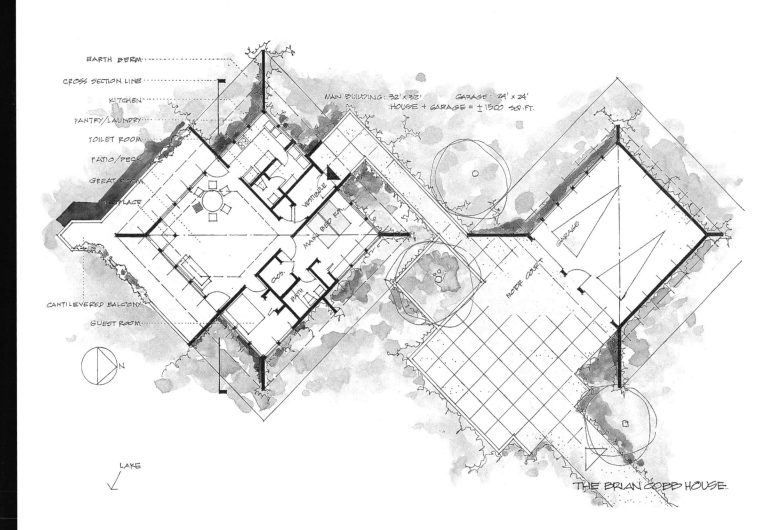

EARTH BERM

CROSS SECTION LINE

KITCHEN

PANTRY/LAUNDRY

TOILET ROOM

PATIO/DECK

GREAT ROOM

FIREPLACE

CANTILEVERED BALCONY

GUEST ROOM

N

LAKE

MAIN BUILDING: 32' x 32'   GARAGE: 24' x 24'
HOUSE + GARAGE = ± 1500 SQ. FT.

VESTIBULE

MAIN BED RM.

CLO.

PATH

GARAGE

MOTOR COURT

THE BRIAN COBB HOUSE

CROSS SECTION

ENTRANCE ELEVATION

THE BRIAN COBB HOUSE

A COUNTRY RESIDENCE FOR MR. & MRS. STANTON J. FREEMAN

NATURAL ARCHITECTURE / JOHN J. MARTIN, ARCHITECT
CHARLES G. WOODS DESIGN

A COUNTRY RESIDENCE FOR MR. AND MRS. STAN FREEMAN

(WITH ARCHITECT JOHN J. MARTIN) 4

THIS WAS DESIGNED FOR STAN FREEMAN, A NOTED FINANCIER, HIS WIFE JACQUELINE, A MODEL (NOW A STUDENT), AND THEIR TWO CHILDREN. STAN KNEW ERROL FLYNN SHORTLY BEFORE HIS DEATH, WHEN STAN WAS QUITE YOUNG. AS FLYNN IS ONE OF MY FANTASY HEROES, I FELT AS IF I HAD "TOUCHED THE HAND THAT TOUCHED THE HAND"! I LIKED STAN INSTANTLY, AND HE REMINDED ME OF A SOMEWHAT OLDER VERSION OF MYSELF. HE WANTED A "MASTERPIECE."

THIS HOUSE IS DESIGNED ON MY USUAL 4' SQUARE MODULE AND ALSO ON LARGER SQUARE MODULES TURNED 45°. IT IS 4500 SQUARE FEET (LOWER LEVEL IS NOT SHOWN) AND IT IS QUITE EXCITING—IT EXPLODES FROM A CENTRAL POINT LIKE A KABBALISTIC SYMBOL OF CREATION OR A TANTRIC SYMBOL OF THE SOUL-UNIVERSE. THE DECKS LITERALLY WRAP AROUND THE HOUSE. MUCH OF THE DRAMA OF THE HOUSE IS CREATED BY THE LIFTED CLERESTORY ROOFS. THE HOUSE IS ALSO EARTH-BERMED.

STAN WAS LIVING PART-TIME IN MY TOWN OF HONESDALE, PENNSYLVANIA, AND PART-TIME IN NEW YORK CITY, THREE HOURS AWAY. AFTER STARTING CONSTRUCTION DRAWINGS, HE MOVED TO FLORIDA. I DID ANOTHER ONE-STORY DESIGN FOR HIM (SEE CRAGGED ROCK) AS A VACATION HOUSE. THIS ONE IS STILL UP IN THE AIR, WHICH HAPPENS TO ARCHITECTS A LOT!

MAC'S DRAWINGS ARE GREAT—I COULD SEE THE INTERIOR PERSPECTIVE HANGING IN THE MUSEUM OF MODERN ART.

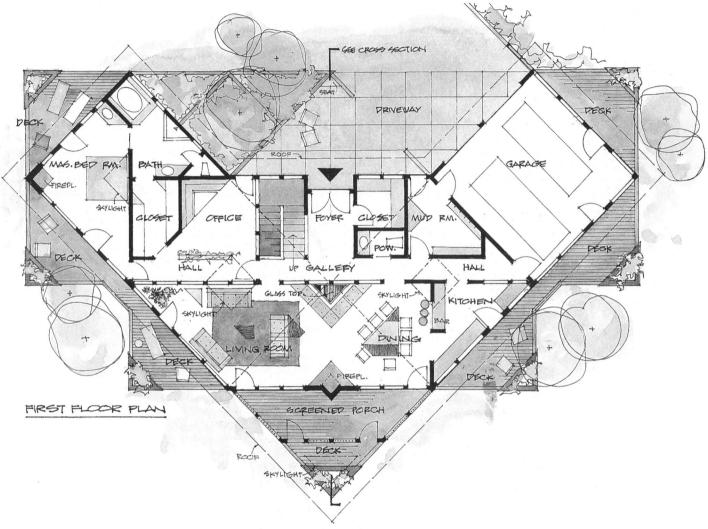

FIRST FLOOR PLAN

A COUNTRY RESIDENCE FOR MR. & MRS. STANTON J. FREEMAN
NATURAL ARCHITECTURE / JOHN J. MARTIN, ARCHITECT   CHARLES G. WOODS DESIGN

A COUNTRY RESIDENCE FOR
MR. AND MRS. STAN FREEMAN
4

INTERIOR PERSPECTIVE OF THE FREEMAN RESIDENCE

NATURAL ARCHITECTURE / JOHN J. MARTIN, ARCHITECT
CHARLES G. WOODS DESIGN

59

A COUNTRY RESIDENCE FOR MR. & MRS. STANTON J. FREEMAN

NATURAL ARCHITECTURE / JOHN J. MARTIN, ARCHITECT
CHARLES G. WOODS DESIGN

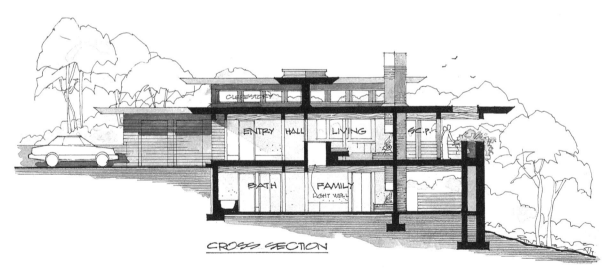

CLERESTORY

ENTRY HALL   LIVING   SC.P.

BATH   FAMILY
LIGHT WELL

CROSS SECTION

A COUNTRY RESIDENCE FOR MR. & MRS. STANTON J. FREEMAN
NATURAL ARCHITECTURE / JOHN J. MARTIN, ARCHITECT   CHARLES G. WOODS DESIGN

THIS HOUSE WAS DESIGNED FOR BOB AND LINDA TERRY AND FAMILY OF ITHACA, NEW YORK. IT IS A 3600-SQUARE-FOOT, TWO-AND-A-HALF-STORY UNDERGROUND HOUSE. SINCE MAC IS "THE FATHER OF UNDERGROUND ARCHITECTURE," HE LIKED THIS ONE, AS DID I. THE HOUSE WAS TO HAVE REINFORCED CONCRETE FLOORS AND WALLS, WITH STEEL JOISTS AND DECKING, ROOF AND SUBFLOOR, AND STONE VENEER EXTERIOR WALLS. I LOVE THE HONEY-COLORED STONE. THE HOUSE IS A LARGE SQUARE, TURNED 45°, LIKE THE COBB HOUSE AND A LATER DESIGN, THE LOW-COST PROTOTYPE.

(NOTE: THERE IS A SLIGHT DISCREPANCY BETWEEN THE EXTERIOR PERSPECTIVE ENTRY DETAIL AND THE FLOOR PLAN.) THERE IS A TWO-STORY LIVING AREA WITH A LOFT BEDROOM/TV ROOM. I WOULD HAVE LIKED A LIVING ROOM THAT WAS A LITTLE LARGER. THE PLAN WAS DICTATED A LITTLE MORE BY THE CLIENT THAN IS USUAL FOR ME. THE CLIENTS LOVED IT, BUT WHEN THEY SAW MY MORE-RECENT CURVED DESIGNS, THEY ASKED FOR SOMETHING SIMILAR (SEE NAUTILUS).

I ADD A LOT OF IDEAS TO MAC'S RENDERINGS, BUT THE ADORABLE FLAT DOG ON THE RUG ON THE INTERIOR PERSPECTIVE IS PURE MAC.

THE TERRY RESIDENCE 1
5

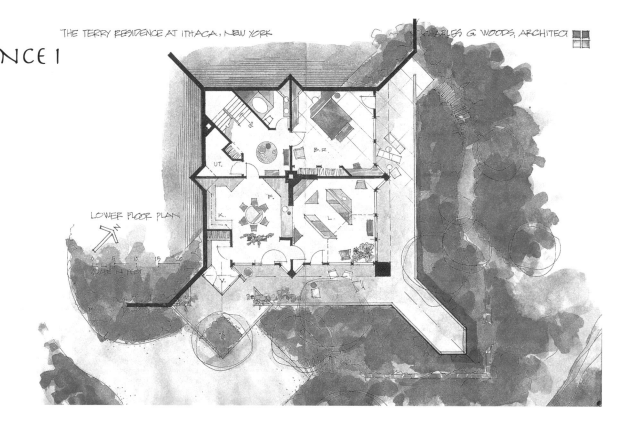

LOWER FLOOR PLAN

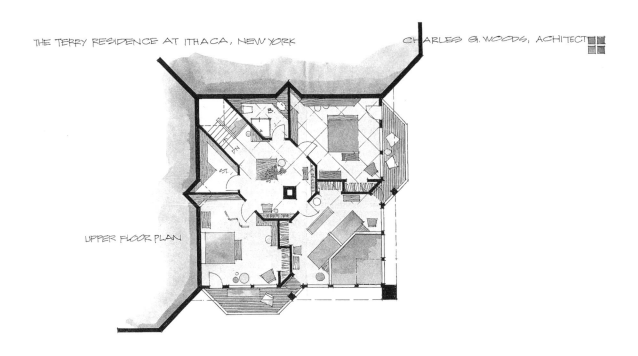

UPPER FLOOR PLAN

THE TERRY RESIDENCE AT ITHACA, NEW YORK

CHARLES G. WOODS, ARCHITECT

"SNOWFLAKE"

THE SISSON HOUSE / AERIAL VIEW FROM THE SOUTH   CHARLES G. WOODS, AIA, ARCHITECT

ALTHOUGH MY WORK HAS BEEN IN MAGAZINES SINCE 1979 AND I WAS A JUNIOR PARTNER IN A FIRM CALLED NATURAL ARCHITECTURE, I FINALLY PASSED ALL OF MY ARCHITECTURE TESTS AND RECEIVED REGISTRATION ONLY IN 1993. SO THIS HOUSE AND THE TERRY RESIDENCE WERE MY FIRST DESIGNS AS A REGISTERED ARCHITECT.

THIS HOUSE IS DESIGNED ON MY 4' BY 4' SQUARE MODULE BUT CUTS ACROSS IT (LIKE THE COUNTY RESIDENCE FOR MR. AND MRS. STAN FREEMAN), CREATING A 45° ANGLE. THAT MEANS THE ANGLED GLASS IS NO LONGER 4'0" O.C., BUT 5'-SOMETHING (PYTHAGOREAN THEOREM). MY EARLIER STULTZ RESIDENCE IS A SIMILAR SHAPE, BUT ON THAT DESIGN ALL GLASS COLUMNS ARE ON THE 4' MODULE BY A TRICK I NO LONGER USE. IMAGINE THREE SHOE BOXES WITH COLUMN LINES DRAWN AT 4'0" O.C. AT ¼" SCALE. I CAN THEN CONNECT THEM AT THE CORNERS TO CREATE A 30° OR 45° (OR ANY ANGLE) PLAN. YOU CAN EASILY SEE THAT THIS DOES NOT INFLUENCE THE GLASS MODULE, BUT THERE IS AN AWKWARD POLYGON CREATED IN THE REAR AND WHEN THE REAR WALL IS BUILT AND THE GLASS IS ON THE 4' MODULE—THE LAST WINDOW ON EACH SIDE IS NOT ON THE MODULE. ALSO, FLOOR MODULES IN CONCRETE DON'T WORK WELL IN THIS SAME INTERSECTION. IT'S NOT UNSIGHTLY AND, ON THE STULTZ'S HOUSE, IT WORKED WELL. BUT THE SISSON RESIDENCE IS A STILL MORE COMPLEX DESIGN—IN PLAN, ELEVATION, AND ROOFS—SO I NEEDED A CONSISTENT USE OF THE MODULE. THE WHOLE COMPLEX PLAN SUPERIMPOSES PERFECTLY OVER A LARGE GRID OF SQUARE MODULES.

* CONSTRUCTION DRAWINGS AVAILABLE.

SNOWFLAKE

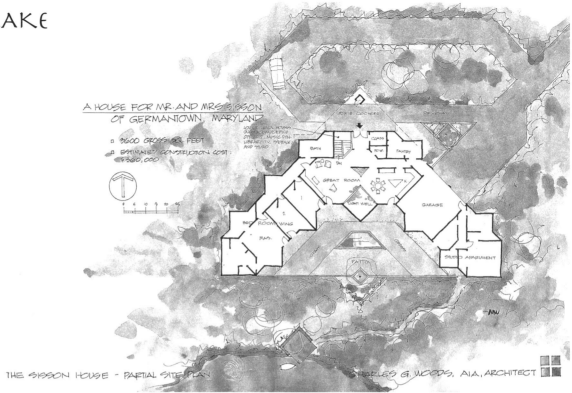

A HOUSE FOR MR. AND MRS. SISSON
OF GERMANTOWN, MARYLAND

□ 3600 GROSS SQ. FEET
□ ESTIMATED CONSTRUCTION COST:
  $360,000

THE SISSON HOUSE - PARTIAL SITE PLAN   CHARLES G. WOODS, AIA, ARCHITECT

THE PLAN HAS A LOWER LEVEL IN THE MIDDLE OF THE HOUSE (NOT SHOWN), LIGHTED BY THE

LIGHTWELL AND AN ADDED FIRE EXIT ON THE NORTH SIDE. I TEND TO THINK NOW, THOUGH, THAT

THE RECTANGULAR SOLAR COLLECTORS ON CENTER ROOFS LOOK OUT OF PLACE IN THE DESIGN.

MAC'S BIRD'S-EYE PERSPECTIVE IS BEAUTIFUL. BIRD'S-EYE PERSPECTIVES ARE OFTEN USED BY

ARCHITECTS BECAUSE A WHOLE COMPLEX SHAPE CAN BE TAKEN IN—IN ONE DRAWING—BUT

IT DOES <u>NOT</u> ALLOW YOU TO SEE THE BUILDING AS IT IS USUALLY SEEN.

PARTLY BECAUSE OF THIS BOOK, I DECIDED TO START ADDING SOME EYE-LEVEL AND

NIGHTTIME DRAWINGS. THE FIRST WAS MAC'S MAGNIFICENT NORTHSIDE DRAWING. HE ALSO

DID A GREAT JOB ON THE DIFFICULT INTERIOR PERSPECTIVES. THE SISSONS ARE COMPUTER
EXPERTS AND MIGHT CONVINCE ME TO USE SOME COMPUTER GRAPHICS IN THE FUTURE—
THEY HAVE SENT ME SOME NICE COMPUTER DRAWINGS OF THE HOUSE—BUT I THINK THEY
WOULD AGREE THAT MAC'S HAND ADDS SOMETHING EXTRA THAT IS HARD TO QUANTIFY.

THOUGH THE PLAN HAS STAYED REMARKABLY THE SAME (IT HAS BEEN FLIPPED) AND NO
EXTERIOR WALLS HAVE CHANGED, IT HAS DEVELOPED AND BEEN IMPROVED IN INNUMERABLE
WAYS BY THE CLIENT'S INPUT TO IT AS A HOME. I TOLD THEM THEY COULD MAKE ANY
REASONABLE CHANGES, PER MY APPROVAL AND ON THE MODULE, AND THEY TOOK ME AT
MY WORD. THIS WAS DONE REASONABLY PAINLESSLY—EVEN THOUGH WE MET ONLY
ONCE—BY THE COMMUNICATION EASE MADE AVAILABLE BY THE MODULE SYSTEM.

PRELIMINARY BIDS HAVE COME IN AT ONLY $75 PER SQUARE FOOT (WITH VERY SIMPLE
FINISHES). BETTER-QUALITY FINISHES ARE AROUND $100 TO $125 PER SQUARE FOOT. THIS IS
STILL GOOD, SINCE I BELIEVE THE AVERAGE NATIONAL PRICE FOR AN ARCHITECT-DESIGNED
HOUSE IS QUOTED AT AROUND $125 PER SQUARE FOOT.

THE SISSONS HAVE BEEN ALMOST PERFECT CLIENTS. IF THEY WANTED TO CHANGE SOMETHING,
THEY FUNNELED IT THROUGH ME AND DID NOT TRY TO IMPOSE IT FROM THE OUTSIDE. THE
HOUSE IS CURRENTLY BEING BUILT, IN A SLIGHTLY REVISED FORM, BY A.I.A. AWARD-
WINNING BUILDER, GREG CURREY.

SNOWFLAKE
6

FOR MR. & MRS. SISSON, GERMANTOWN, MD.

THE SISSON HOUSE / GREAT ROOM PERSPECTIVE

CHARLES G. WOODS, AIA, ARCHITECT

THE SISSON HOUSE

CHARLES G. WOODS, AIA, ARCHITECT

THIS HOUSE WAS DESIGNED FOR EDITOR BOB WILSON AND <u>BETTER HOMES AND GARDEN BUILDING IDEAS</u> MAGAZINE. THEY TOLD ME THAT IF I COULD GET A FAMILY-SIZE HOUSE BUILT FOR $40 PER SQUARE FOOT, THEY WOULD PUBLISH IT. I GOT A BID FROM MY BUILDING CONSULTANT, LARRY WILSON, FOR $40 PER SQUARE FOOT BY USING EVERY TRICK IN THE BOOK. FIRST OFF, THE HOUSE IS MEANT TO LOOK LIKE A "HOUSE" AT A FAST GLANCE, SO, FOR MY INSPIRATION, I WENT BACK TO WRIGHT'S PRAIRIE STYLE (AROUND 1910)—THE ONES HE DID ON THE SMALL PARK RIDGE, ILLINOIS, LOTS. I TURNED THE WHOLE SQUARE PLAN (UPPER AND LOWER PLANS NOT SHOWN) 45° TO THE STREET, CREATING A MORE ANGULAR DESIGN. THE HOUSE ALSO HAS, I BELIEVE, A LITTLE JAPANESE AND EVEN POSTMODERN "GRIDISM" TO IT—THAT'S AS FAR AS I GO WITH POSTMODERNISM.

A UNIQUE ASPECT OF THE DESIGN IS THAT THE HOUSE USES A <u>VERTICAL</u> 4' MODULE, JUST LIKE THE PLAN. THIS NECESSITATED SOME RETHINKING OF THE FLOOR AND WINDOW DETAILS, BUT LOOK HOW NEAT IT IS ON THE EXTERIOR PERSPECTIVE! NO THICK FLOOR LINE. I WANTED THE BALLOONS IN THE DRAWING TO HINT AT EARLY INFLUENCES ON MY THINKING: JULES VERNE AND H. G. WELLS. FOR $40 PER SQUARE FOOT, <u>VERY</u> SIMPLE FINISHES HAD TO BE USED, SUCH AS PLYWOOD SIDING AND VINYL FLOORING, BUT EVEN BETTER FINISHES WOULD STILL BRING UP THE COST TO ONLY $50 TO $60 PER SQUARE FOOT. THIS IS A GOOD RECTILINEAR PLAN FOR UNDERSTANDING THE MODULE.

* CONSTRUCTION PLANS AVAILABLE.

PROTOTYPE LOW-COST HOUSE
AN ALL-WOOD, ENERGY-EFFICIENT FAMILY HOUSE
$40/ SQ·FT.

BUILDING CONSULTANT: LARRY WILSON
CHARLES G. WOODS, A.I.A., ARCHITECT

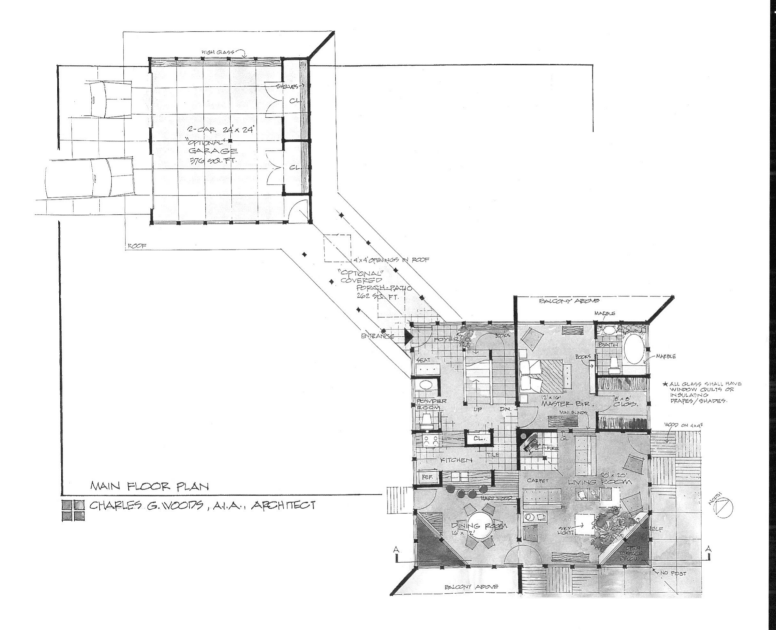

HIGH GLASS

SHELVES
CL.

2-CAR 24' x 24'
"OPTIONAL"
GARAGE
576 SQ. FT.

CL.

ROOF

4'x4' OPENINGS IN ROOF

"OPTIONAL"
COVERED
PORCH-PATIO
262 SQ. FT.

BALCONY ABOVE

MARBLE

ENTRANCE
FOYER
BOOKS
BATH

SEAT
BOOKS
MARBLE

★ ALL GLASS SHALL HAVE
WINDOW QUILTS OR
INSULATING
DRAPES/SHADES.

POWDER
ROOM
UP DN.
12' x 16'
MASTER B.R.
18' x 8'
CLOS.
MINI BLINDS

WOOD ON 4x4s

CL.
FIRE

KITCHEN
TILE
GL
20' x 20'

REF.
CARPET
LIVING ROOM

MAIN FLOOR PLAN

CHARLES G. WOODS, A.I.A., ARCHITECT
HARDWOOD
SKY
LIGHT
SHELF

NORTH

DINING ROOM
16' x 2'
OPEN
TO SPACE BELOW
NO POST

BALCONY ABOVE

LOW-COST PROTOTYPE

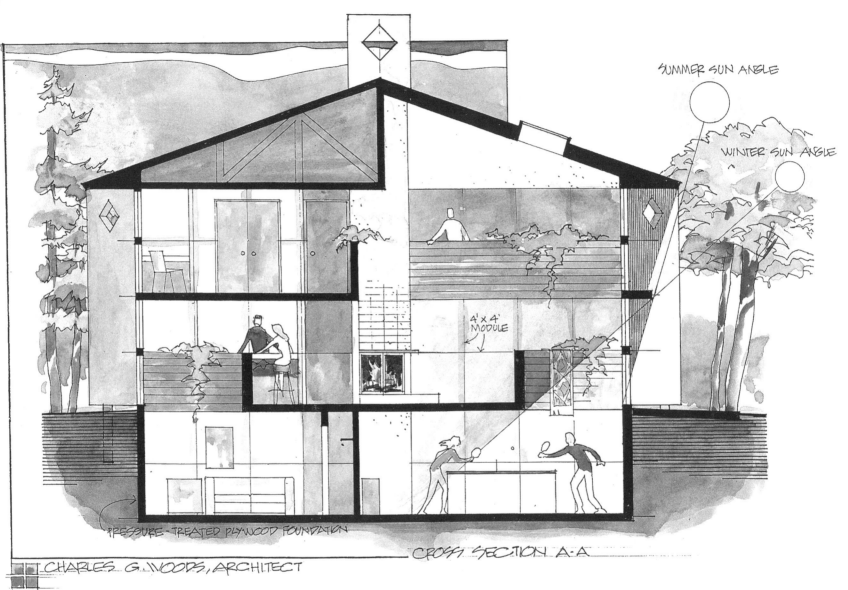

SUMMER SUN ANGLE

WINTER SUN ANGLE

4' X 4' MODULE

PRESSURE-TREATED PLYWOOD FOUNDATION

CROSS SECTION A·A

CHARLES G. WOODS, ARCHITECT

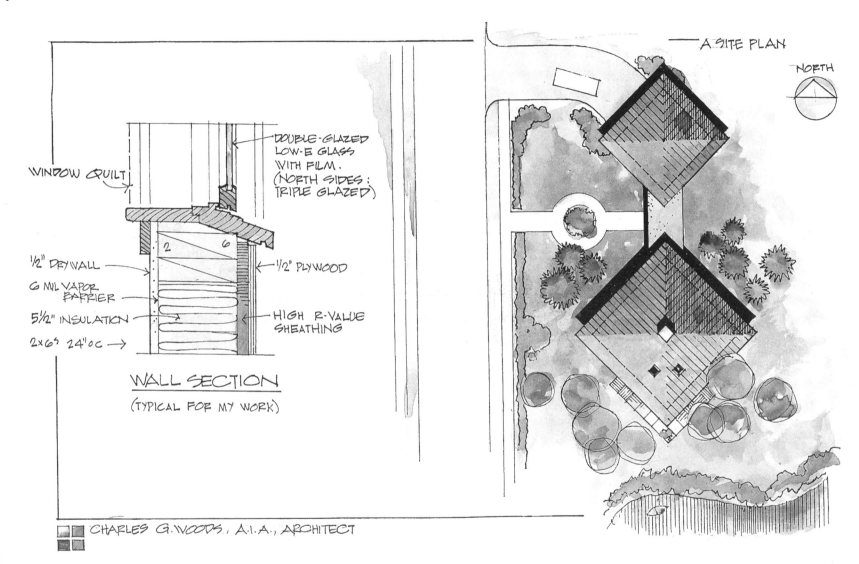

WINDOW QUILT

DOUBLE-GLAZED
LOW-E GLASS
WITH FILM.
(NORTH SIDES:
TRIPLE GLAZED)

½" DRYWALL

6 MIL VAPOR
BARRIER

5½" INSULATION

2×6s 24"OC →

½" PLYWOOD

HIGH R-VALUE
SHEATHING

WALL SECTION
(TYPICAL FOR MY WORK)

A SITE PLAN

NORTH

CHARLES G. WOODS, A.I.A., ARCHITECT

I DESIGNED THE NORTHEAST FITNESS CENTER FOR BARRY AND JANET KANDEL (SEE APPENDIX) AND OVER DINNER ONE NIGHT, BARRY TOLD ME ABOUT A BEAUTIFUL PIECE OF PROPERTY IN MONTEREY PINES, CORROLA, SOUTH CAROLINA. HE TOLD ME ABOUT THE BEAUTIFUL HOUSES BUILT THERE. SOME WERE INDEED BEAUTIFUL, BUT MANY WERE GHASTLY TO MY TASTES (AND PROBABLY TO HIS). WHAT WAS INTERESTING ABOUT THE DESIGNS WAS THAT THEY WERE ALL UP ON STILTS OR PYLONS (TO PREVENT FLOODING) AND WERE OFTEN THREE OR FOUR STORIES HIGH. WHAT I DISLIKED ABOUT MANY OF THE DESIGNS HE SHOWED ME IN THE BROCHURES WAS MAINLY THAT THEY WERE HELD UP BY LITERALLY HUNDREDS OF TWO-BY-FOURS AND -SIXES, AND MUCH OF THE SPACE BELOW WAS USELESS AND UNSIGHTLY.

THE LAND ITSELF WAS BEAUTIFUL: OCEAN ON ONE SIDE (WITHIN VIEW) AND INLAND WATER ON THE OTHER SIDE. BARRY WASN'T QUITE READY TO BUILD YET, BUT HE WAS INTERESTED IN WHAT I'D DO. SO I GAVE HIM A "REDUCED FEE" (A THING OF THE PAST!) ON THE DESIGN DRAWINGS, AND A REGULAR FEE IF HE CONTINUED WITH THE PROJECT. HE LOVED IT, BUT HAS NOT YET GONE ON TO BUILD.

THE FIRST THING I DID WAS LIFT THE WHOLE HOUSE OFF THE GROUND, USING 16 TRIANGULAR PYLONS INSTEAD OF HUNDREDS OF SMALLER MEMBERS. THIS PROVIDED PARKING AND AN ENTRANCE BELOW, AS WELL AS GARDENS.

THE HOUSE ITSELF IS ON MY USUAL 4' SQUARE MODULES, BUT IT ALSO HAS LARGE SQUARES WITH RAISED CLERESTORY ROOFS TURNED 45°. SINCE THE VIEW IS A GOOD 360°, I DESIGNED ALMOST CONTINUOUS (TRIPPLE-GLAZED) GLASS AND DECKS—INSIDE TO AN OPEN CENTRAL

"CRYSTAL" —— A BEACH HOUSE FOR BARRY/JANET KANDEL   MONTEREY PINES, CORROLA, SOUTH CAROLINA
CHARLES G. WOODS, AIA, ARCHITECT.

ATRIUM WITH A TREE AND OUTSIDE OPEN IN ALL DIRECTIONS. THE CENTRAL ATRIUM ALSO ALLOWS LIGHT INTO THE GARDENS AND ENTRY BELOW. THE USE OF THE LARGE REPETITIVE MODULES IS INSPIRED BY MY OWN GREAT TEACHER, ARCHITECT DENNIS BLAIR. I ALSO HAD LE CORBUSIER'S "VILLA SAVOYE" IN THE BACK OF MY MIND WHEN I DESIGNED THE ROOF PATIO AND LOOKOUT. THE PLAN EFFECT WOULD BE DAZZLING IF CONSTRUCTED, ENABLING YOU TO LOOK INTO OTHER PARTS OF THE HOUSE OR FROM A DECK THROUGH ONE MODULE INTO ANOTHER.

THE EXTERIOR PERSPECTIVE WAS ONE OF THE MOST DIFFICULT IN THIS BOOK TO RENDER, WITH, I BELIEVE, 16 VANISHING POINTS. (MAC DID A MARVELOUS JOB!) THE INTERIOR PERSPECTIVE IS ONE OF THE BEST IN THE BOOK. NOTICE THE MOON AND SAILBOATS I REQUESTED OUTSIDE.

AROUND THIS PERIOD, MY WIFE SAID SHE WAS TIRED OF MY "BIRD'S-EYE" PERSPECTIVES. SUCH PERSPECTIVES ARE VERY USEFUL FOR SHOWING A WHOLE, COMPLEX HOUSE IN ONE VIEW, SINCE PERSPECTIVES ARE EXPENSIVE. EVEN WITH MAC WORKING FOR ME AT TIMES AT HALF THE FEE HE COULD GET ELSEWHERE, THESE BOOK RENDERINGS COST THE EQUIVALENT OF A SMALL HOUSE. HOWEVER, I AGREED WITH MY WIFE AND I HAD MAC DO A PARTIAL EYE-LEVEL PERSPECTIVE. THE RESULT IS ANOTHER OF THE BEST DRAWINGS IN THE BOOK AND REFLECTS THE STYLE OF THE GREAT JAPANESE MASTERS. YOU CAN ALMOST FEEL THE SAND BENEATH YOUR FEET.

THE HOUSE CONSISTS OF 4500 SQUARE FEET AND WOULD COST $125 TO $200 PER SQUARE FOOT TO BUILD, DEPENDING ON FINISHES. THIS HIGHLY COMPLEX PLAN IS COMPLETELY ON THE MODULE WITH ALL THE WALLS CENTERED.

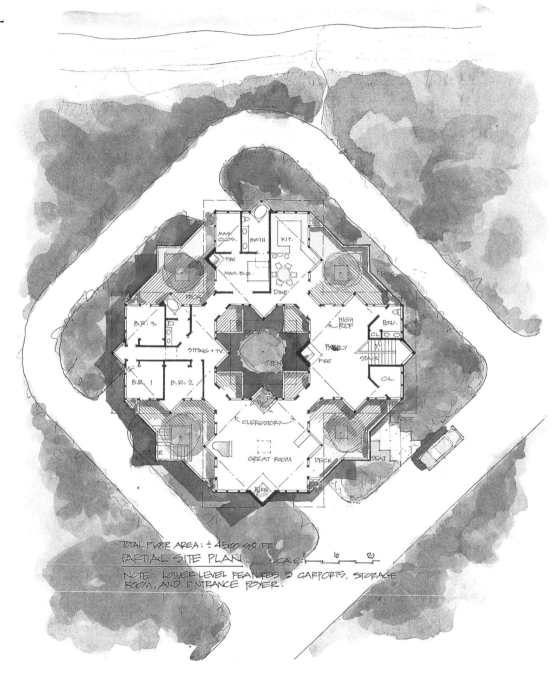

TOTAL FLOOR AREA: ± 4500 SQ. FT.
PARTIAL SITE PLAN   SCALE:
NOTE: LOWER LEVEL FEATURES 3 CARPORTS, STORAGE
ROOM, AND ENTRANCE FOYER.

"CRYSTAL"- A BEACH HOUSE FOR BARRY & JANET KANDEL
CHARLES G. WOODS , AIA, ARCHITECT

"CRYSTAL" - A BEACH HOUSE FOR BARRY/JANET KANDEL.

CHARLES G. WOODS, AIA, ARCHITECT

A CALIFORNIA SINGLES HOUSE*

BRIAN COBB II 9

THIS HOUSE WAS DESIGNED FOR THE SAME BRIAN COBB DESCRIBED EARLIER. WHEN HE SOLD HIS
FIRST HOUSE, HE SAID HE WOULD WANT SOMETHING "WITH CURVES," BUT STILL SMALL, AND
AT A REASONABLE COST. I WANTED TO COMBINE CIRCLES, RECTANGLES, AND TRIANGLES ALL ON
ONE HOUSE AND ALL ON THE MODULE. THE PLAN (WITH LOWER LEVEL NOT SHOWN) IS 2700
GROSS SQUARE FEET, INCLUDING GARAGE AND STORAGE. MAC NOTICED RIGHT AWAY PART OF
WHAT IS INTERESTING ABOUT THE DESIGN. HE SAID, "YOU SCAMP, YOU 'LIT' THE WHOLE
HOUSE WITHOUT CURVED GLASS OR PIERCING THE BARREL-SHAPED WALLS—NOT EVEN A THIN
STRIP WINDOW!" THE CLERESTORY HELPED A LOT. ALTHOUGH MY WORK IS USUALLY
SCULPTURAL, I BELIEVE THAT REVIEWING THE GREAT WORK OF NOTED ARCHITECT MYRON
GOLDFINGER RECENTLY LENT SOME INSPIRATION. ALSO, I HAD CHARLES GWATHMEY'S
STEELHOUSES I AND II IN MIND, WHICH I HAVE LOVED EVER SINCE HIGH SCHOOL.

MAC'S INTERIOR PERSPECTIVE IS ONE OF HIS BEST, AS IS HIS INCREDIBLE EYE-LEVEL DRAWING
ON THE BRIDGE TOWARD THE HOUSE. YOU CAN ALMOST FEEL THE MOIST AIR AND HEAR THE
CRICKETS. IT SHOWS HE IS A MASTER RENDERER. IF YOU LOOK AT IT CLOSELY, THERE ARE
ALMOST NO LINES—IT HAS A QUICK CARTOON-LIKE QUALITY, AND YET, THE COLOR LENDS IT
A REALISM THAT IS NOT EASILY EXPLAINED. THIS HOUSE WAS FEATURED IN <u>BETTER HOMES
AND GARDENS BUILDING IDEAS</u> MAGAZINE (WINTER 1995). ESTIMATED COSTS WERE AT $75
TO $125 PER SQUARE FOOT.

* CONSTRUCTION PLANS AVAILABLE.

A CALIFORNIA SINGLES HOUSE
9

A CALIFORNIA "SINGLES" HOUSE
CHARLES G. WOODS, AIA, ARCHITECT

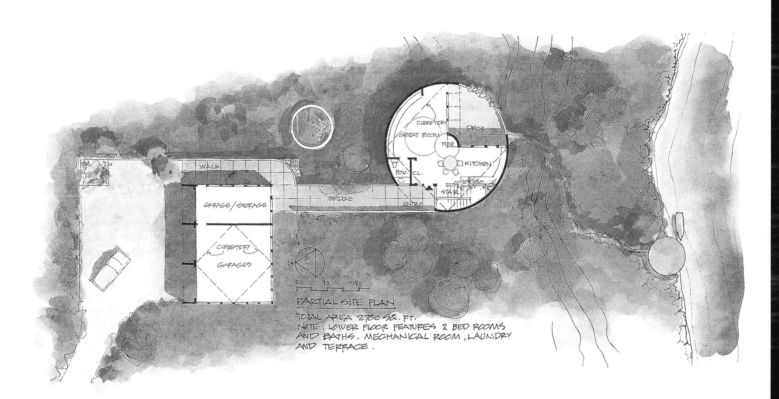

WALK

GARAGE / STORAGE

CLERESTORY
GARAGES

CLERESTORY

GREAT ROOM

FIRE

DECK

KITCHEN

POW. CL.

STAIR

BRIDGE

ENTRY

N

0   10   20

PARTIAL SITE PLAN

TOTAL AREA 2700 SQ. FT.
NOTE: LOWER FLOOR FEATURES 2 BED ROOMS
AND BATHS, MECHANICAL ROOM, LAUNDRY
AND TERRACE.

A CALIFORNIA SINGLES HOUSE
9

A CALIFORNIA "SINGLES" HOUSE
CHARLES G. WOODS, AIA, ARCHITECT

CHARLES G. WOODS, AIA, ARCHITECT
A CALIFORNIA "SINGLES" HOUSE

"TREEHOUSE", A WRITER'S RETREAT, FOR MY WIFE, JULIE K. (BUNNY) GUNDLACH, BY CHARLES G. WOODS, AIA, ARCHITECT.

TREEHOUSE IS A RETREAT FOR MY WIFE, JULIE K. GUNDLACH, AUTHOR OF <u>MY MOTHER BEFORE ME</u> (NEW YORK: BARRICADE BOOKS, 1992). THOUGH SHE LOVES ME, SHE LIKES TO BE ABLE TO GET AWAY FROM ME SOMETIMES (SHE SAYS 'NOT SO'!), SO I DESIGNED HER THIS LITTLE RETREAT AS A BIRTHDAY PRESENT—ONLY 675 SQUARE FEET PLUS DECKS. IT'S UP IN THE AIR ON TELEPHONE POLES BECAUSE SHE LIKES TO BE "UP IN THE TREES" AND WE COULDN'T AFFORD AND DIDN'T NEED THE FIRST FLOOR NECESSARY TO GET HER A SECOND FLOOR. AS IT IS TO BE ON THE END OF THE FOREST, I GAVE IT TWO SCREENED PORCHES AND TWO DECKS. THE INTERIOR IS TO BE AN EXPOSED STRUCTURE (WITH BOARD INSULATION ON THE EXTERIOR) TO GIVE IT A FEEL SIMILAR TO THAT OF HER UNCLE RABBIT'S SUMMER CABIN IN HOUGHTON, MICHIGAN, AND THE "SHACKS" SHE LIVED IN WHILE IN HAWAII.

THIS IS AGAIN A SQUARE PLAN WITH TRIANGULAR DECKS, CREATING A NIFTY-LOOKING SMALL CABIN. I ASKED MAC TO USE SOME PURPLE COLOR IN THE RENDERING AND HE HAS DONE SO NICELY, ON THE TREES. IF THIS BOOK DOES WELL, I MAY BUILD IT FOR HER NEXT YEAR ON HER FIFTIETH BIRTHDAY. ESTIMATED COSTS ARE ONLY $35 TO $50 PER SQUARE FOOT. SURPRISINGLY, WHEN PEOPLE LOOK THROUGH MY PORTFOLIO, THIS SIMPLE DESIGN IS USUALLY ONE OF THEIR FAVORITES.

* CONSTRUCTION PLANS AVAILABLE.

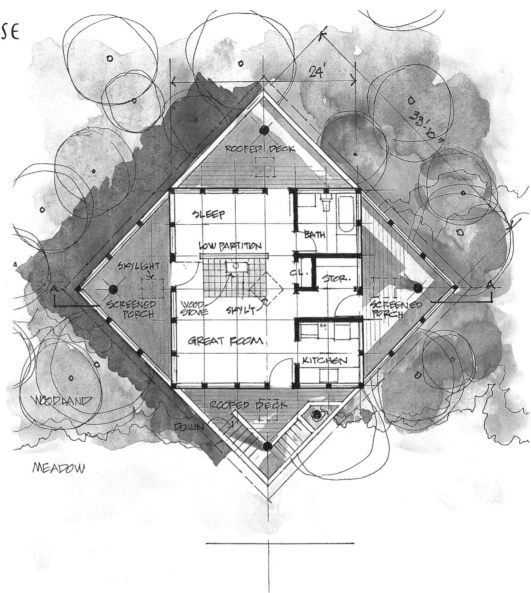

"TREEHOUSE", A WRITER'S RETREAT, FOR MY WIFE, JULIE K. (BUNNY) GUNDLACH
BY CHARLES G. WOODS, AIA, ARCHITECT.

"TREEHOUSE", A WRITER'S RETREAT, FOR MY WIFE, JULIE K. (BUNNY) GUNDLACH, BY CHARLES G. WOODS, AIA, ARCHITECT

FOUNTAINHEAD — A PROPOSED HOUSE OF RADIANT ARCS FOR MR. KEN WILBER

CHARLES G. WOODS, AIA, ARCHITECT

I DESIGNED THIS HOUSE FOR THE BOOK, WITH MY FRIEND, NOTED TRANSPERSONAL PSYCHOLOGIST, KEN WILBER IN MIND, TO SHOW WHAT I WOULD DO ON A MORE EXPENSIVE HOUSE (A MILLION DOLLARS OR MORE)—SAY, ON THE WEST COAST. I GAVE IT TO KEN AS A GIFT.

THIS HOUSE IS DESIGNED COMPLETELY ON A DEGREE MODULE OF 10° OF ARC AND 4' RADIAL CIRCLES, SO IT IS STILL A 4' MODULE BUT NOT A SQUARE ONE. I HAD ALREADY SPENT A LOT OF MONEY ON RENDERINGS AND THE PUBLISHER WAS HAPPY WITH THE BOOK AS IT WAS, BUT I THOUGHT THIS DESIGN WOULD BE A MASTERPIECE IF PROPERLY RENDERED, SO I BEGGED MY WIFE TO HAVE MAC RENDER IT FOR $3000 OR SO. (YES, I DO BEG!) I FELT LIKE DOSTOEVSKY SELLING HIS WIFE'S PEARLS, BUT, LIKE HIM, I FELT INSPIRED. THE SPIRAL-RADIAL PLAN AND TERRACED FLAT ROOFS PRETTY MUCH CAME FROM ME (IF ANYTHING DOES), BUT THE SLOPING SHED ROOF SPINNING IRREGULARLY OVER THE REST WAS GOD'S GIFT. MY WIFE APPROVED "ROUGHS ONLY" FIRST, FROM MAC, AND WHEN THEY CAME BACK AND LOOKED COOL, SHE, WHO IS USUALLY PURPOSELY NONPLUSSED, SAID, "OKAY, ALREADY. HOW DO YOU DO THIS STUFF?!" ULTIMATELY, I DON'T KNOW.

WHEN THE FINAL RENDERINGS CAME BACK AND I SAW THE NIGHTTIME EXTERIOR RENDERING, THE NAME "FOUNTAINHEAD" IMMEDIATELY POPPED INTO MY MIND. I HAD READ AYN RAND'S NOVEL PROBABLY FIVE TIMES, FOR GOOD AND BAD, AND THE DRAWINGS LOOKED AS INTRIGUING, I THOUGHT, AS THE DESCRIPTIONS OF HOWARD ROARK'S DESIGNS IN THE BOOK. I THOUGHT—SOMEWHAT FACETIOUSLY—"I'VE ARRIVED!" I ASKED MAC TO ADD BALLOONS ON THE DAYTIME DRAWING (NOT SHOWN) BECAUSE THE DESIGN ALSO HAD A FANTASY-LIKE UTOPIAN QUALITY THAT REMINDED ME OF H. G. WELLS AND JULES VERNE, WHO, IN A WAY, ARE ARCHITECTURAL INFLUENCES ON ME. I THINK FOUNTAINHEAD COULD BE BUILT FOR $150 TO $200 PER SQUARE FOOT. INTERESTED CLIENTS, PLEASE CALL! IT IS, I BELIEVE, ONE OF THE TOP THREE DESIGNS I'VE DONE TO DATE AND IS MY WIFE JULIE'S ALL-TIME FAVORITE.

FOUNTAINHEAD
11

FOUNTAINHEAD – A PROPOSED HOUSE OF RADIANT ARCS FOR MR. KEN WILBER

CHARLES G. WOODS, ARCHITECT, AIA.

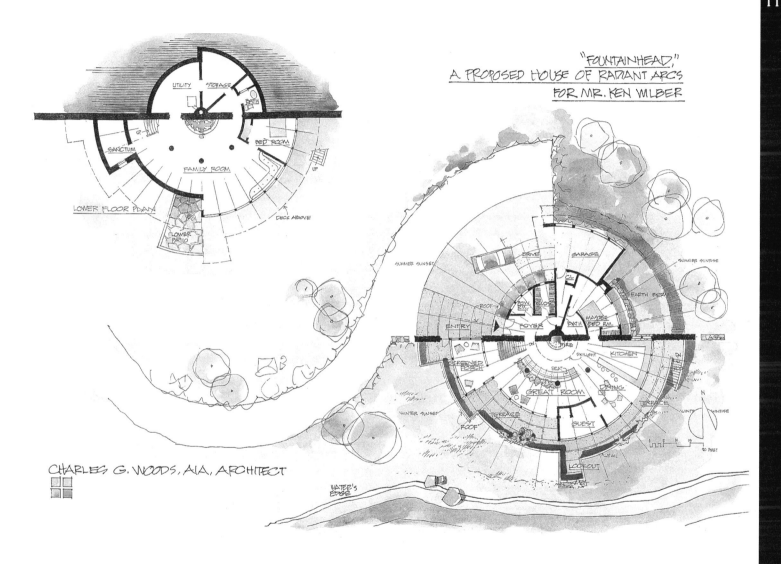

"FOUNTAINHEAD,"
A PROPOSED HOUSE OF RADIANT ARCS
FOR MR. KEN WILBER

CHARLES G. WOODS, AIA, ARCHITECT

"FOUNTAINHEAD", A PROPOSED HOUSE OF RADIANT ARCS FOR MR. KEN WILBER   CHARLES G. WOODS, AIA, ARCHITECT

I DESIGNED THIS HOUSE FOR MY FATHER-IN-LAW, MR. HERMAN GUNDLACH, AS A GIFT. I DESIGNED ONE FOR HIM PREVIOUSLY THAT I THINK WAS ONE OF MY BEST, SO I THOUGHT I'D TRY ANOTHER. "HERMS," AS HE IS KNOWN, IS A HARVARD GRADUATE, CLASS OF 1935, AS WAS HIS WIFE, AND HE IS IN THE HARVARD HALL OF FAME FOR FOOTBALL AS THE FAMOUS "IRONMAN." HE HAS HELPED ME A LOT OVER THE YEARS, AS DID MY DECEASED MOTHER-IN-LAW, BARBARA GUNDLACH. MRS. GUNDLACH TOLD HER DAUGHTER (NOW MY WIFE) BACK WHEN I WAS 21 THAT "HE WILL DO GREAT THINGS ONE DAY!" SINCE MY SITUATION LOOKED PRETTY HOPELESS THEN, I WILL ALWAYS BE GRATEFUL TO HER FOR THAT.

THIS DESIGN, THOUGH NICELY RENDERED, SHOULD BE CONSIDERED ONLY A PRELIMINARY (SCHEMATIC) DESIGN. THE DESIGN USES BOTH 4' SQUARE, AND 5° OF ARC MODULES. IT WAS TO BE ABOUT 10,000 SQUARE FEET AND COST ABOUT $150 TO $200 PER SQUARE FOOT. HERMS COULD HAVE BUILT IT, AS HE AND HIS FATHER HEADED HERMAN GUNDLACH CONSTRUCTION, ONE OF THE 100 OLDEST BUILDING COMPANIES IN THE UNITED STATES AND, FOR A LONG TIME, THE LARGEST IN THE UPPER PENINSULA OF MICHIGAN. NOW, THOUGH STRONG AND HEALTHY IN HIS EARLY EIGHTIES, THIS MANSION MIGHT SEEM A LITTLE MUCH.

THIS HOUSE WAS, NO DOUBT, MORE INSPIRED BY MY EARLY LOVE OF <u>STAR TREK</u> THAN I SHOULD PROBABLY ADMIT. IT REALLY NEEDED ONE MORE STAGE OF RENDERINGS, BUT, FOR ONCE, MAC SAID "NO!" BECAUSE HE WAS RENDERING FOUR HOUSES AT ONCE FOR ME. I DO LIKE IT, THOUGH—ESPECIALLY THE EXTERIOR, PARTIAL EYE-LEVEL VIEW OF THE PAGODA/SCREENED PORCH. ON THE RENDERING, THE RISING "BUBBLES" ARE CLASSIC MAC HUMOR.

A RETIREMENT
RESIDENCE FOR MR. HERMAN GUNDLACH
- SOUTHERN CALIFORNIA
CHARLES G. WOODS, AIA, ARCHITECT

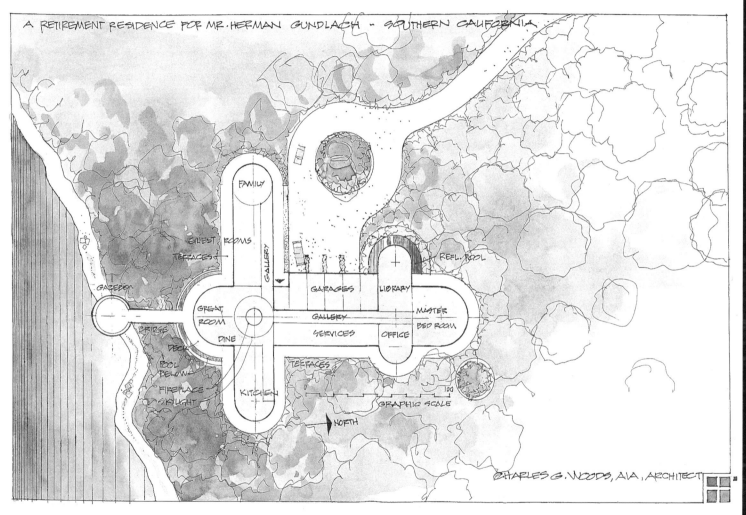

A RETIREMENT RESIDENCE FOR MR. HERMAN GUNDLACH - SOUTHERN CALIFORNIA

FAMILY

GUEST ROOMS

TERRACES

GALLERY

REFL. POOL

GAZEBO

GARAGES

LIBRARY

GREAT ROOM

GALLERY

MASTER BED ROOM

BRIDGE

DINE

SERVICES

OFFICE

DECK

POOL BELOW

TERRACES

FIREPLACE

SKYLIGHT

KITCHEN

100

GRAPHIC SCALE

NORTH

©CHARLES G. WOODS, AIA, ARCHITECT

CHARLES G. WOODS, AIA, ARCHITECT

NAUTILUS A WATERSIDE RESIDENCE FOR BOB AND LINDA TERRY AT ITHACA, N.Y. SCHEME II   CHARLES G. WOODS, AIA, ARCHITECT

NAUTILUS

A HOUSE FOR
BOB AND LINDA TERRY

ITHACA, NEW YORK
(WITH CONSULTING
ARCHITECT, DON
PASSMAN, A.I.A.)

13

NAUTILUS IS A WATERSIDE RESIDENCE FOR BOB AND LINDA TERRY OF 3600 SQUARE FEET, PLUS TERRACES (LOWER LEVEL NOT SHOWN). THIS WAS MY SECOND SCHEME FOR THIS WONDERFUL COUPLE. BOB IS HEAD OF MAINTENANCE FOR CORNELL UNIVERSITY IN ITHACA, NEW YORK. I ALMOST WENT TO ARCHITECTURE SCHOOL THERE. (I WAS HAPPY TO HEAR THAT THEY SELL MY BOOKS THERE NOW!)

SINCE BOB KNOWS A LOT ABOUT CONSTRUCTION, HE HAS BEEN MORE INVOLVED IN THE CONSTRUCTION DETAILS THAN IS USUAL. THIS HAS NOT ALWAYS BEEN A FUN EXPERIENCE FOR THE ARCHITECT OR CLIENT, BUT WE ARE STILL GOOD FRIENDS AND NAUTILUS IS POSSIBLY ONE OF MY BEST DESIGNS TO DATE TO GO TO CONSTRUCTION, SO MAYBE THE CREATIVE COLLABORATION WAS WORTH IT. BOB IS ALSO AN AMATEUR FRANK LLOYD WRIGHT SCHOLAR, SO I WAS PROUD HE CHOSE ME AS HIS ARCHITECT. (ACTUALLY, HIS FIRST CHOICE WAS THE GREAT GUNNAR BIRKERTS.)

THE PLAN IS A SIMPLE ¼ CIRCLE WITH A UNIFORM SHED ROOF. ORIGINALLY, THE TERRACE WAS TO BE CURVED, BUT MY COMPASS WOULDN'T EXTEND FAR ENOUGH, SO I MADE IT A RECTANGLE. ONLY AFTER I DREW IT, DID I REALIZE WHAT A POWERFUL CONTRAST IT WOULD MAKE TO THE CURVING GLASS AREA.

ON THIS SECOND DESIGN, THE TERRYS ASKED IF I COULD USE A NAUTICAL INSPIRATION, BECAUSE OF THE MANY SAILBOATS THAT GO BY THE SITE ON BEAUTIFUL LAKE CAYUGA. THE SIDNEY OPERA HOUSE FLASHED THROUGH MY MIND, BUT AT $75 TO $100 PER SQUARE FOOT, I NEEDED A MUCH SIMPLER TYPE OF SHAPE. MALCOLM'S LAKESIDE PERSPECTIVE WAS

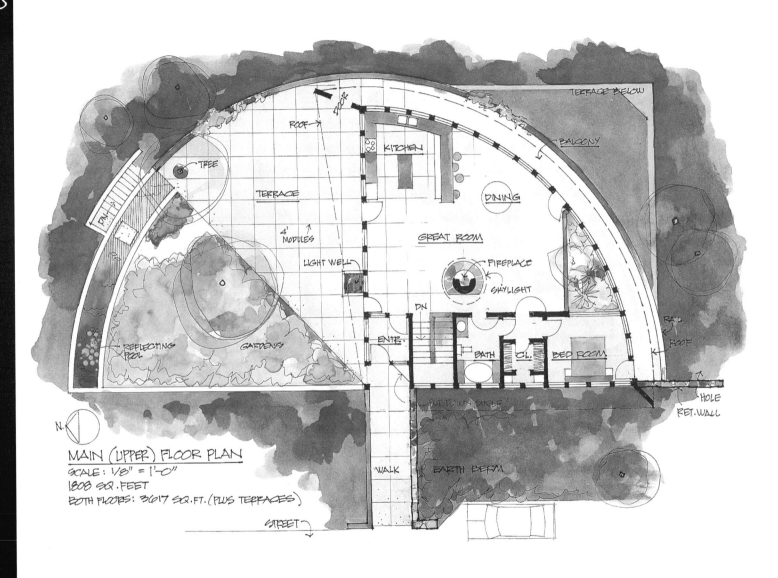

ROOF →

DOOR

TERRACE BELOW

BALCONY

TREE

KITCHEN

TERRACE

DINING

4' MODULES

GREAT ROOM

LIGHT WELL

FIREPLACE

SKYLIGHT

DN

REFLECTING POOL

GARDENS

ENTR.

DN

BATH

CL.

BED ROOM

RAIL

ROOF

HOLE

RET. WALL

PUT-DOWN SHELF

N.

MAIN (UPPER) FLOOR PLAN
SCALE: 1/8" = 1'-0"
1808 SQ. FEET
BOTH FLOORS: 3617 SQ. FT. (PLUS TERRACES)

WALK

EARTH BERM

STREET

EVEN MORE BEAUTIFUL THAN I IMAGINED AND INDEED WAS "NAUTICAL": WITH THE HIGH CURVING GLASS AS A GREAT SAIL AND THE RECTILINEAR TERRACE AS THE PROW, IT LOOKS LIKE A GREAT SHIP MOVING THROUGH THE EARTH. IT REMINDS ME OF ONE MY OF FAVORITE WRIGHT DESIGNS, WHICH HE CREATED FOR HIS SON, LLEWELLYN—THOUGH HIS IS A DIFFERENT SHAPE AND I DID NOT HAVE IT IN MIND WHEN I DESIGNED THIS.

MAC'S RENDERINGS ON THIS SET ARE POSSIBLY THE BEST IN THE BOOK. THE BUILDING COMMISSIONER SAID HE HAD NEVER SEEN ANYTHING LIKE IT. THOUGH SIMPLE IN PLAN AND DETAILS, BIDS HAVE RANGED WILDLY FROM $85 PER SQUARE FOOT FROM MY BUILDING CONSULTANT, LARRY WILSON, TO $150 TO $200 PER SQUARE FOOT. CONSTRUCTION WILL START SOON AT ABOUT $100 PER SQUARE FOOT, WITH THE OWNERS AS CONTRACTOR. I DID TWENTY-TWO 24" BY 36" SHEETS OF CONSTRUCTION DRAWINGS AND WILL ADD "FIELD DETAILS" WHEN I SUPERVISE. THIS HOUSE DESIGN APPEARED IN THE FALL 1995 ISSUE OF BUILDING IDEAS MAGAZINE. (A NOTE ON THE LOWER FLOOR PLAN: THE LIGHT WELL ON THE LEFT SHOULD BE CENTERED ON THE MODULE AND ON THE BOTTOM HALF IT IS NOT.)

NAUTILUS A WATERSIDE RESIDENCE FOR BOB AND LINDA TERRY AT ITHACA, NY

CHARLES G. WOODS
AIA, ARCHITECT

NAUTILUS A WATERSIDE RESIDENCE FOR BOB AND LINDA TERRY AT ITHACA, NEW YORK

CHARLES G. WOODS
AIA, ARCHITECT

 "RED ROCKS" A DESERT HOUSE BY CHARLES G. WOODS, A.I.A., ARCHITECT

RED ROCKS IS A PROTOTYPE DESERT HOUSE. I WANTED TO SHOW THAT I COULD CREATE AN ASYMMETRICAL CURVED STRUCTURE ON A RECTILINEAR GRID. THIS IS HOW I DID IT. THERE ARE THREE RELATED MODULES: MY USUAL 4' SQUARE, A LARGER 16' STRUCTURAL MODULE, AND 5° OF ARC FOR THE CURVING GLASS. ALL CURVES ARE 90° OR ¼ OF A CIRCLE. IT'S A SIMPLE SYSTEM—BUT LOOK AT THE ELEGANT ASYMMETRY OF THE NIGHTTIME EXTERIOR PERSPECTIVE!

THIS HOUSE WAS DESIGNED TO BE CONSTRUCTED OF REINFORCED CONCRETE AND WOULD PROBABLY COST MORE THAN SOME OF THE OTHER DESIGNS IN THE BOOK, OR ABOUT $200 TO $250 PER SQUARE FOOT. THE INTERIOR PERSPECTIVE REQUESTED SHOWING A PARTY SCENE IS ONE OF THE BEST MAC HAS EVER DONE, I BELIEVE. THE PARKING, GARDENS, AND ENTRY ARE FROM BELOW, AS IN THE KANDEL HOUSE, BUT IN A VASTLY DIFFERENT SETTING—DESERT VERSUS BEACH.

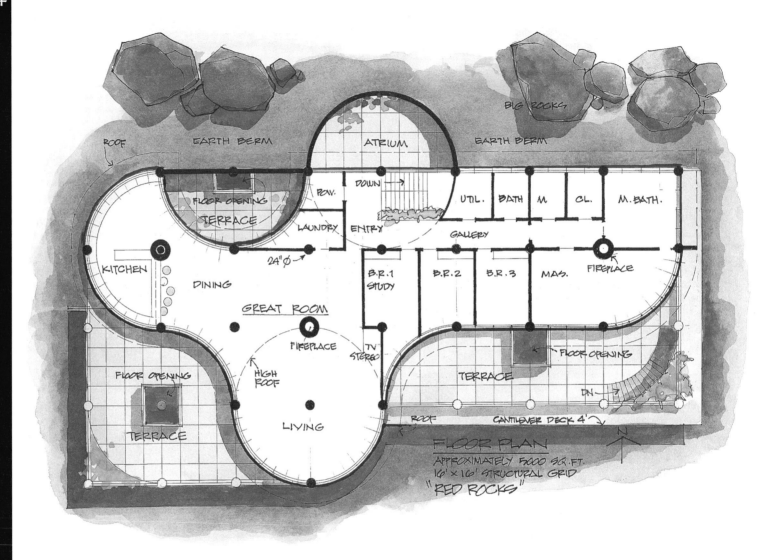

RED ROCKS

EARTH BERM   ATRIUM   EARTH BERM   BIG ROCKS

ROOF

FLOOR OPENING

TERRACE

KITCHEN

DINING

GREAT ROOM

FIREPLACE

HIGH ROOF

FLOOR OPENING

TERRACE

LIVING

POW.   DOWN →

LAUNDRY   ENTRY

24"∅ →

UTIL.   BATH   W   CL.   M. BATH.

GALLERY

B.R.1 STUDY   B.R.2   B.R.3   MAS.   FIREPLACE

TV STEREO

TERRACE   FLOOR OPENING

DN →

ROOF   CANTILEVER DECK 4'

FLOOR PLAN
APPROXIMATELY 5000 SQ. FT.
16' × 16' STRUCTURAL GRID
"RED ROCKS"

RED ROCKS   INTERIOR - LIVING AREA   CHARLES WOODS, AIA ARCHITECT

"HARMONIOUS DISCONJUNCTION" - DEDICATED TO MR. ROBERT ORLOSKI

CHARLES G. WOODS,
AIA
ARCHITECT

114

HARMONIOUS DISCONJUNCTION WAS DESIGNED IN MEMORY OF MY RECENTLY DECEASED STEPFATHER, ROBERT ORLOSKI, A VETERAN AND MASTER SERGEANT IN WORLD WAR II. THE MORE I THOUGHT ABOUT HIS LIFE—AND ALL OUR LIVES—THE MORE I SAW THE CONTRAST OF OUR DISCORDS, FAILURES, AND RAGGED EDGES AGAINST THE SUPPORTING WHOLENESS OF NATURE AND, MORE, GOD. YES, I STILL BELIEVE IN GOD—FOR MANY REASONS, BUT THAT IS ANOTHER BOOK!

ANOTHER INSPIRATION WAS THE DESIRE TO TAKE WHAT WAS VALID IN DECONSTRUCTION THEORY, PHILOSOPHY, AND ARCHITECTURE AND ABSORB IT INTO A "NATURAL ARCHITECTURE." THE GREAT PHILOSOPHER HEGEL CALLS THIS ABSORBING AND <u>TRANSFORMING</u> PROCESS <u>AUFGEHOBEN,</u> WHICH USUALLY BEST TRANSLATES AS "SUBLATED." SO I BELIEVE I HAVE <u>SUBLATED</u> DECONSTRUCTION.

WHAT IS <u>DECONSTRUCTION?</u> IN MY OPINION, AND TO SIMPLIFY IN PHILOSOPHY, IT IS THE VIEW THAT THERE ARE NO "FOUNDATIONS" TO KNOWLEDGE—ONLY ENDLESS "INTERPRETATIONS." ULTIMATELY, IT DOES NOT POSIT A BELIEF IN TRUTH, AND BORDERS, IN MY OPINION, ON NIHILISM BECAUSE IT HAS NO WAY TO SAY WHICH INTERPRETATION IS "TRUER." DECONSTRUCTIONISTS SPEAK OF AN INTERPRETATION BEING "INTERESTING"—BUT WHAT WOULD MAKE ONE VIEW <u>MORE</u> INTERESTING THAN ANOTHER? THEY DO NOT CLEARLY SAY, OF COURSE.

IN ARCHITECTURE, THIS IS MANIFESTED USUALLY IN DISCONJUNCT BUILDINGS, EMPHASIS ON DISCORDS, NONHARMONIOUS ASYMMETRIES, AND BUILDINGS THAT LOOK AS IF THEY DEFY GRAVITY OR APPEAR TO BE FALLING DOWN. I AM RADICALLY OPPOSED IN PRINCIPLE TO DECONSTRUCTIONIST ARCHITECTURE. JUST AS SUCH PHILOSOPHERS DO NOT BELIEVE IN TRUTH, SUCH ARCHITECTS DO NOT APPEAR TO BELIEVE IN BEAUTY.

HARMONIOUS DISCONJUNCTION

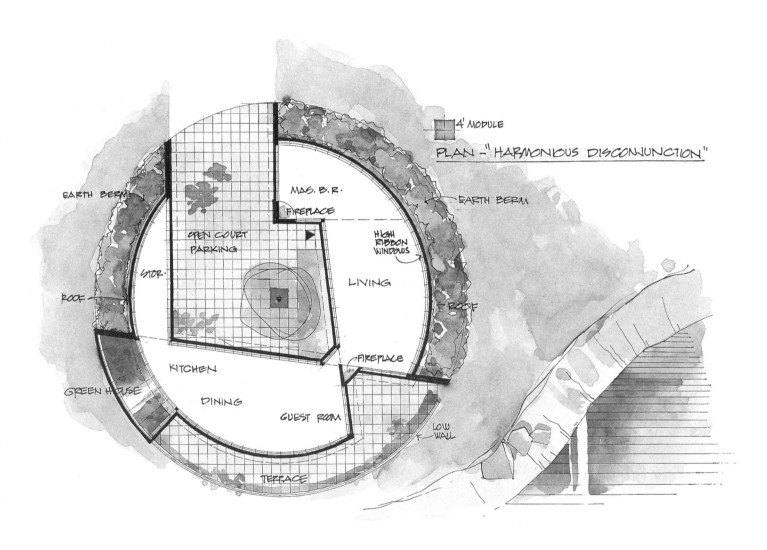

4' MODULE

PLAN – "HARMONIOUS DISCONJUNCTION"

EARTH BERM

MAS. B.R.

FIREPLACE

EARTH BERM

OPEN COURT PARKING

HIGH RIBBON WINDOWS

STOR.

LIVING

ROOF

ROOF

FIREPLACE

KITCHEN

GREEN HOUSE

DINING

GUEST ROOM

LOW WALL

TERRACE

"ROUGH" PLAN ONLY

THESE ARCHITECTS BASE THEIR WORK ON THE CHAOS OF OUR TIMES AND ON THE SEEMING CHAOS OF THE MICROWORLD. BUT EVEN IF SUCH ARTISTS CHOOSE TO MIRROR LIFE AND NOT IMPROVE IT, OUR INDIVIDUAL AND COLLECTIVE LIVES ARE NOT <u>ONLY</u> CHAOTIC, AND THE MICROWORLD IN CHAOS THEORY IS UNFOLDING COMPLEXLY BEAUTIFUL PATTERNS.

IN THIS DESIGN, I TRIED TO KEEP A TENSION BETWEEN CHAOS AND ORDER/BEAUTY, TIPPING THE SCALES JUST SLIGHTLY TOWARD BEAUTY. I BELIEVE IT IS ONE OF MY BEST, MOST INSPIRED DESIGNS EVER—THOUGH THE PLAN IS STILL PRELIMINARY. ANY ARCHITECT READING THIS WILL THINK I MUST BE WRITING OF THE GREAT (AND HE IS GREAT) DECONSTRUCTIONIST ARCHITECT FRANK GEHRY, SO I SHOULD ADDRESS THIS SUBJECT.

GEHRY IS BY FAR THE BEST OF THE DECONSTRUCTIONIST LOT (WITH THE LATE FRANK ISRAEL). HIS EARLY WORK TO ME WAS UGLY. I WOULD NOT BE SEEMINGLY INSULTING TO A GREAT ARCHITECT IN PRINT IF I DID NOT BELIEVE HIS WORK WAS <u>MEANT</u> TO BE SO! HIS NEWEST AND BEST WORK IS SURPRISINGLY BEAUTIFUL AND NOT NEARLY SO DISCORDANT. I BELIEVE HE MIGHT AGREE THAT HIS WORK IS BECOMING LESS DECONSTRUCTIONIST AND MORE EXPRESSIONIST OR ORGANIC. THERE STILL SEEMS TO BE A FEAR OF RECOGNIZABLE GEOMETRIES EXPRESSED IN HIS WORK. WHY? EVEN IF GEOMETRY IS, IN PART, SUBJECTIVE, IT IS PART OF THE GRANDEUR AND FINITUDE OF MAN THAT HE CAN CLEARLY CONCEIVE OF ONLY A FEW LIMITED PLATONIC SHAPES. MY OWN DESIGN HERE HAS SOME—NOT ALL—IRREGULAR ANGLES (ONES NOT EASILY RECOGNIZED AS 30 OR 45°), BUT EVEN THESE ARE CREATED BY CONNECTING CORNERS OF A REGULAR GRID—HINTING AT AN "INTELLIGIBLE BACKGROUND" TO A SEEMINGLY CHAOTIC APPEARANCE. I WILL SAY THIS POSITIVELY: OUT OF CHAOS COMES ORDER. THE 1990S <u>HAVE</u> PRODUCED SOME OF THE BEST ARCHITECTURE IN DECADES.

HARMONIOUS DISCONJUNCTION INTERIOR   CHARLES G. WOODS, AIA - ARCHITECT

I HAD ALWAYS LIKED JOHN LAUTNER'S SAUCER-LIKE HOUSE, SEEN IN THE MOVIE BODY
DOUBLE. AFTER HE DIED, I WANTED TO DO SOMETHING TO HONOR HIM, SO I DESIGNED MY
OWN "SAUCER" VACATION HOUSE. BOTH HOUSES ARE ROUND AND EACH SITS ON A CENTRAL
COLUMN WITH SUPPORT STRUTS. BUT BOTH LOOK QUITE DIFFERENT. YOU CAN ENTER
LOOKOUT FROM THE BRIDGE TO THE ROAD, WHICH IS THE MAIN ENTRY, AND FROM BELOW AT
THE BEACH BY A TWO-STORY SPIRAL STAIR.

THE GAS FIREPLACE IS ABOVE THE STAIR AND CAN BE VIEWED FROM ALL SIDES. THE HOUSE
GLASS SLOPES OUT AWAY FROM THE VIEWER. THIS REMINDED ME OF THE CAPTAIN'S QUARTERS
ON OLD SAILING SHIPS, WHICH IN TURN REMINDED ME OF ONE OF MY EARLIEST PICTURE
BOOKS OF PETER PAN, HENCE THE ALMOST FAIRY-TALE-LIKE RENDERING OF THE INTERIOR
PERSPECTIVE. LOOKOUT ALSO HAS A DECK AND A CENTRAL SKYLIGHT. THE ROOF IS, IN PART,
EARTH COVERED. THE CONSTRUCTION WAS TO BE REINFORCED CONCRETE (CENTRAL COLUMN)
WITH STONE VENEER, WITH STEEL SUPPORT STRUTS, WOOD ROOF, FLOOR, AND WINDOW DETAILS.

THE HOUSE WOULD NOT BE INEXPENSIVE, BUT I BELIEVE IT COULD BE BUILT FOR AROUND
$150 TO $200 PER SQUARE FOOT, OR FOR A TOTAL OF $300,000 AT ITS 1500 GROSS SQUARE
FEET. IT WOULD OFFER A MARVELOUS SENSE OF SPACE—I IMAGINED IT ON THE WEST COAST.
THE HOUSE IS DESIGNED ON 4' AND 5° OF ARC MODULES, AS ARE THE ROOF AND SUPPORT
STRUTS.

LOOKOUT
16

CHARLES G. WOODS, AIA ARCHITECT

"**LOOKOUT**" SAUCER VACATION STUDIO IN MEMORY OF JOHN LAUTNER

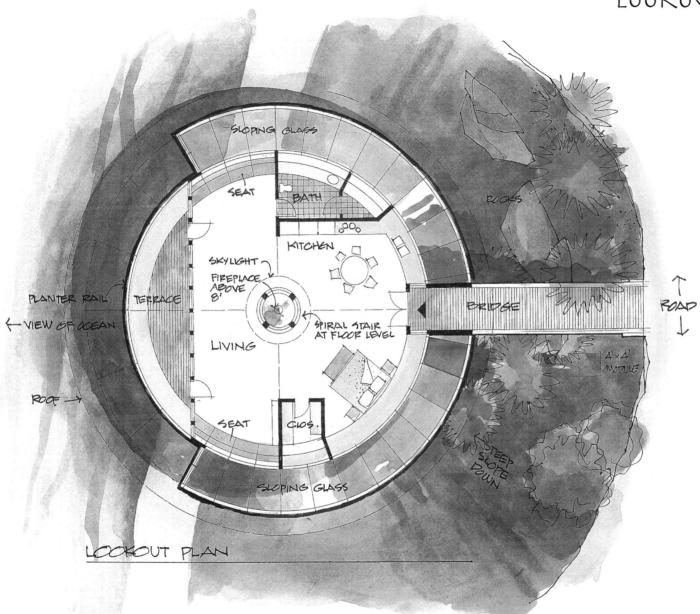

SLOPING GLASS

SEAT

BATH

ROCKS

KITCHEN

SKYLIGHT

FIREPLACE ABOVE 8'

PLANTER RAIL

TERRACE

BRIDGE

ROAD

← VIEW OF OCEAN

SPIRAL STAIR AT FLOOR LEVEL

LIVING

4 × 4' MODULE

ROOF →

SEAT

CLOS.

STEEP SLOPE DOWN

SLOPING GLASS

LOOKOUT PLAN

LOOKOUT   INTERIOR   CHARLES G. WOODS, AIA - ARCHITECT

HOBBITAT IS DESIGNED FOR MY MOST UNIQUE FRIEND, BRUCE E. ANKELE, AKA "BONE." BRILLIANT, WIDELY READ, AND UNBELIEVABLY FUNNY, HE WAS COLLEGE FRIENDS WITH THE FAMOUS LATE COMIC, JOHN BELUSHI. BRUCE IS FIVE YEARS MY SENIOR AND TAUGHT ME TO SWIM AND TO ASK PHILOSOPHICAL QUESTIONS. HE ALSO GAVE ME TOLKIEN'S BOOK, THE HOBBIT, AND TOLD ME I SHOULD DESIGN "HOBBIT HOUSES." I WAS GOING TO CALL WHOLE TOWNS OF THEM "HOBBITATS," A TAKEOFF ON MOSHE SAFDIE'S FAMOUS "HABITAT."

IT WAS THE PONDERING OF HOBBIT HOUSES MIXED WITH WRIGHT'S ORGANIC ARCHITECTURE THAT LED TO MY TWENTY-YEAR LOVE OF EARTH-SHELTERING HOUSES. I'VE BEEN TOLD THAT I AM ONE OF THE BEST-KNOWN DESIGNERS OF SUCH HOUSES. BUT I WAS ALREADY IN THE SECOND GENERATION, AND MALCOLM WELLS, DONALD METZ, DAVID WRIGHT, AND JOHN BARNARD HAD ALL DONE GREAT UNDERGROUND HOUSES BEFORE I EVER STARTED, AND I WAS INFLUENCED BY ALL OF THEM. I BELIEVE I HAVE, HOWEVER, DESIGNED MORE EARTH-SHELTERED HOUSES THAN ANYONE NOW THAT I KNOW OF, WITH THE EXCEPTION OF MAC.

THIS HOUSE WAS ORIGINALLY AN ANGULAR DESIGN, AND I DECIDED TO ROUND ITS CORNER TO MAKE IT MORE HOBBITY FOR MY FRIEND'S GIFT. I DIDN'T REALIZE AT THIS TIME THAT THIS WOULD MAKE IT LOOK SO MUCH LIKE A QUESTION MARK FROM ABOVE—BUT SINCE BRUCE IS SOMETHING OF AN ENIGMA, MAYBE THIS IS APPROPRIATE.

THE PLAN IS NOT VERY DETAILED AND SHOULD BE CONSIDERED SCHEMATIC OR PRELIMINARY ONLY. ALSO, THE CENTRAL COURT WITH THE GREAT TREE WOULD BE PARTIALLY PAVED.

CHARLES G. WOODS, A.I.A., ARCHITECT

HOBBITAT – A HOUSE FOR MR. BRUCE – 'BONE' ANKELE

THE MAN IN THE ROBE IS, OF COURSE, GANDALF COMING TO MEET BRUCE FOR A GREAT HOBBIT DINNER. MAC ACTUALLY LOOKS LIKE THE BOOK'S GREAT WIZARD AND WAS, IN FACT, USED AS A MODEL FOR HIM IN ONE OF <u>THE LORD OF THE RINGS</u> ILLUSTRATED EDITIONS.

THE EXTERIOR PERSPECTIVE IS GOOD, BUT IT'S THE INTERIOR PERSPECTIVE THAT SHOWS THE MAGIC OF WHAT I HOPED TO GET ACROSS. MAC IS NOT PERFECT, AS HE WILL HUMBLY BE THE FIRST TO TELL YOU—AND AS A FAILED VERSION OF THE SNOWSTORM REVEALED (NOT SHOWN). WE LAUGHED SO HARD! I KNOW HE <u>COULD</u> DO A BETTER SNOWSTORM DRAWING, THOUGH. THE HOUSE IS DESIGNED ON THE NORMAL MODULE. HOWEVER, THERE ARE SOME PROBLEM DETAILS THAT COULD EASILY BE IMPROVED ON IN THE CONSTRUCTION DRAWINGS. WHEN BUILT, THE HOUSE IS MEANT TO BE OF REINFORCED CONCRETE—STONE VENEER, STEEL, AND WOOD.

HOBBITAT ("ROUGH PLAN")

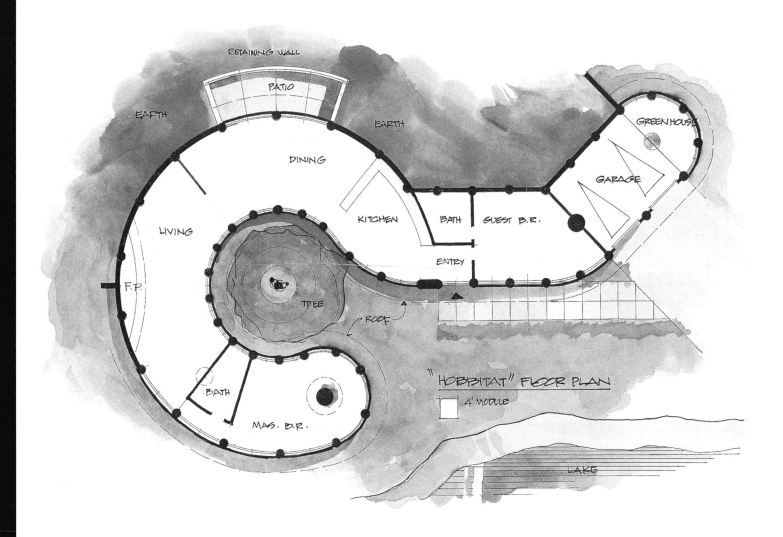

RETAINING WALL

PATIO

EARTH

EARTH

DINING

GREEN HOUSE

GARAGE

LIVING

KITCHEN

BATH

GUEST B.R.

F.P.

ENTRY

TREE

ROOF

"HOBBITAT" FLOOR PLAN

4' MODULE

BATH

MAS. B.R.

LAKE

HOBBITAT - INTERIOR   CHARLES G. WOODS, AIA ARCHITECT

CRAGGED ROCK /FREEMAN HOUSE II...   CHARLES G. WOODS, AIA, ARCHITECT

...AN IRREGULAR HOUSE BASED ON A REGULAR SQUARE GRID

CRAGGED ROCK IS AN <u>IRREGULAR</u> HOUSE BASED ON A <u>REGULAR</u> SQUARE GRID. I THINK THIS DESIGN SHOWS HOW A MODULE NEED NOT BE LIMITED. THIS SYSTEM IS SIMILAR TO THE ONE I. M. PEI HAS USED RECENTLY. THIS IS DEFINITELY ONE OF THE MOST "DIONYSIAN," ASYMMETRICAL, NATURALLY ORGANIC HOUSES IN THE BOOK, AND YET IT IS NOT COMPLETELY UNINTELLIGIBLE. EVERY ANGLE GOES FROM THE CORNER OF ONE SQUARE TO ANOTHER CORNER OF A SECOND—THOUGH WHERE THIS IS ON THE PLAN IS NOT ALWAYS APPARENT. HOWEVER, I BELIEVE THAT THIS APPROACH WOULD MAKE THIS ORGANIC HOUSE MUCH EASIER AND LESS EXPENSIVE TO BUILD. THE HOUSE IS TO BE OF REINFORCED CONCRETE AND STONE VENEER, WITH EARTH-COVERED ROOFS. SOME OF THE BACK WALLS HAVE HIGH RIBBON WINDOWS UP ABOVE, INCLUDING THE HALL REAR WALL. (PLEASE NOTE THAT A BATHROOM DOOR OFF THE HALL IS MISSING.) THE HOUSE CONSISTS OF ABOUT 3500 SQUARE FEET.

I JUST LOVE MAC'S RENDERING—YOU CAN ALMOST FEEL THE COOL MOIST AIR ON THE NIGHTTIME PERSPECTIVE, AND LOOK AT THE NIFTY LIGHT REFLECTIONS ON THIS INTERIOR DRAWING! THIS DESIGN WAS DONE FOR THIS BOOK AS A "PROTOTYPE" AS WELL, BUT I HOPE TO BUILD SUCH STRUCTURES WITH INTERESTED CLIENTS.

THIS TYPE OF DESIGN IS AS IRREGULAR AS DECONSTRUCTIONIST DESIGNS, <u>BUT</u> IT DOES NOT TURN AWAY FROM BEAUTY. ITS HISTORICAL ANCESTORS ARE FOUND IN GAUDI, MENDELSOHN, STEINER, AND FINSTERLIN. I BEGAN DESIGNING FREE-FORM HOUSES AS EARLY AS TWENTY-ONE YEARS OF AGE.

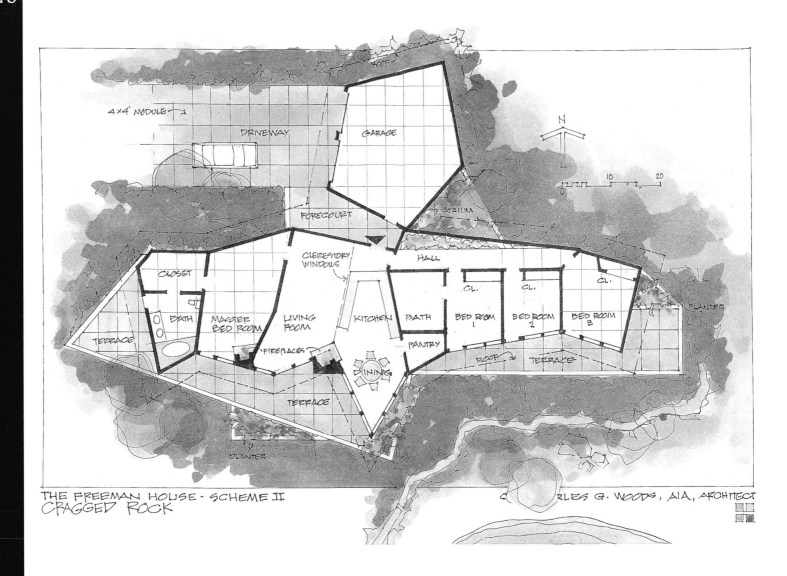

THE FREEMAN HOUSE - SCHEME II
CRAGGED ROCK

CHARLES G. WOODS, AIA, ARCHITECT

CRAGGED ROCK / FREEMAN HOUSE II

AN IRREGULAR HOUSE BASED ON A REGULAR SQUARE GRID

CHARLES G. WOODS, AIA, ARCHITECT

"WEBER HOUSE, SCHE[...]E "D"
"SOLAR ARC"

CHARLES G. WOODS, AIA,
ARCHITECT

THE WEBERS ARE MARVELOUS PEOPLE WITH GOOD TASTE, AND THEY HAVE BEEN FUN TO WORK WITH. I HAVE TO SAY IT, THOUGH: PART OF WHAT IS SO GREAT ABOUT THEM IS THAT THEY KNOW NOTHING ABOUT CONSTRUCTION AND TRUST ME COMPLETELY! IT SEEMS THAT ONLY IN ARCHITECTURE ARE PROFESSIONALS SO OFTEN SECOND-GUESSED AND ADVISED. THERE ARE REASONS FOR THIS, OF COURSE, BUT OFTEN (NOT ALWAYS) CLIENTS PREVENT ARCHITECTS FROM DOING THEIR BEST WORK. THE WEBERS ARE THE OPPOSITE: "GO FOR IT!" THEY SAY, "BUT COME IN AT BUDGET OR ELSE!"

THIS WAS MY FOURTH SCHEME FOR THEM—NOT BECAUSE THEY ASKED FOR MORE, BUT BECAUSE I WAS HAVING A HARD TIME VISUALIZING THE LOT. AFTER VISITING IT ON MY BIRTHDAY WITH THE WEBERS, I SCRIBBLED THE PLAN SHAPE AFTER MY SECOND AND LAST DRINK. I THINK IT HELPED. THE LOT IS LIKE ROLLING WAVES AND THE HOUSE LIKE A SAILING SHIP—SORT OF. (I NOTICE THAT I USE SHIP METAPHORS LATELY—SEE NAUTILUS, GUNDLACH, EARTHSHIP, AND CRAGGED ROCK.) THIS HOUSE STARTED A GLASS-BLOCK PHASE ALSO, NOW THAT YOU CAN GET CLEAR BLOCKS. THE FLAT ROOF IS EARTH-COVERED, AND WATERPROOFED WITH SHEETS OF BUTYL RUBBER.

* CONSTRUCTION PLANS AVAILABLE.

TO GARAGE/BARN/STUDIO

N

5 10 15 20 25 FT.

TERRACE

MAS. BED ROOM

CLOS.

CL.

STOR.

BATH

BATH
+UTIL.

GREAT ROOM

TERRACE

KIT.

CL.

FIREPL.

GUEST

TERRACE

WEBER HOUSE, SCHEME "D" 2000 SQ. FT.   CHARLES G. WOODS   AIA, ARCHITECT

CHARLES G. WOODS, ARCHITECT, AIA   WEBER HOUSE, SCHEME "D" - SOLAR ARC

TWO VIEWS

PRAIRIE HOUSE: RAGSDALE-MACDONALD RESIDENCE
CHARLES G. WOODS, AIA, ARCHITECT

THIS HOUSE WAS DESIGNED FOR THE CHARMING PROFESSIONAL COUPLE OF RAGSDALE AND MACDONALD. I WAS SOMEWHAT RELIEVED WHEN THESE CLIENTS WANTED A RECTILINEAR PLAN. THEY LIKE ANGLES AND CURVES, BUT DIDN'T WANT THE EXTRA EXPENSE. THE 4' SQUARE MODULE IS EASIER TO SPOT ON A PLAN LIKE THIS!

I GAVE THEM AN ANGULAR ROOF AND A CIRCLE TERRACE ANYWAY. THE HOUSE IS PARTLY INSPIRED BY WRIGHT'S ZIMMERMAN HOUSE AND SOME OF FAY E. JONES' HOUSES, BUT IT IS INDIVIDUAL, NEVERTHELESS. THERE ARE A LOT OF TORNADOES AROUND THIS AREA IN MISSOURI, SO WE ADDED ONE—A SMALL NON-THREATENING ONE—TO OUR EXTERIOR RENDERINGS. HOWEVER, THE HOUSE WILL HAVE A STORM ROOM. MAC DID A FINE JOB ON THESE DRAWINGS. I ESPECIALLY LIKE THE INTERIOR SECTIONAL PERSPECTIVE I REQUESTED.

* CONSTRUCTION PLANS AVAILABLE.

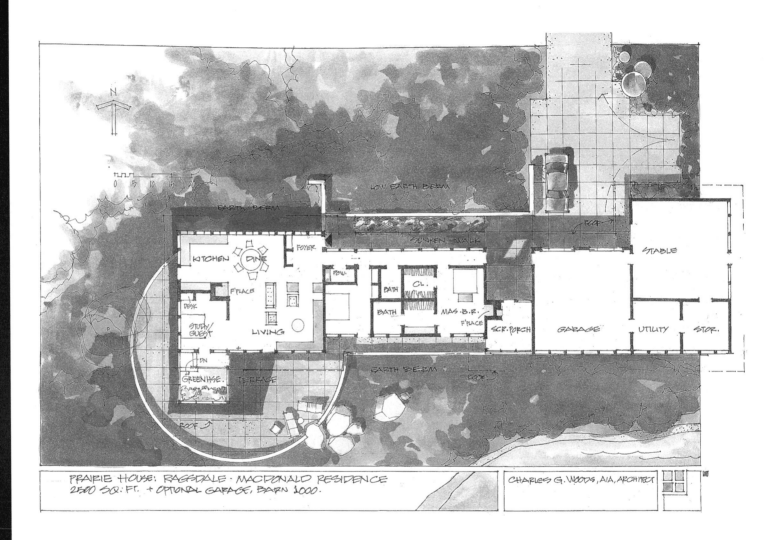

PRAIRIE HOUSE: RAGSDALE · MACDONALD RESIDENCE
2500 SQ. FT. + OPTIONAL GARAGE, BARN 1000.

CHARLES G. WOODS, AIA, ARCHITECT

SECTIONAL PERSPECTIVE,
PRAIRIE HOUSE : RAGSDALE · MACDONALD RESIDENCE

CHARLES G. WOODS, AIA, ARCHITECT

"SPIRAL" - A CALIFORNIA HOUSE   CHARLES G. WOODS, AIA, ARCHITECT

This house should be considered only a preliminary or schematic stage design. The house, completely built of reinforced concrete, is spiral-shaped with a steel-cable-suspended roof so as to have an uninterrupted curving glass-block wall.

The exterior perspective, though nice, is not quite as elegant as I imagined and needed another drawing stage to complete. This was not possible within the deadline for this book.

The plan is, I believe, close to a logarithmic spiral, but it was not consciously designed that way. Though not detailed, the plan is based on a series of circles in 4' increments and 45° angles. The interior perspective, however, <u>is</u> how I imagined it and the sunset I requested of Mac is perfect. The light flowing down on the right wall, however, is incorrect from the position of the sun. This is my fault, not Mac's—an inside rendering joke!

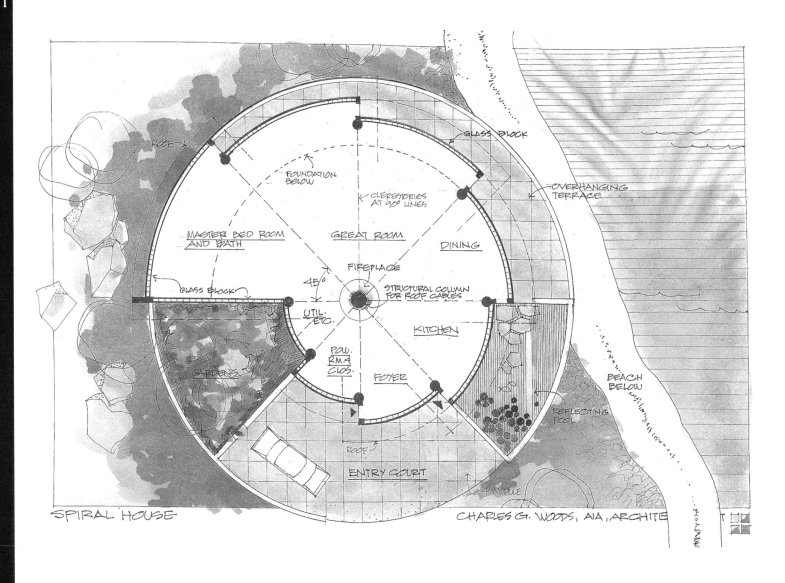

SPIRAL HOUSE   CHARLES G. WOODS, AIA, ARCHITECT

SPIRAL HOUSE — CHARLES G. WOODS, AIA, ARCHITECT

A TERRACED
UNDERGROUND HOUSE

CHARLES G. WOODS, AIA, ARCHITECT

THIS HOUSE SHOWS SOMETHING ABOUT MAC'S SKILL (AND I SUPPOSE ANY I MIGHT HAVE) AND THE MODULE SYSTEM. WITH ONLY TWO WEEKS TO GO TILL CONTRACT TIME, MAC AND I WERE EXHAUSTED, BUT I STILL WANTED TO GET A FEW FINAL HOUSES INTO THE BOOK. MAC, WHO IS CONSIDERED "THE FATHER OF UNDERGROUND ARCHITECTURE," HAS AT TIMES WANTED MORE EARTH ON MY ROOFS (OR SOME AT ALL). I USE EARTH ROOFS WHEREVER I CAN, BUT OCCASIONALLY I WANT SOMETHING MORE VISUALLY STRIKING—SLOPING, CURVED, OR THE LIKE.

SINCE THESE ARE "MY" DESIGNS, MAC WENT ALONG WITH ME MOST OF THE TIME, SO I WANTED TO GIVE HIM A REAL UNDERGROUND HOUSE IN THE BOOK, WITH 3' OF EARTH AND NO ROOF PARAPETS, WHICH I LIKE AND HE HATES. ANYWAY, THOUGH EXHAUSTED, HE SAID HE WOULD RENDER IT IF IT REALLY WAS UNDERGROUND. I DREW FREEHAND ON LARGE GRAPH PAPER ON THE MODULE SYSTEM AND SENT IT TO HIM VIA ONE-DAY MAIL. HE ASKED SOME QUESTIONS AND—VROOM!—THIS ARRIVED, COMPLETELY DONE, WITH NO ROUGHS EVEN. THIS IS NOT OUR USUAL WAY OF WORKING. I DO NOT BELIEVE THAT THIS LEVEL OF COMMUNICATION COULD BE ACCOMPLISHED SO EASILY LONG DISTANCE WITHOUT THIS MODULE SYSTEM. THOUGH A DETAILED PLAN WAS DESIGNED, ALL THAT POOR, TIRED MAC HAD TIME FOR WAS A QUICK ROOF/PARTIAL SITE PLAN. (THE FIRST FLOOR CONSISTS OF GARAGES, STORAGE/UTILITY, ENTRY, AND GARDEN. THE SECOND FLOOR CONSISTS OF LIVING AREA, KITCHEN, AND BEDROOMS.)

DESIGNS DON'T USUALLY COME TO ME THIS QUICKLY—THIS WAS CONCEIVED, DRAWN, AND OUT IN THE MAIL IN ONLY TWO TO THREE HOURS. THOUGH IT COULD BE IMPROVED, I REALLY

UNDERGROUND HOUSE

LIGHT WELL   LIGHT WELL

TERRACE   12' GRID

ROOF AT UPPER LEVEL   TERRACE

ROOF AT LOWER LEVEL

SKYLT.

ENTRANCE
TERRACE

N

SITE PLAN

0   10   20   30   40   50 FT.

LOVE IT, AND MAC'S EXTERIOR PERSPECTIVE IS SO CLOSE TO MY IMAGINED VIEW, IT'S ALMOST
SCARY!

THE HOUSE IS MEANT TO BE CONSTRUCTED OF REINFORCED CONCRETE, WITH SQUARE
STRUCTURAL COLUMNS OF 12' O.C. TURNED 45°, AND ALSO "ROCK-CONCRETE," AS IN
WRIGHT'S FAMOUS TALIESIN WEST. THE WHOLE STRUCTURE WOULD BE INSULATED ON THE
OUTSIDE AND COMPLETELY WATERPROOFED WITH BUTYL RUBBER SHEETS. AS YOU CAN SEE, THE
DESIGN IS TERRACED ON THE CROSS-SECTIONAL PERSPECTIVE. I IMAGINED THE HOUSE AS
HAVING A FUTURISTIC OR TIMELESS ("UTOPIAN") LOOK, À LA JULES VERNE OR
H. G. WELLS, AND I THINK THAT COMES ACROSS IN THE RENDERINGS.

A TERRACED UNDERGROUND HOUSE

CHARLES G. WOODS, AIA, ARCHITECT

EARTHSHIP IS A PRELIMINARY DESIGN FOR MYSELF IN MAYBE FIVE YEARS OR SO—IF I CAN AFFORD IT. I ALREADY LIVE IN A LOVELY LITTLE UNDERGROUND HOUSE OF MY OWN DESIGN, BUT IT IS A VERY SIMPLE SHAPE—A RECTANGLE—AND IT'S VERY SMALL—1100 SQUARE FEET. WE HAVE NO CHILDREN, BUT EVEN SO, WE MOVED OUR OFFICES OUT AND THE HOUSE IS STILL TOO SMALL.

THE SHAPE OF THIS HOUSE IS A SACRED SYMBOL: THAT OF PISCES, THE FISH, AND CHRIST. THE CELTS CALL IT THE "SEED THOUGHT." SINCE I AM A "BAD" CHRISTIAN AND LOVE JOHN SCOTUS ERIUGENA (THE NINTH-CENTURY IRISH CHRISTIAN PHILOSOPHER), IT WOULD BE AN APPROPRIATE SHAPE FOR A NEW HOUSE OR POSSIBLY JUST AN OFFICE.

THE ORIGINAL ROOF WAS MUCH MORE STRIKING—DOUBLE-CURVED ROOFS, CREATING AN ASYMPTOTIC GLASS CLERESTORY, BUT MAC WOULDN'T DRAW IT. HE THOUGHT I WAS GOING MAD—OR FLAMBOYANT. WOULDN'T DRAW IT?! I AM IN A UNIQUE SITUATION HERE: IF I AM EVEN A LITTLE BIT LIKE FRANK LLOYD WRIGHT, THEN MAC IS LIKE LOUIS SULLIVAN DOING MY RENDERINGS. BECAUSE MAC IS A VERY FAMOUS MAN IN HIS OWN RIGHT, I DIDN'T FIGHT HIM ON THIS. THE HOUSE IS <u>STILL</u> STRIKING, AND IT IS LESS EXPENSIVE AND MORE ENERGY EFFICIENT AS I REDESIGNED IT.

NOTE THE GLASS PORTHOLES ON THE RIGHT SIDE OF THE EXTERIOR PERSPECTIVE. I BELIEVE THAT ANOTHER ENVIRONMENTAL ARCHITECT CALLS <u>ALL</u> HIS HOUSES "EARTHSHIPS." I WON'T USE <u>HIS</u> IDEA, EXCEPT ON THIS ONE! AS I HAVE SAID, MY HOUSES HAVE BEEN LOOKING MORE AND MORE LIKE SHIPS OF SORTS. WHY? WELL . . . OUR HOUSES REALLY ARE LIKE SHIPS IF YOU THINK ABOUT IT. THEY DO TRAVEL—NOT THROUGH SEA OR AIR, BUT THROUGH TIME AND SPACE.

NO DETAILED PLAN WAS DONE FOR THIS DESIGN, BUT I HOPE THE ROOF/SITE PLAN AND INTERIOR SECTIONAL PERSPECTIVE HELP.

NEXT: **EARTHSHIP**

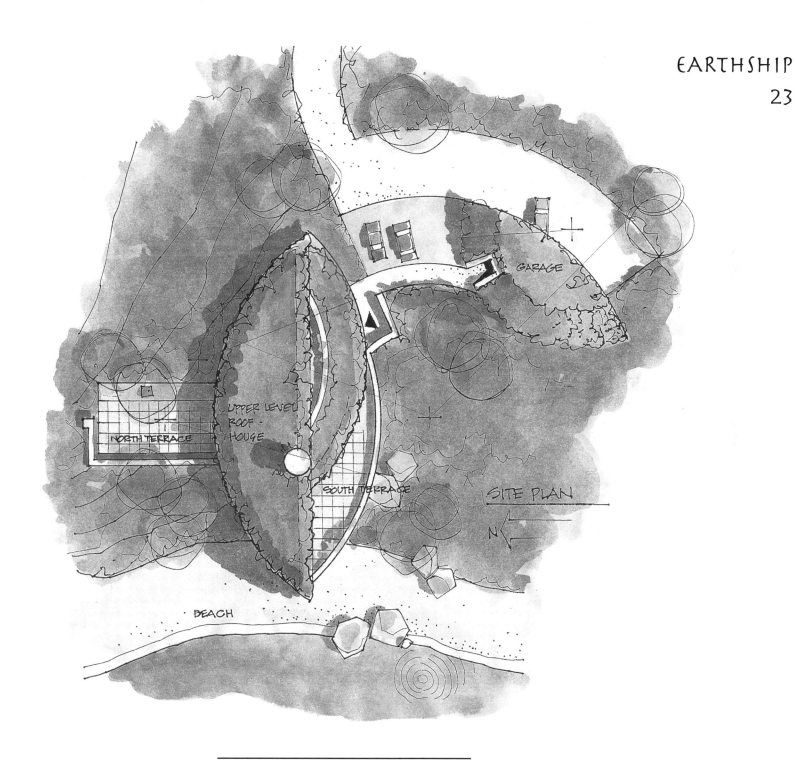

GARAGE

NORTH TERRACE

UPPER LEVEL
ROOF -
HOUSE

SOUTH TERRACE

SITE PLAN

N

BEACH

EARTHSHIP : ARCHITECT'S STUDIO
CHARLES G. WOODS, AIA, ARCHITECT

THIS HOUSE FOR NOTED PHOTOGRAPHER MICHAEL KELLAR (MISSPELLED ON THE DRAWING) IS OBVIOUSLY NOT IN MY USUAL STYLE. IT IS ONE OF ONLY FIVE TRADITIONAL-LOOKING HOUSES THAT I HAVE DONE TO DATE. MY HEART IS JUST NOT IN IT, BUT MIKE'S A SLY MAN. HE CAME TO MY OFFICE AND TOLD ME HE <u>LOVES</u> MY WORK, THEN PROCEEDED TO ASK ME TO DO SOMETHING COMPLETELY CONTRARY TO IT. I REFUSED HIM; HE BEGGED. I STILL TOLD HIM NO, AND HIS GIRLFRIEND MANAGED TO FLATTER ME INTO TAKING THE COMMISSION.

I HAVE TOLD YOU THIS SLIGHTLY EMBARRASSING STORY SO ALL YOU MALE AND FEMALE ARCHITECTS OUT THERE LEARN SOMETHING FROM THIS: "PRIDE GOES BEFORE THE FALL." ACTUALLY, I DID NOT COMPLETELY GIVE UP MY ETHICS. I HAD THIS BOOK IN THE BACK OF MY MIND AND TOLD MIKE I WOULD DO THIS DESIGN FOR HIM ONLY IF I COULD DO IT ON MY MODULE AND IN THE CRAFTSMAN STYLE WITH NO FAKE TRIM OR DETAILS AND IF HE WOULD PAY FOR AT LEAST ONE RENDERING (ACTUALLY, WE SPLIT IT BECAUSE IT GOT EXPENSIVE—$800).

I THOUGHT IT WOULD BE INTERESTING TO SHOW MY READERS THAT DESIGNS BASED ON MY MODULE SYSTEM NEED NOT LOOK PARTICULARLY "MODULAR" OR "MODERN," OR "ORGANIC." THIS DESIGN CAME OUT GREAT AND LOOKS MORE LIKE A TYPICAL HOUSE THAN ANYTHING ELSE I'VE DESIGNED. AFTER MONTHS OF MEETINGS, CALLS, LETTERS, AND ENDLESS LATE-NIGHT FAXES, MIKE CHANGED IT SOMEWHAT HIMSELF. BUT HE WAS HAPPY WITH MY WORK, AND HE PAID ME FAIRLY, SO WE ARE STILL FRIENDS.

THIS MIGHT BE A GOOD PLACE TO MENTION THAT THERE ARE AT LEAST THREE TYPES OF ARCHITECTS. ONE TYPE WORKS LIKE A DRAFTSMAN (OR -WOMAN)—EITHER BECAUSE OF A

LACK OF EXTRAORDINARY DESIGN SKILLS OR PERHAPS JUST TO SUPPORT THE FAMILY. THERE IS A SECOND TYPE, WHICH I HAVE COME TO RESPECT A LOT MORE, THAT DOES NOT HAVE A "STYLE" AS SUCH BUT CAN COMBINE THE CLIENT'S WISHES INTO TRULY UNIQUE DESIGNS—BUT ONES THAT BEAR LITTLE SIMILARITY TO PREVIOUS WORK. SOME OF THE BEST FIRMS NOW DO THIS AND WIN MAJOR AWARDS.

I AM OF THE THIRD TYPE, THE "ARTIST/ARCHITECT," OR WHAT IS KNOWN AS A SIGNATURE/ARCHITECT. MOST FAMOUS ARCHITECTS ARE OF THIS TYPE. (I MIGHT AS WELL MENTION THIS FOR POTENTIAL CLIENTS.) THIS BOOK IS A GOOD EXAMPLE OF THE WORK OF SUCH AN ARCHITECT, FOR WITH ALL THESE VARIOUS GEOMETRIES AND FORMS, THERE IS, I BELIEVE, A CONSISTENCY AND "SIGNATURE" OF SORTS IN MY WORK. ALTHOUGH I DO WANT TO KNOW MY CLIENTS' WISHES AND DESIRES FOR THEIR HOMES, I WANT EVERYTHING TO FILTER THROUGH MY MIND. I DON'T THINK IT'S A MATTER OF ARROGANCE—IT'S THE ONLY WAY I KNOW HOW TO WORK. ALSO, I HAVE A STRONG CONVICTION THAT I REALLY CAN DESIGN BETTER THAN MY CLIENTS. THIS IS NOT TO DENIGRATE THE INTELLIGENCE AND IMAGINATION OF MY CLIENTS, WHICH IS OFTEN EQUAL OR SUPERIOR TO MY OWN—IT IS A MATTER OF "TRAINED" SKILL.

IF MY CLIENTS (OR THOSE OF ANY ARCHITECT) DO NOT BELIEVE WE ARE MORE SKILLED THAN THEY ARE IN ARCHITECTURE, THEN THE SYSTEM JUST DOES NOT WORK. THAT IS WHY I FIND THAT PROFESSIONALS OFTEN (BUT NOT EXCLUSIVELY) MAKE THE BEST CLIENTS FOR ARCHITECTS, SINCE PEOPLE PAY THEM AND TRUST THEM FOR THEIR JUDGMENTS. THEY TEND TO TRUST OTHER PROFESSIONALS TO DO THEIR JOBS, UNLESS IT HAS BEEN DEMONSTRATED OTHERWISE.

ARCHITECTURE AS ART IS A VERY PAINFUL PROCESS AND USUALLY, AT THE END, THE ARCHITECT HEARS THAT DREADFUL QUESTION, "WHOSE HOUSE IS IT ANYWAY?" ONE BAD MAILBOX, GARAGE DOOR, OR OUT-OF-PLACE COLOR OR WINDOW CAN WRECK YEARS OF AN ARCHITECT'S WORK. ARCHITECTS ARE, IF ANYTHING, UNDERPAID—EVEN CONSIDERING THE "HIGH" FEES OF SOME. THERE ARE MUCH EASIER WAYS TO MAKE MONEY!

ONE THING I DO AGREE WITH AYN RAND'S FICTIONAL ARCHITECT, HOWARD ROARK, ABOUT, THOUGH, IS WHEN HE SAID, "I DON'T BUILD IN ORDER TO HAVE CLIENTS—I HAVE CLIENTS IN ORDER TO BUILD" (I QUOTE FROM MEMORY WITH DUE RESPECT TO THE AUTHOR).

A CRAFTSMAN STYLE HOUSE/STUDIO FOR MICHAEL KELLER BASED ON THE MODULE SYSTEM
BEACH LAKE, PENNSYLVANIA   CHARLES WOODS, AIA, ARCHITECT

CONSTRUCTION DRAWINGS

THIS IS THE ONLY HOUSE IN THIS BOOK THAT IS OLDER THAN FOUR YEARS. I DESIGNED THIS OVER TEN YEARS AGO WITH MAC. THE REASON I INCLUDE IT IS TO SHOW A SET OF CONSTRUCTION DRAWINGS THAT MAC DID FOR ME ON THE MODULE, IN INK, AND WITH GREAT DETAIL FOR A 500-SQUARE-FOOT HOUSE. IT ALSO SHOWS THE AMOUNT OF WORK THAT GOES INTO A GOOD SET OF PLANS.

THIS SET WAS SOLD TO <u>POPULAR SCIENCE</u> MAGAZINE READERS IN AN EDITORIAL ARTICLE BY AL LEES (WHO GAVE ME A CHANCE) IN 1983. THE ONE THING I WOULD DO DIFFERENTLY NOW IS TO SHOW EVERY MODULE LINE ENDING ON A CIRCLE WITH A LETTER OR NUMBER IN IT— SAY, A, B, C, ETC., ACROSS AND 1, 2, 3, ETC., DOWN. THIS WAY, ANY PART OF A COMPLEX PLAN OR STRUCTURE COULD BE EASILY LOCATED. INSTEAD OF VAGUE AND SUBJECTIVE ATTEMPTS TO IDENTIFY A PART, YOU WOULD REFER TO "THE WINDOW AT E, 5." THIS IS REALLY SIMPLE FOR IDENTIFYING DETAILS, TOO.

I DID NOT INVENT THIS SYSTEM BUT IT IS USUALLY USED FOR LARGER STRUCTURES. FOR A MORE COMPLEX EXAMPLE, SEE THE SENALIK RESIDENCE SHOWN IN MY PREVIOUS BOOK (WITH MAC), <u>DESIGNING YOUR NATURAL HOUSE</u> (VNR, 1992). THIS ALSO SHOWS THE AMOUNT OF WORK THAT GOES INTO EVEN AN ARCHITECTURALLY DESIGNED CABIN.

* CONSTRUCTION PLANS, AS SHOWN, AVAILABLE.

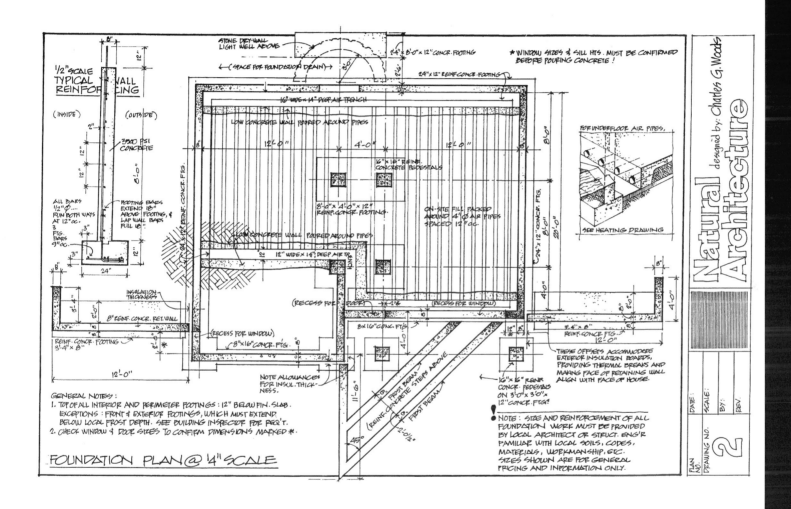

FOUNDATION PLAN @ ¼" SCALE

½" SCALE TYPICAL WALL REINFORCING

GENERAL NOTES:
1. TOP OF ALL INTERIOR AND PERIMETER FOOTINGS : 12" BELOW FIN. SLAB. EXCEPTIONS : FRONT & EXTERIOR FOOTINGS, WHICH MUST EXTEND BELOW LOCAL FROST DEPTH. SEE BUILDING INSPECTOR FOR REQ'T.
2. CHECK WINDOW & DOOR SIZES TO CONFIRM DIMENSIONS MARKED *.

NOTE: SIZE AND REINFORCEMENT OF ALL FOUNDATION WORK MUST BE PROVIDED BY LOCAL ARCHITECT OR STRUCT. ENG'R FAMILIAR WITH LOCAL SOILS, CODES, MATERIALS, WORKMANSHIP, ETC. SIZES SHOWN ARE FOR GENERAL PRICING AND INFORMATION ONLY.

Natural Architecture

designed by: Charles G. Woods

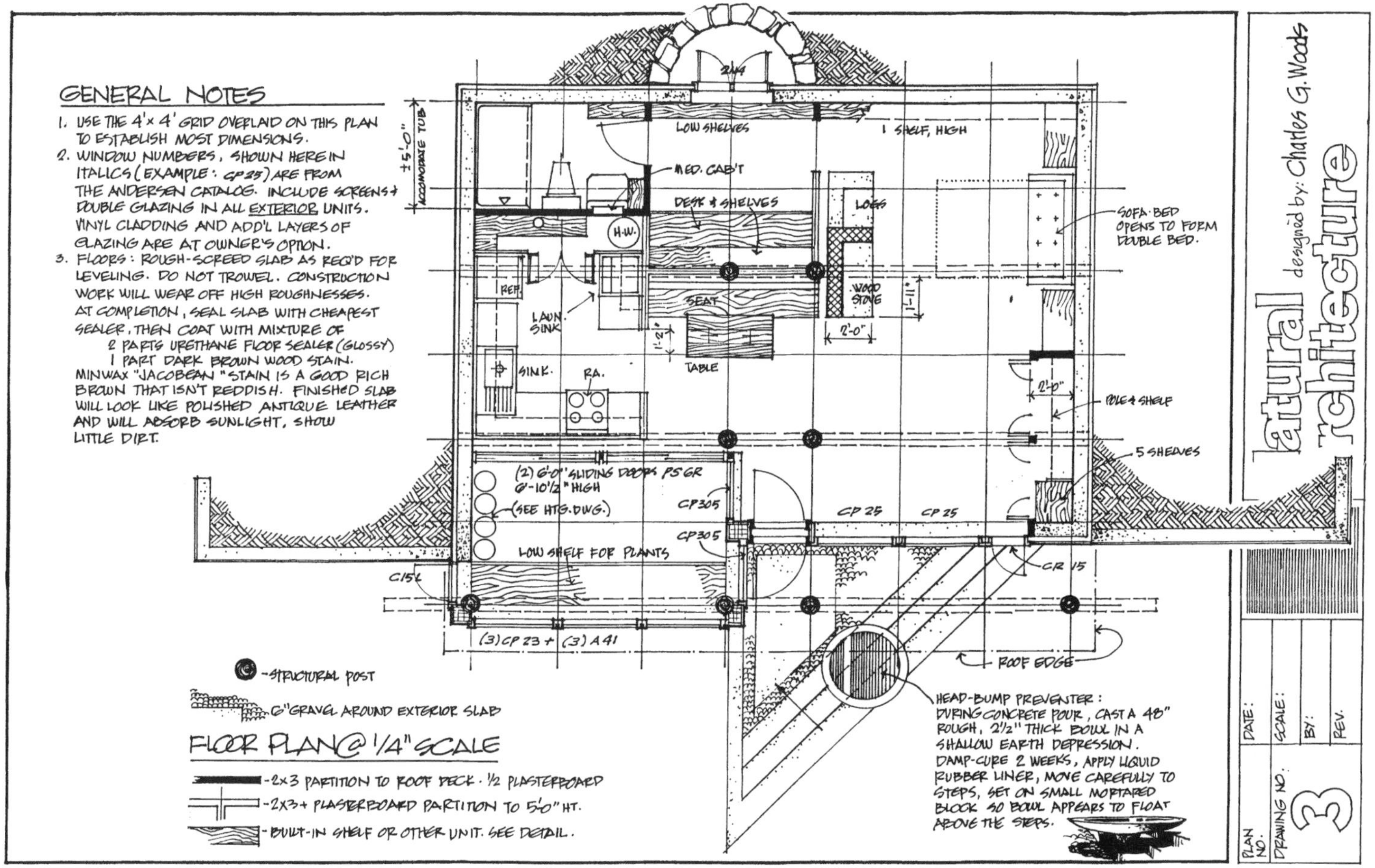
GENERAL NOTES
1. USE THE 4'× 4' GRID OVERLAID ON THIS PLAN TO ESTABLISH MOST DIMENSIONS.
2. WINDOW NUMBERS, SHOWN HERE IN ITALICS (EXAMPLE: CP23) ARE FROM THE ANDERSEN CATALOG. INCLUDE SCREENS + DOUBLE GLAZING IN ALL EXTERIOR UNITS. VINYL CLADDING AND ADD'L LAYERS OF GLAZING ARE AT OWNER'S OPTION.
3. FLOORS: ROUGH-SCREED SLAB AS REQ'D FOR LEVELING. DO NOT TROWEL. CONSTRUCTION WORK WILL WEAR OFF HIGH ROUGHNESSES. AT COMPLETION, SEAL SLAB WITH CHEAPEST SEALER, THEN COAT WITH MIXTURE OF 2 PARTS URETHANE FLOOR SEALER (GLOSSY) 1 PART DARK BROWN WOOD STAIN. MINWAX "JACOBEAN" STAIN IS A GOOD RICH BROWN THAT ISN'T REDDISH. FINISHED SLAB WILL LOOK LIKE POLISHED ANTIQUE LEATHER AND WILL ABSORB SUNLIGHT, SHOW LITTLE DIRT.
±5'-0" ACCOMMODATE TUB
LOW SHELVES
1 SHELF, HIGH
MED. CAB'T
DESK & SHELVES
LOGS
H.W.
SOFA-BED OPENS TO FORM DOUBLE BED.
REF.
LAUN. SINK
SEAT
WOOD STOVE
1'-11"
2'-0"
1'-2"
TABLE
SINK.
RA.
2'-0"
POLE & SHELF
5 SHELVES
(2) 6'-0" SLIDING DOORS PS GR 6'-10½" HIGH
(SEE HTG. DWG.)
CP305
CP305
CP 25
CP 25
LOW SHELF FOR PLANTS
C15
CR 15
(3) CP 23 + (3) A 41
ROOF EDGE
-STRUCTURAL POST
-6" GRAVEL AROUND EXTERIOR SLAB
FLOOR PLAN @ 1/4" SCALE
-2x3 PARTITION TO ROOF DECK · ½ PLASTERBOARD
-2x3 + PLASTERBOARD PARTITION TO 5'-0" HT.
-BUILT-IN SHELF OR OTHER UNIT. SEE DETAIL.
HEAD-BUMP PREVENTER: DURING CONCRETE POUR, CAST A 48" ROUGH, 2½" THICK BOWL IN A SHALLOW EARTH DEPRESSION. DAMP-CURE 2 WEEKS, APPLY LIQUID RUBBER LINER, MOVE CAREFULLY TO STEPS, SET ON SMALL MORTARED BLOCK SO BOWL APPEARS TO FLOAT ABOVE THE STEPS.
natural architecture
designed by: Charles G. Woods
DATE:
SCALE:
BY:
REV.
PLAN NO.
DRAWING NO.: 3

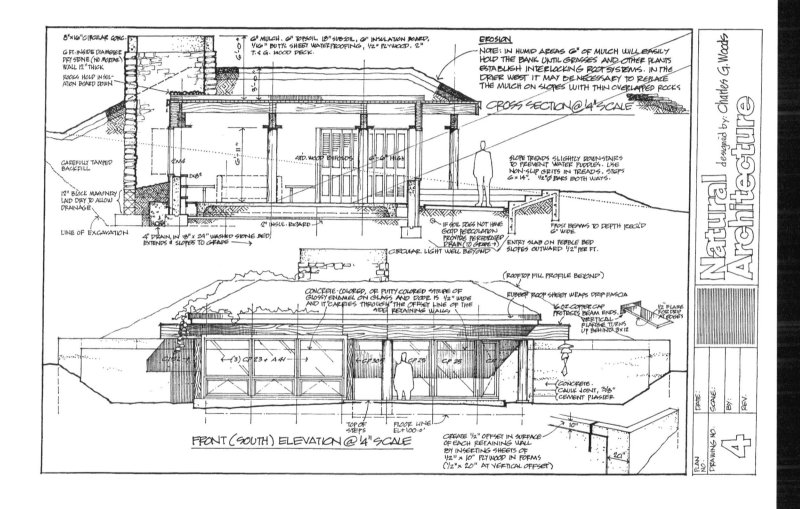

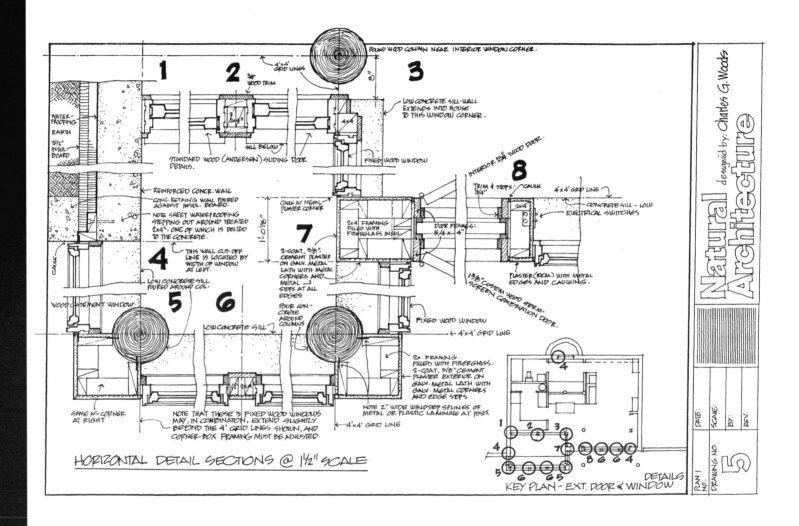

ROUND WOOD COLUMN NEAR INTERIOR WINDOW CORNER.

1 **2** **3**

4'x4' GRID LINES

34" WOOD TRIM

LOW CONCRETE SILL-WALL EXTENDS INTO HOUSE TO THIS WINDOW CORNER.

8"

WATER-PROOFING

EARTH

3 1/2" INSUL BOARD

4x4

SILL BELOW

STANDARD WOOD (ANDERSEN) SLIDING DOOR DETAILS.

FIXED WOOD WINDOW

INTERIOR 1 3/4" WOOD DOOR.

8

TRIM & STOPS: CAULK

3/4"

4'x4' GRID LINE

2x4

CONCRETE SILL - LOW ELECTRICAL SWITCHES

REINFORCED CONCR. WALL

CONC. RETAIN'G WALL POURED AGAINST INSUL. BOARD.

NOTE SHEET WATERPROOFING STEPPING OUT AROUND TREATED 2x4's, ONE OF WHICH IS BOLTED TO THE CONCRETE.

CAULK AT METAL PLASTER CORNER

11'-0 1/8"

7

2x4 FRAMING FILLED WITH FIBERGLASS INSUL.

DOOR FRAMES: 5/4 x 4"

THIS WALL CUT-OFF LINE IS LOCATED BY WIDTH OF WINDOW AT LEFT.

2-COAT, 5/8" CEMENT PLASTER ON GALV. METAL LATH WITH METAL CORNERS AND METAL STOPS AT ALL EDGES

13/8" CUSTOM WOOD STORM-SCREEN COMBINATION DOOR.

PLASTER (CEM.) WITH METAL EDGES AND CAULKING.

CAULK

4

LOW CONCRETE SILL POURED AROUND COL.

WOOD CASEMENT WINDOW.

5 **6**

LOW CONCRETE SILL

POUR CONCRETE AROUND COLUMNS

FIXED WOOD WINDOW

← 4'x4' GRID LINE

2x4

2x FRAMING FILLED WITH FIBERGLASS.

2-COAT, 5/8" CEMENT PLASTER EXTERIOR ON GALV. METAL LATH WITH GALV. METAL CORNERS AND EDGE STOPS

SAME AS CORNER AT RIGHT

NOTE THAT THESE 3 FIXED WOOD WINDOWS MAY, IN COMBINATION, EXTEND SLIGHTLY BEYOND THE 4' GRID LINES SHOWN, AND CORNER-BOX FRAMING MUST BE ADJUSTED.

NOTE 2" WIDE WINDSTOP SPLINES OF METAL OR PLASTIC LAMINATE AT POSTS.

← 4'x4' GRID LINE

HORIZONTAL DETAIL SECTIONS @ 1 1/2" SCALE

KEY PLAN - EXT. DOOR & WINDOW

DETAILS

Natural **Architecture**

designed by: Charles G. Woods

DATE:

SCALE:

BY:

REV.

PLAN NO.

DRAWING NO. **5**

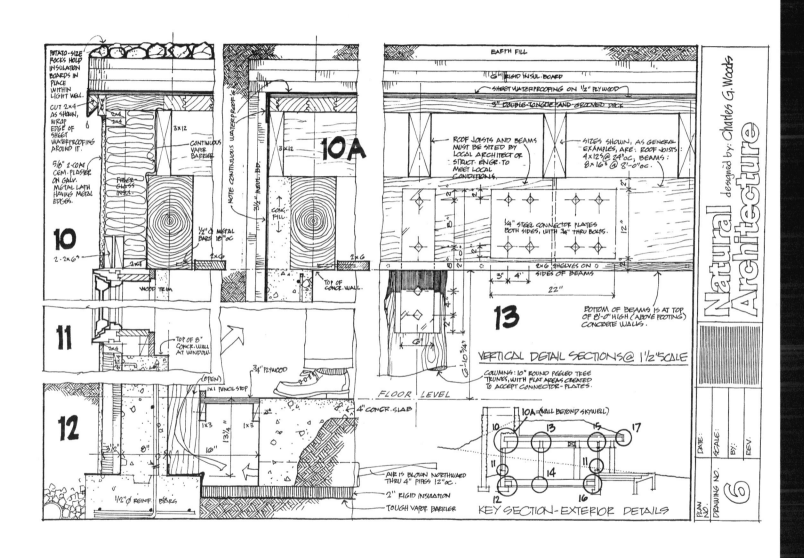

10
PITATO-SIZE ROCKS HOLD INSULATION BOARDS IN PLACE WITHIN LIGHT WELL.

CUT 2×4 AS SHOWN, WRAP EDGE OF SHEET WATERPROOFING AROUND IT.

5/8" 2-COAT CEM. PLASTER ON GALV. METAL LATH HAVING METAL EDGES.

2-2×6's

2×4 2×4

3×12

FIBER-GLASS INSUL.

CONTINUOUS VAPOR BARRIER

1/2" Ø METAL BARS 18"OC

2×4

2×6

WOOD TRIM

10A
NOTE CONTINUOUS WATERPROOF.

3×12

3 1/2" INSUL. BD.

CONC. FILL.

2×6

TOP OF CONC. WALL

EARTH FILL

RIGID INSUL. BOARD

SHEET WATERPROOFING ON 1/2" PLYWOOD

3" DOUBLE-TONGUE AND-GROOVED DECK

ROOF JOISTS AND BEAMS MUST BE SIZED BY LOCAL ARCHITECT OR STRUCT. ENGR. TO MEET LOCAL CONDITIONS.

SIZES SHOWN, AS GENERAL EXAMPLES, ARE: ROOF JOISTS: 4×12's @ 24"OC; BEAMS: 8×16's @ 8'-0"OC.

1/4" STEEL CONNECTOR PLATES BOTH SIDES, WITH 3/4" THRU BOLTS.

2×6 SHELVES ON SIDES OF BEAMS

3' 4'

12"

22"

13

BOTTOM OF BEAMS IS AT TOP OF 8'-0" HIGH (ABOVE FOOTING) CONCRETE WALLS.

6'-10 3/4"

VERTICAL DETAIL SECTIONS @ 1 1/2" SCALE

COLUMNS: 10" ROUND PEELED TREE TRUNKS, WITH FLAT AREAS CREATED TO ACCEPT CONNECTOR-PLATES.

11
2×4

TOP OF 8" CONC. WALL AT WINDOW.

(OPEN)

1×1 PENCIL STOP

3/4" PLYWOOD

1×3 1×3

13 3/4"

12"

FLOOR LEVEL

4" CONCR. SLAB

12
3 1/2"

8"

1/2" Ø REINF. BARS

AIR IS BLOWN NORTHWARD THRU 4" PIPES 12"OC.

2" RIGID INSULATION

TOUGH VAPOR BARRIER

10A=(WALL BEYOND SKYWELL)

10 13 15 17

11 11

14

12 16

KEY SECTION-EXTERIOR DETAILS

Natural Architecture
designed by: Charles G. Woods

DATE:
SCALE:
BY:
REV.

PLAN NO.
DRAWING NO. **6**

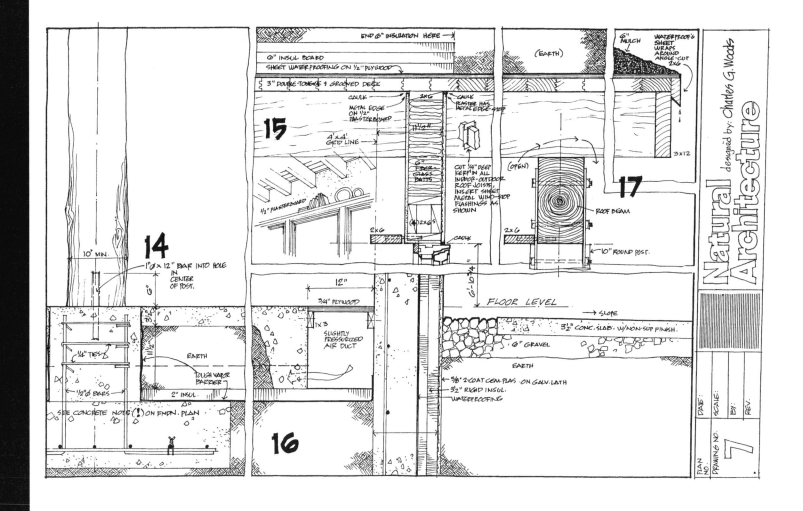

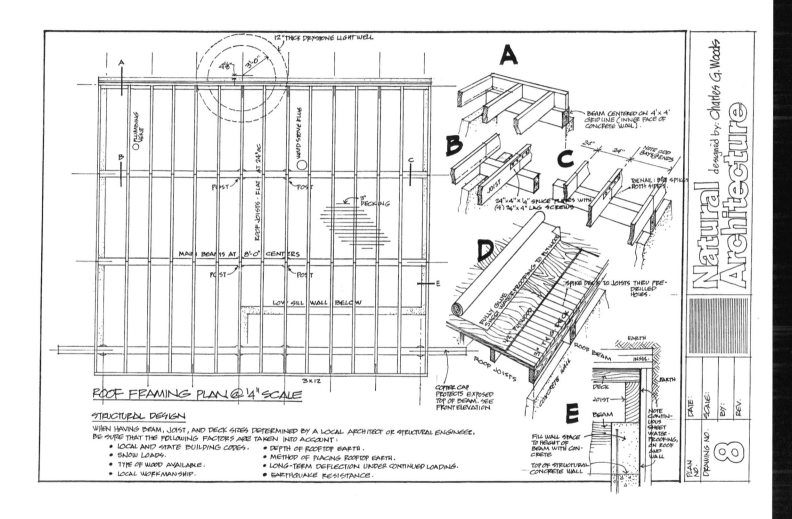

12" THICK DRYSTONE LIGHTWELL

4'8" 3'-0"

A

BEAM CENTERED ON 4'x 4'
GRID LINE (INNER FACE OF
CONCRETE WALL)

PLUMBING VENT

WOOD STOVE FLUE

B

C

POST

ROOF JOISTS - FLAT AT 24" OC

POST

24" 24" NOTE ODD
BAYS/ENDS

3" DECKING

JOIST

TOENAIL: 8 d" SPIKES
BOTH SIDES

MAIN BEAMS AT 8'-0" CENTERS

24"x 4"x 4" SPLICE PLATES WITH
(4) 3/4"x 4" LAG SCREWS

POST

POST

D

FULLY GLUE
SHEET WATERPROOFING TO PLYWOOD

SPIKE DECK TO JOISTS THRU PRE-
DRILLED HOLES.

E

LOW SILL WALL BELOW

1/2" T+G PLYWOOD

3" T+G DECK

ROOF JOISTS

EARTH

ROOF BEAM

INSUL.

EARTH

3x12

DECK

JOIST

ROOF JOISTS

CONCRETE WALL

BEAM

COPPER CAP
PROTECTS EXPOSED
TOP OF BEAM. SEE
FRONT ELEVATION

NOTE CONTIN-
UOUS
SHEET
WATER-
PROOFING
ON ROOF
AND
WALL

ROOF FRAMING PLAN @ 1/4" SCALE

STRUCTURAL DESIGN

WHEN HAVING BEAM, JOIST, AND DECK SIZES DETERMINED BY A LOCAL ARCHITECT OR STRUCTURAL ENGINEER,
BE SURE THAT THE FOLLOWING FACTORS ARE TAKEN INTO ACCOUNT:
- LOCAL AND STATE BUILDING CODES.
- SNOW LOADS.
- TYPE OF WOOD AVAILABLE.
- LOCAL WORKMANSHIP.
- DEPTH OF ROOFTOP EARTH.
- METHOD OF PLACING ROOFTOP EARTH.
- LONG-TERM DEFLECTION UNDER CONTINUED LOADING.
- EARTHQUAKE RESISTANCE.

FILL WALL SPACE
TO HEIGHT OF
BEAM WITH CON-
CRETE

TOP OF STRUCTURAL
CONCRETE WALL

Natural Architecture

designed by: Charles G. Woods

DATE:

SCALE:

BY:

REV.:

PLAN NO:

DRAWING NO. 8

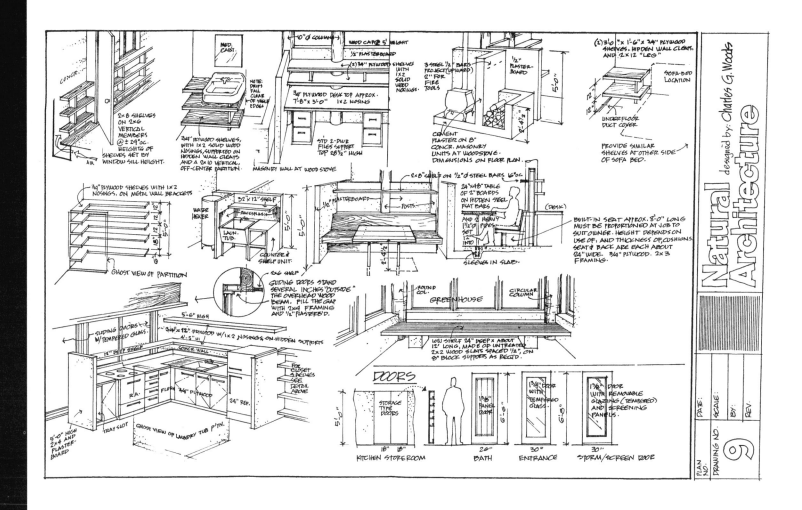

Natural **Architecture**
designed by: Charles G. Woods

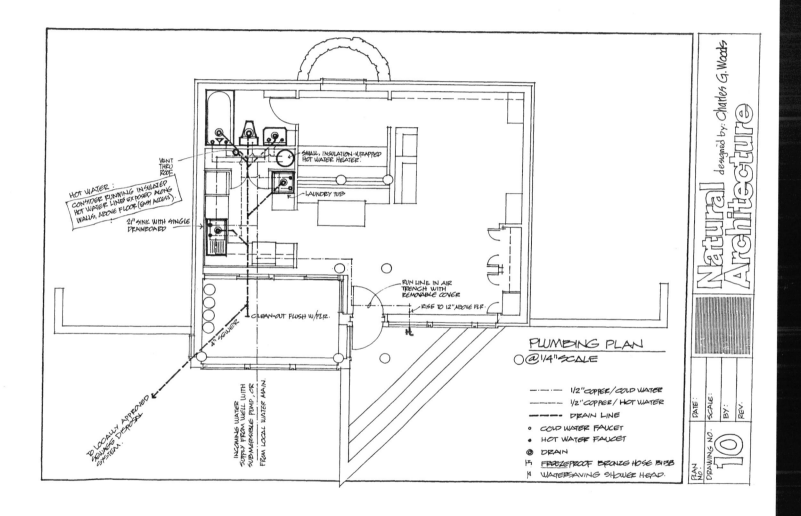

VENT
THRU
ROOF

SMALL, INSULATION-WRAPPED
HOT WATER HEATER.

HOT WATER:
CONSIDER RUNNING INSULATED
HOT WATER LINE EXPOSED ALONG
WALLS, ABOVE FLOOR (EASY ACCESS).

— LAUNDRY TUB

24" SINK WITH SINGLE
DRAINBOARD

RUN LINE IN AIR
TRENCH WITH
REMOVABLE COVER

— RISE TO 12" ABOVE FLR.

4" SEWER CLEAN-OUT FLUSH W/FLR.

TO LOCALLY APPROVED
SEWAGE DISPOSAL
SYSTEM

INCOMING WATER
SUPPLY FROM WELL WITH
SUBMERSIBLE PUMP, OR
FROM LOCAL WATER MAIN.

PLUMBING PLAN
@ 1/4" SCALE

– – –	1/2" COPPER / COLD WATER
— —	1/2" COPPER / HOT WATER
– · – ·	DRAIN LINE
○	COLD WATER FAUCET
●	HOT WATER FAUCET
◉	DRAIN
⊢	FREEZEPROOF BRONZE HOSE BIBB
⊬	WATERSAVING SHOWER HEAD.

designed by: Charles G. Woods

Natural Architecture

DATE:
SCALE:
BY:
REV:

PLAN NO.
DRAWING NO. 10

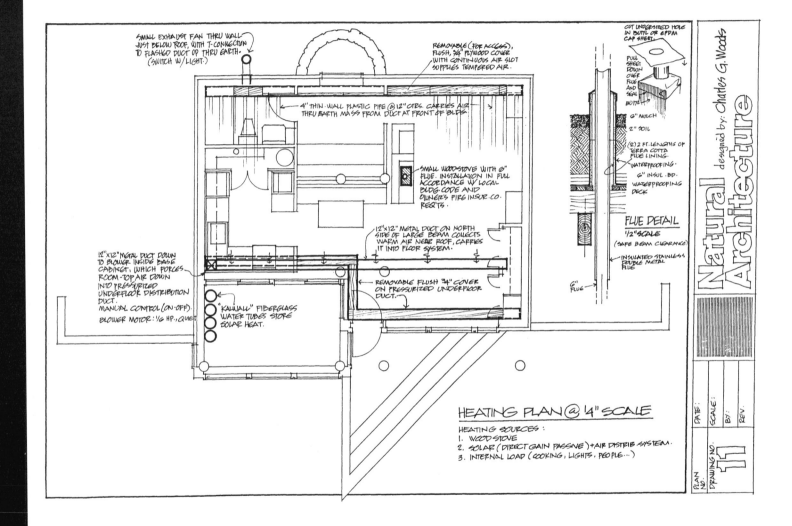

SMALL EXHAUST FAN THRU WALL
JUST BELOW ROOF, WITH T-CONNECTION
TO FLASHED DUCT UP THRU EARTH.
(SWITCH W/LIGHT.)

REMOVABLE (FOR ACCESS),
FLUSH, ¾" PLYWOOD COVER
WITH CONTINUOUS AIR SLOT
SUPPLIES TEMPERED AIR.

CUT UNDERSIZED HOLE
IN BUTYL OR EPDM
CAP SHEET.

PULL
SHEET
DOWN
OVER
FLUE
AND
SEAL
BUTYL

4" THIN-WALL PLASTIC PIPE @ 12" CTRS. CARRIES AIR
THRU EARTH MASS FROM DUCT AT FRONT OF BLDG.

6" MULCH

2" SOIL

(2) 2 FT. LENGTHS OF
TERRA COTTA
FLUE LINING.

WATERPROOFING.

6" INSUL. BD.

WATERPROOFING
DECK

SMALL WOODSTOVE WITH 6"
FLUE. INSTALLATION IN FULL
ACCORDANCE W/ LOCAL
BLDG. CODE AND
OWNER'S FIRE INSUR. CO.
REQ'TS.

FLUE DETAIL
½" SCALE
(SAFE BEAM CLEARANCE)

12"x12" METAL DUCT ON NORTH
SIDE OF LARGE BEAM COLLECTS
WARM AIR NEAR ROOF, CARRIES
IT INTO FLOOR SYSTEM.

INSULATED STAINLESS
DOUBLE METAL
FLUE

6" FLUE

12"x12" METAL DUCT DOWN
TO BLOWER INSIDE BASE
CABINET, WHICH FORCES
ROOM-TOP AIR DOWN
INTO PRESSURIZED
UNDERFLOOR DISTRIBUTION
DUCT.
MANUAL CONTROL (ON-OFF).

BLOWER MOTOR: ⅙ HP., QUIET.

REMOVABLE FLUSH ¾" COVER
ON PRESSURIZED UNDERFLOOR
DUCT.

"KALWALL" FIBERGLASS
WATER TUBES STORE
SOLAR HEAT.

HEATING PLAN @ ¼" SCALE

HEATING SOURCES:
1. WOOD STOVE
2. SOLAR (DIRECT GAIN PASSIVE) + AIR DISTRIB. SYSTEM.
3. INTERNAL LOAD (COOKING, LIGHTS, PEOPLE...)

Natural
Architecture

designed by: Charles G. Woods

DATE:
SCALE:
BY:
REV.

PLAN NO.
DRAWING NO. 11

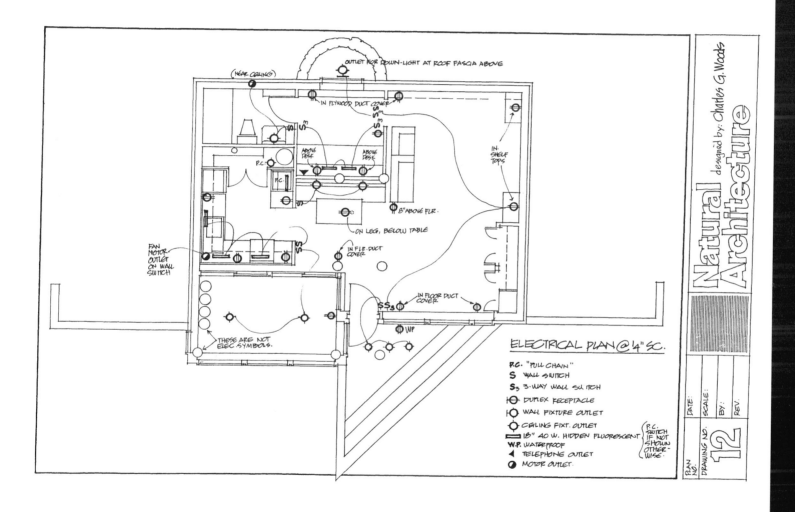

OUTLET FOR DOWN-LIGHT AT ROOF FASCIA ABOVE

(NEAR CEILING)

IN PLYWOOD DUCT COVER

ABOVE DESK

ABOVE DESK

P.C.

P.C.

IN SHELF TOPS

8" ABOVE FLR.

ON LEG, BELOW TABLE

IN FLR. DUCT COVER

FAN MOTOR OUTLET ON WALL SWITCH

IN FLOOR DUCT COVER

THESE ARE NOT ELEC. SYMBOLS.

WP

ELECTRICAL PLAN @ ¼" SC.

P.C. "PULL CHAIN"
S WALL SWITCH
S3 3-WAY WALL SWITCH
⊖ DUPLEX RECEPTACLE
⟜O WALL FIXTURE OUTLET
O CEILING FIXT. OUTLET
▭ 18" 40 W. HIDDEN FLUORESCENT
W.P. WATERPROOF
▲ TELEPHONE OUTLET
⊙ MOTOR OUTLET.

(P.C. SWITCH IF NOT SHOWN OTHER-WISE.)

Natural Architecture designed by: Charles G. Woods

PLAN NO:
DRAWING NO. 12
DATE:
SCALE:
BY:
REV.

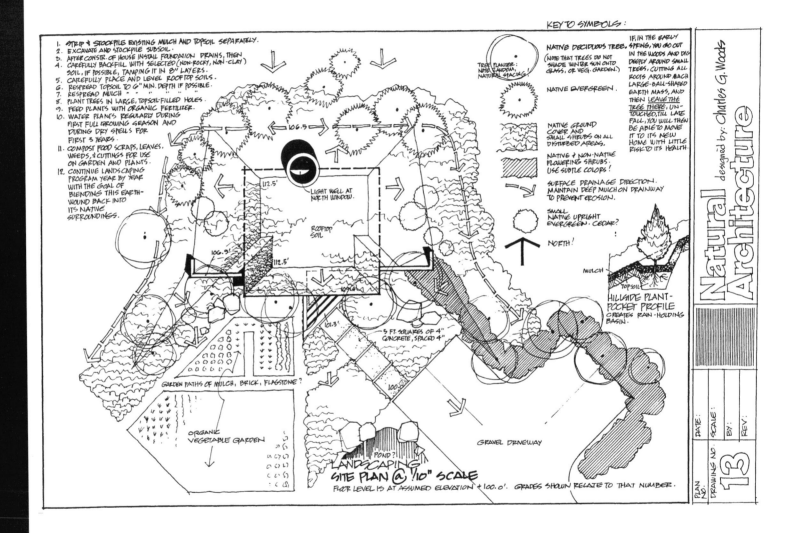

KEY TO SYMBOLS:

1. STRIP & STOCKPILE EXISTING MULCH AND TOPSOIL SEPARATELY.
2. EXCAVATE AND STOCKPILE SUBSOIL.
3. AFTER CONSTR. OF HOUSE INSTALL FOUNDATION DRAINS, THEN
4. CAREFULLY BACKFILL WITH SELECTED (NON-ROCKY, NON-CLAY) SOIL, IF POSSIBLE, TAMPING IT IN 8" LAYERS.
5. CAREFULLY PLACE AND LEVEL ROOFTOP SOILS.
6. RESPREAD TOPSOIL TO 6" MIN. DEPTH IF POSSIBLE.
7. RESPREAD MULCH " " " " .
8. PLANT TREES IN LARGE, TOPSOIL-FILLED HOLES.
9. FEED PLANTS WITH ORGANIC FERTILIZER.
10. WATER PLANTS REGULARLY DURING FIRST FULL GROWING SEASON AND DURING DRY SPELLS FOR FIRST 3 YEARS.
11. COMPOST FOOD SCRAPS, LEAVES, WEEDS, & CUTTINGS FOR USE ON GARDEN AND PLANTS.
12. CONTINUE LANDSCAPING PROGRAM YEAR BY YEAR WITH THE GOAL OF BLENDING THIS EARTH-WOUND BACK INTO ITS NATIVE SURROUNDINGS.

NATIVE DECIDUOUS TREE.
(NOTE THAT TREES DO NOT SHADE WINTER SUN ONTO GLASS, OR VEG. GARDEN.)

NATIVE EVERGREEN.

NATIVE GROUND COVER AND SMALL SHRUBS ON ALL DISTURBED AREAS.

NATIVE & NON-NATIVE FLOWERING SHRUBS. USE SUBTLE COLORS!

SURFACE DRAINAGE DIRECTION. MAINTAIN DEEP MULCH ON DRAINWAY TO PREVENT EROSION.

SMALL NATIVE UPRIGHT EVERGREEN. CEDAR?

NORTH!

IF, IN THE EARLY SPRING, YOU GO OUT IN THE WOODS AND DIG DEEPLY AROUND SMALL TREES, CUTTING ALL ROOTS AROUND EACH LARGE-BALL-SHAPED EARTH MASS, AND THEN LEAVE THE TREE THERE, UN-TOUCHED, TILL LATE FALL, YOU WILL THEN BE ABLE TO MOVE IT TO ITS NEW HOME WITH LITTLE RISK TO ITS HEALTH.

TREE PLANTER: NOTE RANDOM, NATURAL SPACING!

LIGHT WELL AT NORTH WINDOW.

ROOFTOP SOIL

112.5'
106.5'
106.9'
112.5'
101.3'
100.0'

5 FT. SQUARES OF 4" CONCRETE, SPACED 4"

GARDEN PATHS OF MULCH, BRICK, FLAGSTONE?

ORGANIC VEGETABLE GARDEN

POND?

GRAVEL DRIVEWAY

MULCH
TOPSOIL

HILLSIDE PLANT-POCKET PROFILE
CREATES RAIN-HOLDING BASIN.

LANDSCAPING
SITE PLAN @ 1/10" SCALE
FLOOR LEVEL IS AT ASSUMED ELEVATION ± 100.0'. GRADES SHOWN RELATE TO THAT NUMBER.

Natural Architecture
designed by: Charles G. Woods

DATE:
SCALE:
BY:
REV:

PLAN NO.
DRAWING NO.
13

OUTLINE SPECIFICATIONS FOR THE HERMIT CABIN

I. GENERAL REQUIREMENTS

A. THIS CONTRACT SHALL BE WRITTEN ON AIA FORM NO._____ WITH AIA "GENERAL CONDITIONS", AIA 201, IN EFFECT AS IF WRITTEN OUT IN FULL. THE SCOPE OF THE WORK SHALL INCLUDE A COMPLETED BUILDING, READY FOR OCCUPANCY.

B. ALL WORK MUST COMPLY WITH STATE AND LOCAL CODES AND ORDINANCES, AND SHALL BE DONE TO GOOD STANDARDS OF CRAFTSMANSHIP BY JOURNEYMEN OF THE RESPECTIVE TRADES.

C. TEMPORARY FACILITIES FOR THE PROTECTION OF TOOLS AND EQUIPMENT SHALL CONFORM TO LOCAL REGULATIONS, AND SHALL BE THE CONTRACTOR'S RESPONSIBILITY.

D. CONTRACTOR SHALL PRESENT THE BUILDING FOR ACCEPTANCE, CLEAN AND READY FOR OCCUPANCY, INTERIOR AND EXTERIOR.

E. CONTRACTOR SHALL BE RESPONSIBLE FOR WINTER PROTECTION, HEAT, AND SNOW REMOVAL.

F. CONTRACTOR SHALL FURNISH ALL BONDS REQUIRED FOR HIMSELF AND HIS SUBCONTRACTORS.

G. CONTRACTOR SHALL CARRY BUILDER'S RISK "ALL RISK" INSURANCE TO COVER COST OF THIS WORK AS DEFINED IN ARTICLE 11 OF THE GENERAL CONDITIONS. HE SHALL PRESENT COPIES OF CERTIFICATES OF INSURANCE TO THE OWNER AT THE TIME OF SIGNING OF THE CONTRACT.

II. SITE WORK

A. STRIP SITE OF EXISTING TOPSOIL, IF ANY, AND STOCKPILE FOR RE-USE IN LANDSCAPING. ALL TREES DESIGNATED TO BE SAVED SHALL BE PROTECTED FROM ANY AND ALL DAMAGE.

B. GRADE DRIVE AND PARKING AREA AND PROVIDE A 12" COMPACTED BED OF APPROVED PIT-RUN GRAVEL OR CRUSHED STONE.

C. EXCAVATE, FILL, AND REGRADE SITE AS REQUIRED BY SITE PLAN AND OTHER DRAWINGS.

D. ALL UTILITIES SHALL BE EXTENDED FROM THE BUILDING, UNDERGROUND, TO THE UTILITY CONNECTIONS.

E. PROVIDE ALL EXTERIOR WALLS, WALKS, GARDENS, TREES, PLANTINGS, AND LIGHTING AS SHOWN.

III. CONCRETE

A. SEE REQ'TS ON DRAWINGS.

B. BE SURE CONCRETE IS MIXED, POURED, AND FINISHED AS DRY AS POSSIBLE, AND ALLOWED TO CURE, UNDISTURBED, UNDER DAMP CONDITIONS FOR AT LEAST 7 DAYS.

IV. BLOCK MASONRY (OPTION)

A. REMEMBER THAT EARTH PRESSURES ARE SURPRISINGLY GREAT AND THAT BLOCK MASONRY IS GENERALLY WEAKER THAN CONCRETE. IF BLOCK MASONRY IS USED TO REPLACE CONCRETE WALLS BE SURE IT IS PROPERLY DESIGNED, CONSTRUCTED, AND BRACED UNTIL ROOF LOADS HELP HOLD IT IN PLACE.

V. METALS

A. SEE REQ'TS ON DRAWINGS.

VI. CARPENTRY

A. FRAMING LUMBER SHALL BE STRESS GRADE, KILN-DRIED DOUGLAS FIR OR LARCH OF SIZES AS NOTED OR REQ'D BY THE WORK.

B. ROOF FRAMING SHALL BE PLACED WITH GREAT CARE, ALLOWING FULL BEARING OF EACH MEMBER. BOLT & SPIKE AS SHOWN.

C. ALL WOOD UNDERFLOOR AND/OR IN PROXIMITY TO EARTH SHALL BE PRESSURE TREATED.

D. PLYWOOD: EXTERIOR GRADE IN ALL CASES.

E. WOOD BLOCKING: SOLID, AS REQ'D, WHETHER SPECIFICALLY SHOWN OR NOT.

F. FINISHED WOODWORK FOR EXTERIOR AND INTERIOR USE, SHALL BE OF WESTERN RED CEDAR.

VII. THERMAL & MOISTURE

A. BATT INSULATION SHALL BE FIBERGLASS IN THICKNESSES AS SHOWN.

B. RIGID INSULATION: CLOSED-CELL POLYSTYRENE.

C. ROOF & WALL WATERPROOFING: 1/16" BUTYL SHEETING IN A COMPLETE SYSTEM (AS FURNISHED BY CONSTR. MATL'S DIVISION, CARLISLE TIRE AND RUBBER CO., CARLISLE PA 17013, OR EQUAL). NO WATERPROOFING ON CURVED STONE WALL OR CONCRETE WING WALLS. ALL WORK IN ACCORDANCE WITH MFR'S SPECS.

D. UNDERFLOOR VAPOR BARRIER: HEAVY, FIBERGLASS REINFORCED SHEETS (MOISTOP OR EQUAL) FULLY SEALED AT ALL SEAMS & EDGES.

E. FRENCH DRAIN AROUND FOUNDATION MUST SLOPE AND EXTEND OUT TO GRADE FOR GOOD POSITIVE DRAINAGE VIA GRAVITY.

F. PROVIDE CONTINUOUS 6 MIL POLYETHYLENE VAPOR BARRIER ON WARM SIDE OF ALL EXTERIOR WOOD FRAMED WALLS, CORNERS, ETC.

G. CAULK ALL JOINTS BETWEEN DIFFERENT MATERIALS AND ABUTTING SAME MATERIALS WITH G.E. (OR EQUAL) SILICONE CAULKING.

VIII. DOORS, WINDOWS, GLASS

A. PROVIDE DOORS WITH GOOD QUALITY HARDWARE.

B. SEAL TOPS & BOTTOMS OF ALL DOORS.

C. WEATHERSTRIP EXTERIOR DOORS USING HEAVY DUTY METAL + PLASTIC COMPRESSION GASKETS.

D. WINDOWS: ANDERSEN, PELLA, OR EQUAL, WITH SCREENS ON ALL UNITS EXCEPT INTERIOR SLIDERS.

E. DOUBLE GLAZE ALL OPENINGS. TEMPERED GLASS: AT FULL-HEIGHT GLASS: SINGLE GLAZING IS OK.

F. MEDICINE CABT'.: FLUSH 18x24 MIRRORED FRONT.

IX. MILLWORK

A. SEE INTERIOR CABINETRY DRAWINGS. USE HARDWOOD VENEERS ON ALL CABINET PLYWOOD - WITH SOLID NOSINGS ON ALL EXPOSED EDGES.

X. FINISHES

A. DRYWALL: 1/2" THICK, TAPED, SANDED TO A COMPLETELY SMOOTH FINISH. METAL EDGES AND EXT. CORNERS. PAINT: 2 COATS.

B. PLASTIC LAMINATE ON KIT. COUNTERS AND BACKSPLASHES: FORMICA, WILSONART, OR EQUAL

C. ALL PAINTING: 2 COAT WORK (OR MORE AS NEEDED FOR FULL COVERAGE. STAINS: 1 COAT.

Natural Architecture

designed by: Charles G. Woods

14

.... MORE OUTLINE SPECIFICATIONS... AND A MATERIALS LIST....

XI. LANDSCAPING

A. AVOID HARD EDGES AT BOUNDARIES OF THE WORK. LET THE LANDSCAPE APPEAR TO FLOW NATURALLY FROM ITS SURROUNDINGS.

XII. APPLIANCES

A. BE SURE THESE ARE PROVIDED FOR; MAKE SURE, BEFORE SIGNING CONTRACT, WHETHER OWNER OR CONTRACTOR IS TO SUPPLY THEM. INSTALLATION IS TO BE BY CONTRACTOR.

XIII. PLUMBING

A. SOIL VENTS: PVC, WATER PIPING: COPPER.
B. FIXTURES: AMERICAN STANDARD, CRANE, KOHLER, OR EQUAL.
C. HOT WATER HEATER: 40 GALLON GLASS-LINED, SUPERINSULATED. FUEL: OWNER'S OPTION.

XIV. HEATING, VENTILATING

A. IF THE HOUSE IS VERY TIGHTLY BUILT, IT WILL BE NECESSARY TO INSTALL AN AIR-TO-AIR HEAT EXCHANGER (MINIMUM SIZE) FOR ADEQUATE VENTILATION.
B. BASIC SYSTEM SHOWN IS SOLAR + WOOD. THIS MAY HAVE TO VARY DEPENDING ON QTY'S OF BOTH. A GROUND WATER HEAT PUMP MAY BE MORE EFFICIENT IN SOME REGIONS.
C. EXHAUST FAN: BROAN, NUTONE, OR EQUAL.
D. WOODSTOVE: BY OWNER, INSTALL BY CONTR.
E. WATER TUBES: KALWALL CORP., MANCHESTER, N.H.

XV. ELECTRICAL

A. MAIN SERVICE: 100 AMPS.
B. ALL WIRING: ROMEX COPPER.
C. INSTALL FIXTURES (FURNISHED BY OWNER).
D. FULLY GROUND ENTIRE SYSTEM.

SPECIAL NOTE:

EVERY ATTEMPT HAS BEEN MADE IN THE PREPARATION OF THESE DRAWINGS TO AVOID MISTAKES, BUT THE MAKER CANNOT GUARANTEE AGAINST HUMAN ERROR. THE CONTRACTOR ON THE JOB MUST CHECK ALL DIMENSIONS AND OTHER DETAILS AND BE RESPONSIBLE FOR SAME.

MATERIALS NEEDED

NOTE: THAT CONCRETE AND TIMBER STRUCTURES MUST BE DESIGNED BY A LOCAL ARCHITECT OR ENGINEER, TO MEET LOCAL CONDITIONS AND REQUIREMENTS. THE STRUCTURAL QTY'S SHOWN HERE ARE, LIKE ALL OTHER QUANTITIES, FOR ESTIMATING PURPOSES ONLY.

1. BATTER BOARDS FOR LAYOUT, 2x4'S — 80 BD. FT.
2. FOUNDATION DRAIN
   A. PIPE, 4" — ± 150 LIN. FT.
   B. CRUSHED STONE (3/4"-1 1/2") — 11 CU. YDS.
   C. HAY COVERING — 4 BALES
3. CONCRETE
   A. WALL FTGS, INCL. RET. WALLS — 9 CU. YDS.
   B. INTERIOR FTG'S & PEDESTALS — 4 " "
   C. 8" THICK WALLS, INCL. RET. — 26 " "
   D. FILL AT TOP OF WALLS — 2 " "
   E. INTERIOR FLOOR SLAB — 7 1/2 " "
   F. EXTERIOR SLABS — 1 1/4 " "
   G. EXTERIOR STEPS — 4 " "
   H. 1/2" Ø BARS — 750 LIN. FT.
4. MISC. METAL
   A. 1/4" PLATE, VARIOUS SIZES — 60 SQ. FT.
   B. 3/4" x 4" GALV. LAG SCREWS — 120
   C. 3/4" x 10" GALV. THRU-BOLTS — 80
5. CARPENTRY
   A. 3" DOUBLE-TONGUE ROOF DECK, DRILLED — 2600 BD. FT.
   B. 4 x 12 ROOF JOISTS — 1560 " "
   C. 1/2" PLYWOOD DECK (+ NAILS) — 840 SQ. FT.
   D. 8 x 16 ROOF BEAMS — 960 BD. FT.
   E. 3 x 12 JOIST HEADERS — 180 " "
   F. COLUMNS, 10" Ø x 7'-0" — 8
   G. 8" GALV. SPIKES FOR 4 x 12'S — 160
   H. DECK SPIKES — SUPPLIED WITH DECK
   I. NAILS — VARIOUS SIZES
   J. 2 x 6 FASCIA / DRIP PC'S — 40 BD. FT.
   K. 2 x 3 STUDS FOR PTNS. — 300 " "
   L. 2 x 4 STUDS, MISC. FRAMING — AS REQ'D.
   M. BLOCKING — " "
   N. SMALL GALV. BOLTS, MISC. — " "
6. MILLWORK
   A. INT. DOOR, BATH — 1
   B. EXT. DOOR, ENTRANCE — 1
   C. EXT. STORM / SCREEN DOOR — 1

D. WINDOWS, AS SHOWN — 11 UNITS.
E. CABTS, COUNTERS, BUILT-INS — AS DETAILED
F. 2 x 8 SHELVES, NORTH WALL — 60 BD. FT.
G. 2 x 6 SUPPORTS FOR SAME — 30 " "
H. 2 x 6 SHELVES ON BEAMS — 210 " "
I. 1/2" Ø BARS FOR SAME: — 105 LIN. FT.
7. ROOFING, WATERPROOFING.
   A. 1/16" BUTYL OR EPDM — 1800 SQ. FT.
   B. FIBERGL. REINF. VAP. BARR. — 750 " "
   C. 6 MIL. VAP. BARR — 200 " "
8. INSULATION
   A. 6" FIBERGL. BATTS — 1 ROLL
   B. POLYSTYRENE BOARD, EXTRUDED
      ROOF — 4000 BD. FT.
      WALLS — 3500 " "
      UNDERFLOOR — 1200 " "
9. CEM. PLASTER, GALV. LATH, 5/8" — 17 SQ. YDS.
10. W' STRIPPING @ ENTRANCE — 20 LIN. FT.
11. FLAGSTONE FOR SKYWELL, FACE AREA: 120 SQ. FT.
12. GRAVEL FOR ENTRY AREA — 1/3 CU. YD.
13. COPPER CAPS, 16 OZ, PROJECTING BMS. — 6 SQ. FT.
14. GLASS, GLAZING, MIRRORED MED. CAB — AS SHOWN.
15. FINISHES
    A WALLS, CONCRETE --- — NONE
       PLASTERBOARD --- — 2 COAT LATEX, FLAT
    B. TIMBERS & DECK — NONE
       (PAINT DUCT SIMILAR COLOR)
    C. FLOOR: STAIN / SEALER
    D. MILLWORK: STAIN & SEAL
    E. CABINETS: GLOSSY ENAMEL.
    F. EXTERIOR MATLS. — NONE
16. PLUMBING — AS SHOWN
    WATERSAVING HEAD, FAUCETS.
17. HEATING, VENTILATING — AS SHOWN
18. ELECTRICAL — AS SHOWN
19. LANDSCAPING — AS SHOWN.

designed by: Charles G. Woods

Natural Architecture

15

PRELIMINARY DESIGN

NINETY PERCENT OF THE TOTAL CREATIVITY OF A DESIGN COMES, I BELIEVE, IN THE PRELIMINARY "PARTI" OR SKETCH. TO HAVE A DESIGN COME TO PROPER FRUITION, THE OTHER 10 PERCENT, UNFORTUNATELY AND PARADOXICALLY, WEIGHS IN THE BALANCE. GUNNAR BIRKERTS SPEAKS OF THE "ECSTASY" OF THE ORIGINAL VISION AND THE PAIN OF THE DETAILS. I AGREE. WITHOUT GOOD DETAILS, EVEN THE BEST FORM BECOMES HEAVY-HANDED. AS MIES SUPPOSEDLY SAID, "GOD IS IN THE DETAILS." ONE OF THE BEST DETAILERS I KNOW IS YOUNG, AWARD-WINNING ARCHITECT, JOSEPH N. BIONDO.

MY OWN DETAILS ARE COMING ALONG—THEY ARE NOT YET AS CREATIVE AS FAY JONES', BUT HIS OWN DETAILS, I SUSPECT, WERE MORE CREATIVE AND COMPLEX AT AGE 60 THAN 40. IN ANY CASE, THE MODULE SYSTEM HELPS EVEN HERE. IT ALSO HELPS TO ORGANIZE SMALL-SCALE PLANS.

MY ORIGINAL IDEAS COME FROM NOWHERE AND EVERYWHERE—FROM NATURE, OTHER ARCHITECTS' WORK, AND ESPECIALLY GEOMETRY. MANY PEOPLE'S DOODLES ON GRAPH PAPER COULD BE NIFTY HOUSE PLANS, WITH THE APPROPRIATE SKILL APPLIED. MY "PRELIMINARY STAGE" DESIGNS FOR CLIENTS CONSIST OF ONE TO FIVE DESIGNS (USUALLY TWO).

THE SITE AND THE CLIENT'S PROGRAM AND IDEAS, OF COURSE, DO INFLUENCE MY GEOMETRY'S PURITY AT TIMES—SOMETIMES FOR THE BETTER. TO DO A GOOD DESIGN, THOUGH, YOU DO NEED AN IDEA—MAYBE EVERY DETAIL WILL NOT BE IN PLACE, BUT YOU NEED A GREAT, IF HAZY, IDEA.

FINAL DESIGN

ALTHOUGH THEY REQUIRE SKILL, FINAL DESIGN DRAWINGS ARE IN PART PROSAIC, INVOLVING SITING THE HOUSE MORE CAREFULLY, IMPROVING THE PLANS, ADDING A TERRACE, AND SO ON. WHAT HAS MADE IT FUN FOR ME RECENTLY HAS BEEN MAC'S GREAT RENDERINGS. I HAVE INCLUDED A LARGE NUMBER OF FINAL DESIGN DRAWINGS BECAUSE THEY EASILY SHOW THE CLARITY OF THE MODULE AND ARE MORE FUN FOR THE READER TO LOOK AT.

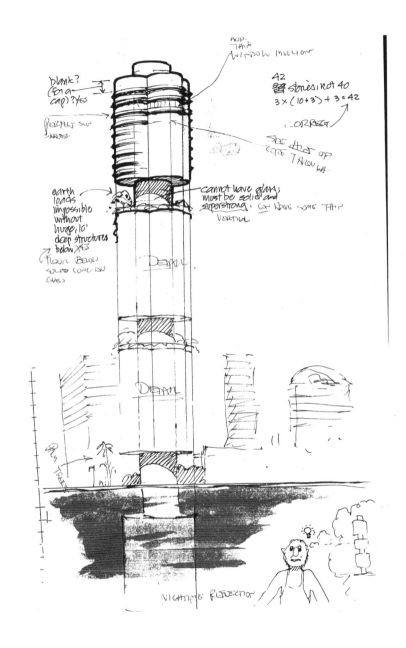

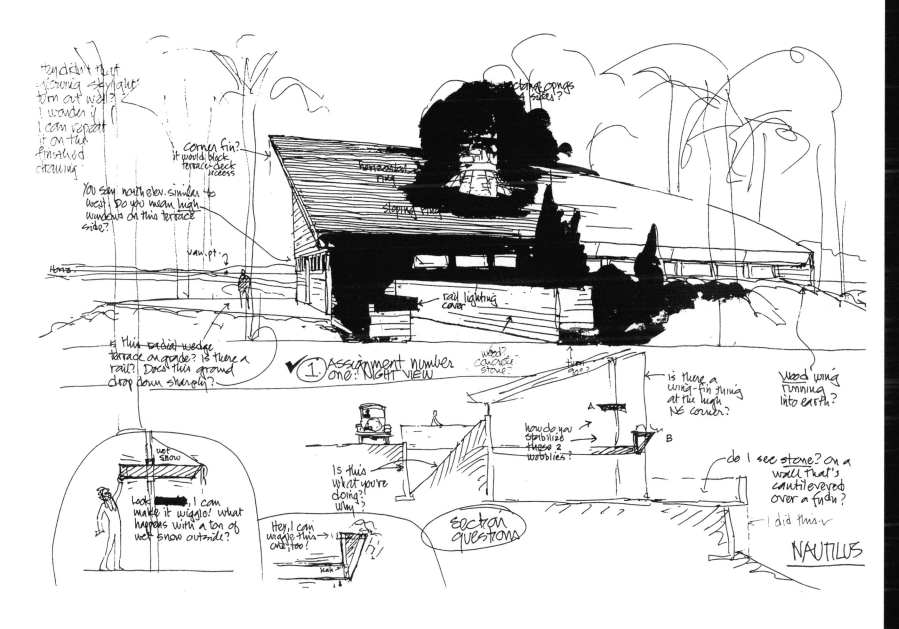

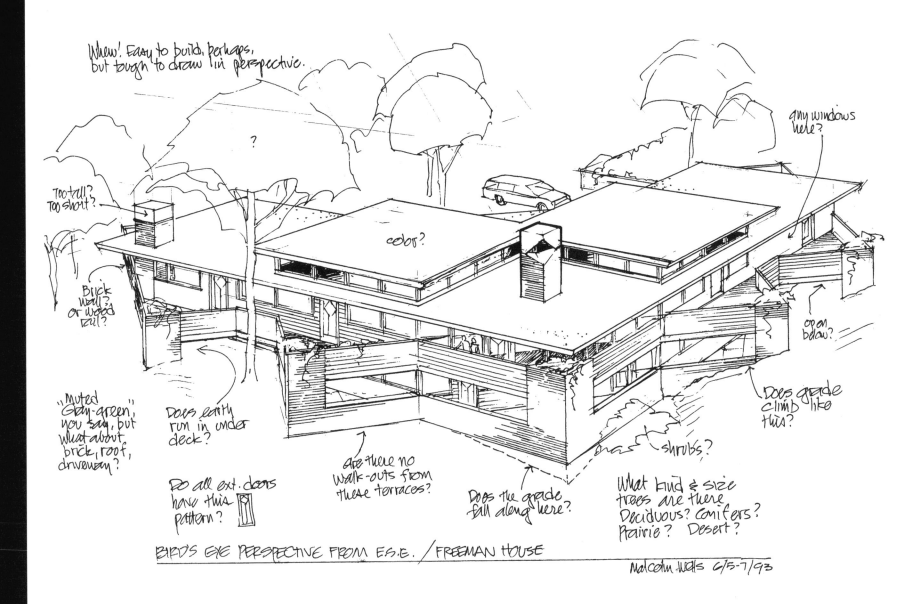

Whew! Easy to build, perhaps, but tough to draw in perspective.

?

any windows here?

Too tall? Too short?

color?

Brick wall? or wood rail?

open below?

"Muted Gray-green" you say, but what about brick, roof, driveway?

Does earth run in under deck?

Does grade climb like this?

Do all ext. doors have this pattern?

are there no walk-outs from these terraces?

Does the grade fall along here?

shrubs?

What kind & size trees are there. Deciduous? Conifers? Prairie? Desert?

BIRD'S EYE PERSPECTIVE FROM E.S.E. / FREEMAN HOUSE

Malcolm Wells 6/5-7/93

glass?

finish?

wood finish or plas'bd?

office beyond

glass to floor or to 3' sill?

seat? cushions

sill ht?

Do the porch openings have 3' sills or floor level sills

cabt?

flat glass top on "skylight" to Children/Family below?

Why is the dining area remote from the kitchen? Wouldn't a big triangular table fit the space near the kitchen?

I know: it's carpet. I show the grid only for orientation.

INTERIOR PERSPECTIVE / FREEMAN HOUSE

Malcolm Wells 6/8/93

SISSON HOUSE ("ROUGH")

any windows in this elegant blank wall?

my aerial persp. shows a hole in the roof right where this closet occurs. Which is right?

5·18/19·94
SISSON ROUGH

CRAGGED ROCK ("ROUGH")

The building is shown as being about 9 or 10' high.

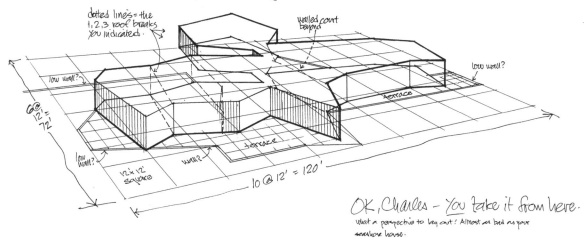

dotted lines = the 1,2,3 roof breaks you indicated.

walled court beyond

low wall?

low wall?

6 @ 12' = 72'

low wall?

12'x 12' square

wall?

terrace

terrace

10 @ 12' = 120'

OK, Charles — you take it from here.

What a perspective to lay out! Almost as bad as your seashore house.

Irving Schwartkhorst's new car, designed by Charles G. Woods, AUCRAA, to complement his new house.

SOME OF MY <u>MOST</u> UNIQUE, CURVILINEAR (AND, UNFORTUNATELY, EXPENSIVE) HOUSES ARE STILL TO BE CONSTRUCTED OR ARE IN CONSTRUCTION NOW. BUT SO THAT THE NUMBER OF SUCH DESIGNS DOES NOT LEAD SOME READERS TO THINK THEY COULD NOT BE BUILT, I HAVE INCLUDED SOME OF MY PAST WORK SUCH AS:

<u>STULTZ RESIDENCE</u>—$500,000. FINISHED EXCEPT FOR PATIO, RED GRAVEL IN DRIVE, LANDSCAPING, AND FURNISHING. (4200 SQUARE FEET.)

<u>AUGELLO</u>—FINISHED AND BUILT FOR THE LOW COST OF LESS THAN $150,000. (3700 SQUARE FEET.)

<u>COOPER</u>—ABOUT $75 PER SQUARE FOOT. THE MS. ELFREDE COOPER HOUSE WAS BUILT FROM A STOCK PLAN OF MINE. THE PLAN WAS SLIGHTLY MODIFIED AT THE SITE BY ARCHITECT GLEN STRAIGHT. BOTH MRS. COOPER AND STRAIGHT DID A GREAT JOB, THOUGH, OF NECESSITY, THEY DID SOME THINGS DIFFERENTLY THAN I WOULD HAVE IF I HAD SUPERVISED. NEVERTHELESS, SINCE THE LANDSCAPING IS ALMOST DONE AND THE HOUSE IS BEAUTIFULLY FURNISHED, IT IS MY BEST MEDIUM-SIZE HOUSE COMPLETED TO DATE. (4500 SQUARE FEET.)

<u>CODY HOUSE</u>—$500,000. SHOWN UNDER CONSTRUCTION IS A 3500-SQUARE-FOOT TERRACED HOUSE. SHOULD BE MAGNIFICENT WHEN FINISHED PROPERLY!

<u>SNOWFLAKE</u> AND <u>NAUTILUS</u> ARE NOW UNDER CONSTRUCTION.

FROM AN ARCHITECT'S STANDPOINT, I THINK MANY CLIENTS BUILD TOO LARGE AND UNDERSTANDABLY RUN OUT OF MONEY FOR THE IMPORTANT LANDSCAPING AND PROPER FURNISHING. FOR INSTANCE, AN ARCHITECT CANNOT DO MORE ARTISTICALLY ON A $500,000 HOUSE THAN ON A $100,000 ONE, <u>IF</u> ALL THE EXTRA MONEY IS USED UP ON EXTRA SQUARE FOOTAGE—THAT EXTRA DESIGN QUALITY REQUIRES <u>MORE</u> MONEY OR <u>LESS</u> SQUARE FOOTAGE. FURTHERMORE, IT SEEMS THAT, AT THE END OF THE PROJECT, THE CLIENT FEELS LESS IN NEED OF THE ARCHITECT AND OFTEN DOES NOT LISTEN TO HER OR HIM REGARDING SMALL DETAILS. TO BE BRUTALLY HONEST, THIS CAN WRECK TWO TO FOUR YEARS OF THE ARCHITECT'S WORK, OFTEN IN AS LITTLE AS A WEEK, BY, FOR EXAMPLE, PAINTING THE HOUSE THE WRONG COLOR. MY SUGGESTION IS TO LISTEN TO YOUR ARCHITECT UNTIL THE PROJECT'S COMPLETION, AFTER WHICH YOU COULD MAKE MINOR CHANGES.

GUNDLACH WOODS RESIDENCE

COOPER HOUSE

COOPER HOUSE

COOPER HOUSE

COOPER HOUSE

I HAD A POTENTIAL CLIENT CALL AND SAY, "I WANT YOU AND I AM WILLING TO PAY FOR YOU, SO I DON'T HAVE PROBLEMS OF ANY SORT!" I WAS FLATTERED BUT TOLD HIM, "IT'S NOT QUITE SUCH A FOOLPROOF SYSTEM." THE BEST METHOD OF WORKING WITH AN ARCHITECT IS TO LET THE BUILDER BE RESPONSIBLE TO THE ARCHITECT AND THE ARCHITECT TO THE CLIENT. OTHERWISE, IF PROBLEMS ARISE, THE BUILDER WILL SOMETIMES TRY TO SEPARATE THE OWNER FROM THE ARCHITECT. MIKE AUGELLO GAVE ME FULL CONTROL WITH HIS HOUSE PROJECT. THOUGH THE BUILDER, JERRY DULAY, HAD SOME EARLY PROBLEMS WITH THE MODULE SYSTEM, HE STUCK WITH IT AND CREATED A BEAUTIFUL AND LOW-COST ($40 PER SQUARE FOOT) HOUSE IN 1992.

CREATING A "PERFECT" PROJECT IS DIFFICULT, BUT IT'S GETTING EASIER FOR ME. I ONCE ASKED MAC HOW WRIGHT GOT HIS GENERALLY MORE COMPLEX HOUSES BUILT SO NICELY. MAC RESPONDED LACONICALLY, "HE WAS MEANER THAN WE ARE, I GUESS!" I HATE TO SAY IT, BUT I THINK THERE WAS SOME TRUTH TO HIS JOKE. IT'S BEST TO ALL CONCERNED TO LISTEN TO THE ARCHITECT (WHICH MEANS "CHIEF BUILDER") UNLESS HE OR SHE IS PROVEN TO BE NOT COMPETENT.

COOPER HOUSE

COOPER HOUSE

AUGELLO HOUSE

AUGELLO HOUSE

AUGELLO HOUSE

COBB HOUSE BEFORE LANDSCAPING

CODY HOUSE UNDER CONSTRUCTION

STULTZ HOUSE

I BELIEVE I COINED THE TERM "NATURAL ARCHITECTURE" IN ABOUT 1977. POSSIBLY OTHERS ALREADY USED THE TERM, BUT I THOUGHT I INVENTED IT. SINCE THEN I'VE USED IT AS THE NAME OF MY FIRM, MY FIRST BOOK (WHICH WAS A SERIES OF HOUSE DESIGNS), AND MY ARCHITECTURE IN GENERAL. FRANK LLOYD WRIGHT, OF COURSE, CALLED HIS STYLE "ORGANIC" ARCHITECTURE. I WAS THEREFORE HAPPY TO SEE IN A RECENT BOOK ON FAY JONES THAT THE AUTHOR DESCRIBED JONES' GREAT ARCHITECTURE AS "ORGANIC—THAT IS NATURAL ARCHITECTURE." I BELIEVE THAT WRIGHT GOT THE TERM IN PART FROM THE PHILOSOPHIES OF AMERICAN TRANSCENDENTALISM AND EVEN FROM GERMAN IDEALISM. I ALSO RECEIVED MY IDEA FROM PHILOSOPHY. I WAS TRYING TO COME UP WITH A NAME FOR MY FIRM, WHICH SPECIALIZED IN DESIGNING EARTH-SHELTERED HOUSES. I LOVED ZEN BUDDHISM AND THE TAOISM OF LAO-TZU, AND I HAD STUDIED THE DUTCH PHILOSOPHER SPINOZA FOR YEARS. EVERY OTHER BOOK TITLE WAS "THE TAO OF . . ." OR "ZEN AND THE . . . ," AND I WANTED SOMETHING DIFFERENT. "GOD ARCHITECTURE," "TAO ARCHITECTURE," AND "ZEN ARCHITECTURE" SEEMED PRETTY PRESUMPTUOUS! BUT LAO-TZU'S "TAO" IS OFTEN TRANSLATED AS "NATURE," ZEN

PHILOSOPHY SPEAKS OF THE "BUDDHA-NATURE," AND SPINOZA WROTE IN LATIN OF "DEUS SIVE NATURA," TRANSLATED AS "GOD OR NATURE" (WITH A CAPITAL "N"). SO "NATURAL ARCHITECTURE" SEEMED MORE HUMBLE—NOT MUCH MORE, OF COURSE, BUT I THINK OF "NATURAL ARCHITECTURE" AS AN ASYMPTOTIC GOAL, OR UNREACHABLE IDEAL, NOT AS MY PERSONAL ACCOMPLISHMENT. I PREFER THE TERM TO "ORGANIC ARCHITECTURE" FOR SEVERAL REASONS.

ORGANIC ARCHITECTURE AT THIS POINT IN HISTORY IS PRETTY WELL TIED TO WRIGHT'S MAGNIFICENT WORK. FURTHERMORE, "ORGANIC" MEANS "DERIVED FROM LIVING ORGANISMS," AND I CAN IMAGINE AN ARCHITECTURE THAT IS "NATURAL" WITHOUT MIMICKING LIFE FORMS. I AM NOT SUGGESTING THAT WRIGHT'S WORK DID MIMIC OFTEN, BUT GOFF'S OR BART PRINCE'S ARCHITECTURE MIGHT BE MORE "ORGANIC" THAN SOME OF WRIGHT'S OWN—THOUGH NOT NECESSARILY MORE NATURAL.

MY OWN BEGINNINGS IN ARCHITECTURE WERE AS FOLLOWS. AS A CHILD, I LOVED BUILDING BLOCKS AND MODULE BUILDING SETS. I THOUGHT I WOULD BE AN ARTIST, A PRIEST, OR A COMEDIAN LIKE JERRY LEWIS.

THE TEACHERS SAID I WAS "HYPERACTIVE" (NOW THEY WOULD SAY ADHD).

IN THE FIRST WEEKS OF HIGH SCHOOL ART CLASS, IN A RARE MOMENT OF SERIOUSNESS, I DREW A BOWLING BALL–LIKE SHAPE WITH SMALLER BOWLING BALLS COMING OUT FROM IT AND CALLED IT "BIRTH." MY TEACHER THOUGHT I WAS BEING A "MORON" AND THREW ME OUT INTO THE HALL— FOREVER! NO DOUBT, I WAS A LITTLE PROBLEM. I HEARD PEOPLE TALKING AND LAUGHING IN THE CLASS NEXT DOOR. I WALKED INTO THE ARCHITECTURAL DRAFTING CLASS. WHEN NOT HAVING A LECTURE, WE WERE ALLOWED TO TALK AND JOKE IN CLASS AS LONG AS WE WORKED. THIS WAS VERY HELPFUL TO MY HYPERACTIVE MIND.

I FLOURISHED! IN MY SOPHOMORE YEAR, I STARTED ARCHITECTURE. MR. EPERSON, MY DRAFTING TEACHER, WAS WONDERFUL, AND I THINK HE MUST HAVE HAD EXPERIENCES WITH OTHER ADHD CHILDREN. HE DIDN'T MAKE ME DRAW "WALL SECTIONS," HE WOULD JUST TELL ME A WALL WOULD BE 4" TO 12" THICK AND LET ME DESIGN. IF I WANTED TO DRAW A CIRCLE HOUSE OR A BANANA HOUSE, HE WOULD SAY, "GO FOR IT!" HE HOOKED ME UP WITH A YOUNGER

TEACHER, MR. KNUDSEN, WHO SEEMED TO BE INSPIRED BY MODERN ARCHITECTURE. MR. KNUDSEN WAS A GOOD DESIGNER AND RENDERER, AND HE WORKED WITH ME.

AN IMPORTANT EVENT IN MY LIFE HAPPENED WHEN A VERY TALENTED SENIOR STUDENT, KEN BRAINARD, SHOWED ME SOME OF FRANK LLOYD WRIGHT'S WORK IN BOOKS. I REMEMBER KEN SHOWING ME HOW TO DRAW STONE HORIZONTALLY, LIKE WRIGHT DID. SOMETHING CLICKED, LIKE A MINOR ZEN "SATORI," AND I STARTED DESIGNING LIKE CRAZY. I WOULD COMPETE WITH KEN, WHO WAS A WONDERFUL DESIGNER.

BY AGE FIFTEEN-AND-A-HALF, I WAS AS A LITTLE PRODIGY. MY DESIGNS THEN WERE ALMOST AS GOOD AS THEY ARE NOW. OF COURSE, I "KNOW" A LOT MORE NOW, BUT THE DESIGN TALENT WAS DEVELOPED. WITHIN A YEAR, I WON SOME COLLEGE DESIGN AWARDS FOR MY CHURCHES, BUT I COULD NOT WIN THE PRESTIGIOUS IIT (ILLINOIS INSTITUTE OF TECHNOLOGY) AWARDS. MY WORK WAS TOO "ORGANIC."

I WAS SOON UNOFFICIALLY ASSISTANT-TEACHING, WITH REAL HUMILITY. I WOULD WALK FROM DESK TO DESK BEFORE A

CONTEST, SUGGESTING THAT STUDENTS WIDEN A FIREPLACE OR CHANGE A WINDOW. I MISSED GRADUATING FROM HIGH SCHOOL BY ONE CREDIT AND I DID NOT, IN FACT, GET MY DIPLOMA UNTIL EIGHT YEARS LATER WHILE I WAS IN GRADUATE SCHOOL!

THE ARCHITECTURE AND PHILOSOPHY OF FRANK LLOYD WRIGHT HAS BEEN A PRIMARY INFLUENCE ON ME. BUT I READ PETER BLAKE'S THE MASTER BUILDERS IN HIGH SCHOOL AND COULD NOT HOLD MIES VAN DER ROHE AND LE CORBUSIER IN RIGID OPPOSITION TO WRIGHT. BOTH HAD ALSO BEEN INFLUENCED BY WRIGHT AND I BELIEVE THEIR INFLUENCE AFFECTED WRIGHT AS WELL.

ERICH MENDELSOHN AND RICHARD JOSEF NEUTRA WERE ALSO POWERFUL INFLUENCES AND LATER SO WERE THE EXPRESSIONISTIC ARCHITECTS, FINSTERLIN AND STEINER. IN MY OPINION, WRIGHT IS THE GREATEST ARCHITECT OF ALL TIME, BUT HE WAS NOT PERFECT IN HIS OWN LIFE, NOR PROBABLY IN HIS ARCHITECTURE. BOTH HIS BROADACRE CITY FOR SUBURBAN DESIGN AND HIS MILE HIGH SKYSCRAPER FOR THE CITY WERE HORRIBLE MISTAKES. HIS WORK SUFFERS FROM OVERORNAMENTATION AT TIMES, AND HIS UNDERSTANDING OF

MATERIALS WAS OFTEN MORE "POETIC" THAN ACTUAL.

NO DOUBT, WRIGHT WAS A GREAT TEACHER OF SORTS AND REALLY MEANT TO GIVE FREEDOM TO HIS STUDENTS, BUT MANY WHO STAYED MORE THAN A YEAR OR TWO BECAME LITTLE CLONES (AN EXCEPTION WOULD BE THE GREAT JOHN HOWE). HOWEVER, AS A FORM GIVER, WRIGHT WAS ABSOLUTELY UNPARALLELED. YOU FEEL THE VERY FECUNDITY OF NATURE IN HIS DESIGNS. AND AFTER MORE THAN TWENTY-FIVE YEARS OF STUDYING THESE DESIGNS, I AM STILL OVERWHELMED, AWED, AND HUMBLED.

SAMPLE COLOR DRAWINGS (THE LAST WORD)

I SNUCK SOME OF MY NICEST WORK INTO THIS COLOR SECTION (SEE INSERT). DR. MARTIN, WHO MAY BE HIRING ME TO DESIGN HIS ESTATE, DIRECTLY INSPIRED ME TO "PUSH THE ENVELOPE" ON MY "CHAOS" AND "SHARDS" DESIGNS, WHICH, LIKE MY "HARMONIOUS DISCONJUNCTION," ARE INFLUENCED BY A REFORMED USE OF DECONSTRUCTION PHILOSOPHY.

OTHER NEW DESIGNS OF NOTE ARE "OUROBOROS," THE DUTCH CIRCLE HOUSE, AND THE RAMIREZ HOUSE. AS I WRITE THESE LAST LINES—A YEAR LATER THAN THE REST OF THE BOOK AND A FEW WEEKS BEFORE PRESS TIME—I REALIZE, IN RETROSPECT, HOW MUCH THIS BOOK HAS BEEN ABOUT THE NATURE OF CREATIVITY.

I HAVE DESIGNED ABOUT ONE-FIFTH OF ALL MY WORK IN JUST THE LAST TWELVE MONTHS—AND, OF NECESSITY, DID IT QUICKLY, PLAYFULLY, AND, AT TIMES, ALMOST PURELY INTUITIVELY. "X-4," FOR INSTANCE, IS A PINWHEEL-TYPE PLAN, WHICH CAME TO ME FROM A JAPANESE SYMBOL THAT I SAW FLEETINGLY IN A MOVIE. THERE ARE MANY SUCH EXAMPLES OF INSPIRATION; I WON'T BORE THE READER WITH THEM.

NO MATTER THE DEGREE TO WHICH CREATIVITY IS PRIMARILY AN INDIVIDUAL THING, I AM AWARE OF HOW MUCH ALMOST EVERYONE I KNOW "PARTICIPATES" IN MY OWN CREATIVITY, AND, FURTHER, I AM GRATEFUL TO ALL.

THE SAMPLE COLOR DRAWINGS WERE REPRODUCED DIRECTLY FROM MALCOLM WELLS' ORIGINALS THAT WERE DONE ON

VARIOUS WATERCOLOR PAPERS, SOME OF WHICH WRINKLE WHEN THE PAINT DRIES. THIS HAS CAUSED UNINTENTIONAL SHADOWS TO APPEAR ON SOME OF THESE DRAWINGS AS AN UNAVOIDABLE RESULT OF THE REPRODUCTION PROCESS.

BY THE WAY, IF YOU THINK THESE DRAWINGS LOOK BEAUTIFUL IN COLOR—WHICH THEY DO—YOU SHOULD SEE MAC'S ORIGINALS. THE SAND COLOR OF THE STUCCO IN "CONE HOUSE" IS REALLY A ROSE COLOR, AND THE BLUES OF "CHAOS" ARE REALLY SHADES OF A MYSTERIOUS PURPLE COLOR. HOWEVER, THE "REAL" IS ALWAYS PARTLY A CONTRACTION OF THE "IDEAL"—BUT PARADOXICALLY NO LESS IDEAL FOR ALL OF THAT. I WILL LEAVE MY KIND READERS WITH THAT FINAL KOAN.

SOLAR EARTH-SHELTERED HOUSE SECTION.

THERE ARE VARIOUS ASPECTS OF ENERGY EFFICIENCY IN HOUSING THAT NEED TO BE CONSIDERED. WHAT DOES <u>EFFICIENCY</u> MEAN? IF ONE COULD DESIGN A HOUSE THAT DIDN'T NEED ANY HEATING OR COOLING, IS THAT ENERGY EFFICIENT? NO DOUBT! BUT WHAT IF THE HOUSE WOULD COST YOU $100,000 MORE, AND TWICE THAT MUCH WITH MORTGAGE INTEREST, OVER TWENTY OR THIRTY YEARS? THAT CHANGES THINGS, OF COURSE. BUT IS MONEY THE ONLY THING THAT MATTERS?

MAGAZINES AND MANY DESIGNERS USED TO QUOTE THE COST OF UNDERGROUND AND EARTH-SHELTERED HOUSES AT 10 PERCENT LESS THAN THAT OF TRADITIONAL HOUSING. MOST OF THE TIME FOR THE WELL-DESIGNED ONES, THAT WAS <u>NOT</u> TRUE. I DID DESIGN ONE SUCH HOUSE FOR <u>POPULAR SCIENCE</u> IN 1980, WHICH AT THE TIME COULD BE BUILT FOR $25 PER SQUARE FOOT (AND NOW PROBABLY FOR $40 TO $60 PER SQUARE FOOT), WHICH IS PRETTY GOOD—BUT THAT WAS WITH ONLY 6" OF EARTH AND SOD. IF ONE WANTED 2 TO 4' OF EARTH LIKE MALCOLM WELLS DOES, THEN (AS HE HAS LONG ADMITTED) COSTS WOULD BE 10 OR MORE PERCENT HIGHER. BUT THE HOUSES COULD LAST <u>HUNDREDS</u> OF YEARS.

SO THERE IS A DIFFERENCE BETWEEN SIMPLE ENERGY EFFICIENCY, OR EVEN COST SAVINGS, AND ENVIRONMENTAL IMPACT OR <u>PLANET SAVING</u>. ALL OF THIS AND MORE MUST BE TAKEN INTO ACCOUNT IN THE DESIGN DECISION PROCESS. MAC IS, NO DOUBT, STRICTER ON THIS THAN I AM. BUT I THINK I HAVE COME UP WITH A REASONABLE COMPROMISE. I USE EARTH-SHELTERING, OR BERMING, ALMOST ALWAYS, EARTH ON THE ROOF WHEN I CAN, SUPERINSULATION ALWAYS, AND AS MUCH PASSIVE SOLAR GLAZING AS I CAN. AT TIMES, I USE SOLAR COLLECTORS, BUT MORE OFTEN THAN NOT I USE THEM FOR WATER HEATING ONLY. I HAVE NOT BEEN ABLE TO USE WATERLESS TOILETS YET, BUT I WOULD IF IT WAS FEASIBLE. THOUGH SEPTIC SYSTEMS <u>ARE</u> EXPENSIVE, AS I UNDERSTAND THEM, THEY ARE <u>NOT</u> USUALLY TERRIBLY ENVIRONMENTALLY UNSOUND. WATERLESS TOILETS AND THE SMALL ROOMS AND ACCESS SPACE NEEDED TO HOUSE THEM COST, TOO, AND IF YOU ADD ON INTEREST AGAIN . . . BUT THEY ARE A GOOD IDEA, AND MANY THINGS WE ADD TO OUR HOUSES COST EXTRA MONEY. IMPORTANT BUT INEXPENSIVE DETAILS TO CONSIDER ARE THE PROPER USE OF VAPOR BARRIERS AND PROPER INSULATION VENTING.

ALSO, ATTENTION SHOULD BE GIVEN TO UNHEALTHY TOXINS. MORE NATURAL FINISHES SUCH AS STAINS AND PAINTS SHOULD BE CHOSEN WHEREVER POSSIBLE. HOUSES SHOULD BE TESTED FOR RADON GAS, AND HEAT EXCHANGERS SHOULD BE USED ON ALL HOUSES OR WHEREVER POSSIBLE TO PROVIDE A CONTINUOUS STREAM OF FRESH AIR.

AFTER FIFTEEN YEARS OF RESEARCH, I HAVE CONCLUDED THAT LOW-COST HOUSING COMES DOWN TO A MATTER OF SIMPLE-SHAPED MODULAR DESIGNS, SIMPLE FINISHES, AND REDUCED GLAZING.

THERE IS THE SAYING THAT "WAR IS HELL." WELL, BIDDING CAN BECOME A HELL OF SORTS, TOO! TO AVOID THIS, I USUALLY HAVE "ROUGH" BIDS DONE ON PRELIMINARY (SCHEMATIC) STAGE DESIGN DRAWINGS, BY MY BEST "QUAKER" BUILDER AND BUILDING CONSULTANT, LARRY WILSON. I DO THIS EVEN IF THE HOUSE IS BEING CONSTRUCTED LONG DISTANCE AND HE WILL NOT BE BUILDING IT. I DO THIS BECAUSE HE HAS BUILT MY WORK AND IS ACCURATE. ALTHOUGH BUILDING COSTS DO VARY SOMEWHAT IN DIFFERENT AREAS, QUANTITIES DO NOT. SO IF A BUILDER AT A DISTANT LOCATION SAYS THE GLAZING WILL COST $50,000 AND LARRY SAYS $15,000, SOMETHING IS WRONG SOMEWHERE. MY OWN GUESSTIMATES HAVE USUALLY BEEN CLOSE, TOO, ALTHOUGH OFTEN ON THE LOW SIDE.

FOR FINAL BIDS, YOU NEED DETAILED CONSTRUCTION PLANS/SPECIFICATIONS AND REASONABLE ALLOWANCES FOR KITCHENS, BATHS, LIGHTING, AND SO ON. I HAVE OFTEN SAVED MY WHOLE FEE JUST IN BIDDING CLARIFICATION. I THOUGHT IT WAS MY IMAGINATION, BUT I HAVE READ THAT OTHER NOTED ARCHITECTS SAY THE SAME THING. AN ARCHITECT SHOULD NOT BE HIRED FOR THIS REASON ALONE, HOWEVER,

SINCE IT CAN'T BE COUNTED ON, ESPECIALLY WHEN DEALING LONG DISTANCE MORE THAN TWO TO FOUR HOURS AWAY.

OFTEN THE BUILDERS' BIDS COME IN HIGH OR MYSTERIOUSLY LOW (DON'T TRUST THESE!) AND WE DISCUSS OR ARGUE OUR WAY BACK, CLOSE TO MY OWN BID (UNLESS I'M WRONG).

THE NAUTILUS HOUSE HAS HAD THE GREATEST SWINGS IN BIDS. I GUESSTIMATED $100 OR LESS PER SQUARE FOOT. LARRY WILSON BID IT FOR $75 TO $80 PER SQUARE FOOT IF BUILT IN OUR AREA OF SCRANTON, PENNSYLVANIA. THE LOCAL BIDS HAVE BEEN FROM $125 TO $200 PER SQUARE FOOT. WE HAVE NOW NEGOTIATED (WITH BOB TERRY'S LOCAL HELP) DOWN NEAR MY ORIGINAL ESTIMATE OF $125 PER SQUARE FOOT, BUT WITHOUT THE GARDEN AND SIMPLER FINISHES. I THINK THAT, IN THE FUTURE, I WANT TO GET THE ACTUAL BUILDER INVOLVED EARLIER, ESPECIALLY IF DOING BUSINESS LONG DISTANCE.

MANY BUILDERS SEEM TO WANT TO "REDESIGN" THE HOUSE TO GET TO THE PROPER NUMBER TO MATCH THE ARCHITECT'S ESTIMATE. SOMETIMES THERE ARE VALID CONCERNS, BUT OFTEN A BUILDER JUST

DOESN'T WANT TO FOLLOW THE PLANS AND WANTS AN "OUT." THIS SHOULD BE RIGOROUSLY AVOIDED BY SUCH METHODS AS MODIFYING DETAILS AND USING CHANGE ORDERS. <u>NEVER, EVER MAKE A CHANGE WITHOUT A TYPED "CHANGE ORDER"!</u> THIS ALONE CAN SAVE THE OWNER, BUILDER, AND ARCHITECT PROBABLY 90 PERCENT OF CONSTRUCTION PROBLEMS. WITH THESE SAFEGUARDS, BIDDING NEED NOT BE HELL AND CAN EVEN BE FUN!

APPENDIX C:
NON-RESIDENTIAL DESIGN—NORTHEAST FITNESS AND HEALTH CENTER

(WITH ARCHITECT
DON PASSMAN)

BARRY AND JANET KANDEL, WHO OWN THE HIGHLY SUCCESSFUL NORTHEAST FITNESS CENTERS IN NORTHEASTERN PENNSYLVANIA NEAR SCRANTON, HIRED ME DAYS AFTER I RECEIVED MY REGISTRATION, TO DESIGN THEIR NEW FITNESS CENTER. BARRY ALSO WANTED OFFICES FOR HOLISTIC PHYSICIANS. THE BUILDING HAD TO BE OF REASONABLE COST, ENERGY EFFICIENT, AND A SIMPLE SHAPE—HE SUGGESTED A RECTANGLE. OTHER THAN THAT, I COULD HAVE FUN AND MAKE IT AS STRIKING AS POSSIBLE.

I SUGGESTED THE IDEA OF A RESTAURANT-MALL, AND HE LIKED IT. THE CENTER WAS ONE OF MY FIRST LARGE BUILDINGS (50,000 SQUARE FEET) OTHER THAN CHURCHES, SO I REALLY PUT MYSELF INTO IT. ARCHITECT DON PASSMAN AND BUILDING CONTRACTOR LARRY WILSON HELPED A LOT AS CONSULTANTS, AS DID MY FRIEND, NOTED ARCHITECT JOHN C. LAHEY.

THE BUILDING IS QUITE SIMPLE IN PLAN WITH REPETITIVE LONG-SPAN STRUCTURAL BAYS OF 28'0". THE 45° ANGULAR WALLS

ON THE EXTERIOR AND MALL ROOFS CREATED A STRIKING LOOK, THOUGH THEY COST ONLY $75 PER SQUARE FOOT ON PRELIMINARY BIDS. MAC (AND ARCHITECTS JAY AND TRACY BOYLES) DID SUPERB DRAWINGS AND ARCHITECT VINCE VAN DE VENTER CONSTRUCTED A WONDERFUL MODEL. MR. KANDEL IS IN THE FUND-RAISING STAGE NOW, AND I LOOK FORWARD TO THE BUILDING'S COMPLETION. I INCLUDE THIS DESIGN (AND A FEW OTHERS) IN A BOOK THAT LARGELY FOCUSES ON HOUSES TO SHOW THAT THE MODULE IDEA DOES WORK WELL FOR LARGER STRUCTURES. I DREW THIS DESIGN AT ⅛" SCALE, SO THE LARGE MODULES WERE 8' AND I COULD EASILY EYEBALL THE 4' ONES.

NORTH/EAST FITNESS
AND HEALTH CENTER

CGW '93

ENTRANCE AREA

THE NEW NORTH/EAST FITNESS AND HEALTH CENTER

OWNERS: BARRY AND JANET KANDEL ❖ CHARLES G. WOODS, AIA ARCHITECT

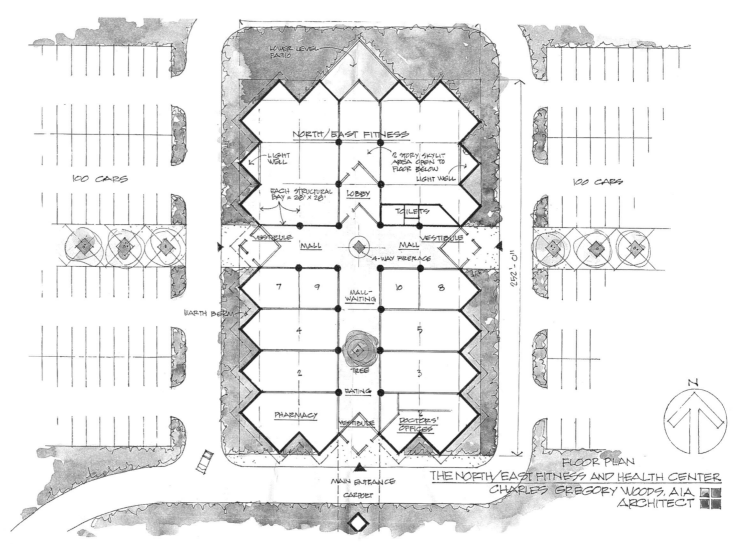

LOWER LEVEL PATIO

100 CARS

NORTH/EAST FITNESS

LIGHT WELL

2 STORY SKYLIT AREA OPEN TO FLOOR BELOW
LIGHT WELL

EACH STRUCTURAL BAY = 28' x 28'

LOBBY

TOILETS

VESTIBULE

MALL

MALL

VESTIBULE

4-WAY FIREPLACE

100 CARS

7   9

MALL WAITING

10   8

EARTH BERM

4

5

2

TREE

3

EATING

PHARMACY

VESTIBULE

DOCTORS' OFFICES

MAIN ENTRANCE
CARPORT

252' - 0"

N

FLOOR PLAN
THE NORTH/EAST FITNESS AND HEALTH CENTER
CHARLES GREGORY WOODS, AIA
ARCHITECT

(LOWER PLAN NOT SHOWN)

LOOKING NORTH FROM THE ENTRANCE

THE NEW NORTH/EAST FITNESS AND HEALTH CENTER

OWNERS: BARRY AND JANET KANDEL   CHARLES G. WOODS, AIA, ARCHITECT

PHARMACY

■ THE NEW NORTH/EAST FITNESS AND HEALTH CENTER

■ OWNERS: BARRY AND JANET KANDEL ■■ CHARLES G. WOODS, AIA ARCHITECT

A DOCTOR'S OFFICE

THE NEW NORTH/EAST FITNESS AND HEALTH CENTER

OWNERS: BARRY AND JANET KANDEL CHARLES G. WOODS, AIA ARCHITECT

LOOKING DOWN THE EAST MALL

THE NEW NORTH/EAST FITNESS AND HEALTH CENTER

OWNERS: BARRY AND JANET KANDEL ■■ CHARLES G. WOODS, AIA, ARCHITECT

THE NEW NORTH/EAST FITNESS AND HEALTH CENTER

OWNERS: BARRY AND JANET KANDEL ▪ CHARLES G. WOODS, AIA ARCHITECT

THE POOLS

■THE NEW NORTH/EAST FITNESS AND HEALTH CENTER
■ OWNERS: BARRY AND JANET KANDEL   ■■ CHARLES G. WOODS, AIA, ARCHITECT

BIBLIOGRAPHY/SUGGESTED READING LIST

Baker, John Milnes. <u>How to Build a House with an Architect.</u> New York: Harper and Row, 1988.

Bower, John. <u>The Healthy House.</u> New York: Lyle Stuart, 1989.

Carmody, John. <u>Underground Space Center, Earth Sheltered Housing Design.</u> New York: VNR, 1979. (Two of my houses are in the second edition.)

De Vido, Alfredo. <u>Designing Your Client's House.</u> New York: Wiley, 1992.

Hale, Jonathan. <u>The Old Way of Seeing.</u> Boston: Houghton Mifflin, 1994.

Jacobson, Max, et al. <u>The Good House.</u> Newtown, CT: Taunton, pr. 1990.

Wade, Alex. <u>30 Energy Efficient Homes You Can Build.</u> Emmaus, PA: Rodale, 1978.

Wells, Malcolm. <u>Gentle Architecture.</u> New York: McGraw-Hill, 1990.

Woods, Charles Gregory. <u>The Complete Earth-Sheltered House.</u> New York: VNR, 1983 (Purchase from author.)

———. <u>Designing Your Natural House.</u> New York: VNR, 1992.

———. <u>Natural Architecture.</u> Element, 1988. (Purchase from author.)

Wright, David. <u>Natural Solar Architecture.</u> New York: VNR, 1981.

Wright, Frank Lloyd. <u>The Natural House.</u> New York: Meridian, 1970.

SELECT BIBLIOGRAPHY/CHRONOLOGY
OF THE WORK OF CHARLES G. WOODS, A.I.A.

(EXCLUDES LECTURES AND EXHIBITS, AND INCLUDES IMPORTANT PROJECTS)

1953	BORN IN CHICAGO, JUNE 24 (SAME BIRTHDAY AS BART PRINCE). RAISED IN BARRINGTON, ILLINOIS.
1967–72	BARRINGTON HIGH SCHOOL (RECEIVED DEGREE IN 1980).
1971–93	APPRENTICED WITH ARCHITECT DENNIS BLAIR A STUDENT OF FRANK LLOYD WRIGHT (1971–1981 AND 1984), AND WITH OTHER ARCHITECTS INCLUDING WRIGHT-TRAINED ALBERT SINCAVAGE, AND DAN LAWRENCE, JOHN J. MARTIN, MALCOLM WELLS (1981–1993).
1972	HONORABLE MENTION FOR CHURCH AND CATHEDRAL, NORTHERN ILLINOIS UNIVERSITY DESIGN CONTEST.
1978	"HOME IMPROVEMENT," BARRINGTON COURIER REVIEW NEWS. (EXACT DATE UNKNOWN.)
1979	B.A. DEGREE IN COMPARATIVE RELIGIOUS PHILOSOPHY (MINOR IN ARCHITECTURE), CAMPUS-FREE COLLEGE.
1979–1980	TAUGHT PHILOSOPHY PART-TIME, WILLIAM RAINEY HARPER JUNIOR COLLEGE.
1979	"HOUSE IN A HILL: A PLAN FOR THE FUTURE?" (WITH ARCHITECT DENNIS BLAIR), CHICAGO SUN-TIMES, MAY 25–26.
1979	"SOUTH FACE-1," HUDSON HOME GUIDE, NOVEMBER, PP. 72–73.
1979	MARRIED TO JULIE KETTLE GUNDLACH.
1980	"EARTH-SHELTERED SOD-ROOFED HOME," POPULAR SCIENCE, SEPTEMBER, PP. 96–97.
1981	M.A. DEGREE IN COMPARATIVE RELIGIOUS PHILOSOPHY, BEACON COLLEGE.
1981	"EARTH-SHELTERED HEAT TRAP," POPULAR SCIENCE, SUMMER, PP. 78–79.
1981	"BETHANY RESIDENT GAINING RECOGNITION," THE WAYNE INDEPENDENT, OCTOBER 22, PP. 12–13.
1981	"PEOPLE REALLY DIG THEIR HOUSE," THE WAYNE INDEPENDENT, OCTOBER 26, PP. 15–16.

1981	"Evolution of an 'Organic' Architect," <u>Earth Shelter Digest,</u> September/October, pp. 56–61.
1981–82	Woods/Gundlach Residence, Honesdale, Pennsylvania.
1982–83	"Taking Shelter," <u>The Scranton Times</u> (2 parts).
1982	"Earth Shelter House Designs 1," <u>Earth Shelter Living,</u> July/August, pp. 58–59.
1982	"Earth-Sheltered Atrium," <u>Popular Science,</u> September, pp. 117–118.
1983	Honorable Mention, Passive Solar Design Awards.
1983	<u>Natural Architecture,</u> Minneapolis: Webco.
1983	"Charles Woods, Natural Architecture," <u>The Wayne Independent,</u> February 10.
1983	"Earth Bermed Wood Foundation," <u>Popular Science,</u> April, pp. 112–113.
1983	"Passive Solar Plus," <u>The Mother Earth News</u> July-August.
1983	"Solar-Earth Retreat," <u>Popular Science,</u> September, pp. 120, 150.
1984	"Rocky Mountain High" (with architect Dennis Blair), <u>Architectural Record,</u> June.
1984	"Woods/Gundlach Residence," in University of Minnesota's <u>Earth Sheltered Housing Design</u> 2d ed. New York: VNR, pp. 268–270.
1984	"Solar Attic," <u>Popular Science,</u> January, pp. 106–107.
1984	"A Designer Looks at His House," <u>Earth Shelter Living,</u> July/August, cover, pp. 14–17.
1984	"Hermit's Cabin," <u>Popular Science,</u> August, pp. 94–95.
1984	<u>Natural Architecture,</u> revised ed., New York: VNR.
1984	Project: Architerra (with architect Dennis Blair).
1984	"The Emperor Has No Clothes!," <u>Architectural Record,</u> published letter to the editor, April.
1985	<u>The Complete Earth Sheltered House</u> (illustrated by Malcolm Wells), New York: VNR.
1985	"Designer's Portfolio," <u>Earth Shelter Living,</u> November/December, p. 27.
1985	Woods Residence, <u>Earth Shelter</u> magazine, cover.
1985	"Solar Cube," <u>Popular Science,</u> May, p. 85.
1985	"Is Earth Shelter Architecture on the Right Track?" <u>Earth Shelter Living,</u> November/December, cover, pp. 21–26.
1986	Ph.D. studies in philosophy.
1986	Woodhaven house design, <u>New Shelter</u> magazine, January, pp. 78–79.
1986	"Earth Bermed Home I and II," <u>Best Selling Home Plans,</u> special edition, pp. 114 and 128.
1986	"Bermed-T," <u>Popular Science,</u> March, pp. 94–95.
1986	"Six Uncommon Houses," 1 house, <u>Popular Science,</u> May, p. 95.

1986   "The Case for Earth-Sheltered Housing," _Better Homes & Gardens' Home Plan Ideas,_ Summer, pp. 69–72, 115–116.

1988   _Natural Architecture,_ 2d revised ed., Warwick, N.Y.: Amity House. (Available from author.)

1988   "Magnificent Seven," 2 houses, _Popular Science,_ February, pp. 82–86.

1989   Radiant and Omega houses, _Popular Science,_ April, pp. 132–136.

1990–1993   Stultz Residence, Clinton, New Jersey.

1990–1995   Cody Residence, Cornwall Bridge, Connecticut.

1990   "State of the Art Houses," _Popular Science_ Magazine, January, pp. 58–62. (One house featured and served as design consultant.]

1992–93   Augello House, Honesdale, Pennsylvania.

1992–94   Cobb House, Honesdale, Pennsylvania.

1992   Project: Notre Dame Cathedral (Vince Van De Venter, R.A., associate designer).

1992   _Designing Your Natural House_ (with Malcolm Wells, R.A.), New York: VNR.

1992   "Seven Deadly Sins of Home Design," _Building Ideas,_ Fall, pp. 81–86.

1993–1994   Cooper House, Kansas.

1993   Project: Northeast Fitness and Health Center.

1993   Became a registered architect (RA-011641-X) in Pennsylvania on September 24, and a member of the A.I.A. shortly thereafter (228459038).

1993–94   Projects: Terry, Sisson, Weber, MacDonald/Ragsdale, (ongoing).

1994   "Out of the Woods—Natural Architecture," Spring, pp. 91–96.

1994   "Wright for the Times," _Building Ideas,_ Spring, pp. 46–51.

1995   _Sacred Spaces,_ architecture book (in progress).

1995   _God, Being, Truth: Essays in the History of Metaphysics_ (unpublished philosophy book).

1995   "No-Thing or nothing," philosophical paper presented to the International Society for NeoPlatonic Studies at Nashville, Tennessee, May 28.

1995   "Throw Your Design Plans a Curve," _Better Homes and Gardens Building Ideas,_ Winter, pp. 68–75.

1996   _Natural System of House Design,_ New York: McGraw-Hill.

<u>Note:</u> Presently Woods is entering more design contests (not having entered any since 1984), and he is seeing projects through to completion.

PHOTOGRAPH BY JULIE K. GUNDLACH

BORN IN CHICAGO IN 1953 OF LARGELY POLISH (BUT ALSO RUSSIAN AND GERMAN) CATHOLIC ANCESTRY, CHARLES G. WOODS IS AN INTERNATIONALLY NOTED AND AWARD-WINNING REGISTERED ARCHITECT/PA AND A MEMBER OF THE AMERICAN INSTITUTE OF ARCHITECTS. HE IS A LONG-TIME SPECIALIST IN EARTH-SHELTERED, ENERGY EFFICIENT, ENVIRONMENTAL AND LOW-MAINTENANCE HOUSING. HE IS THE AUTHOR OF THREE PREVIOUS BOOKS ON ARCHITECTURE AND HIS WORK HAS APPEARED IN 50 RESPECTED JOURNALS AND NEWSPAPERS. HE HAS LECTURED ON ARCHITECTURE AND ON TELEVISION AND RADIO. HE HAS ALSO LECTURED AND TAUGHT COLLEGE PHILOSOPHY. HE APPRENTICED FOR OVER TEN YEARS UNDER TWO DIRECT STUDENTS OF FRANK LLOYD WRIGHT, AND HE HAS A B.A. DEGREE IN COMPARATIVE RELIGION (WITH A MINOR IN ARCHITECTURE) AND AN M.A. DEGREE IN COMPARATIVE RELIGIOUS PHILOSOPHY. HE IS CURRENTLY WRITING HIS DOCTORAL DISSERTATION IN PHILOSOPHY ON THE PHILOSOPHER SPINOZA. HE HAS ALSO WRITTEN AN (AS YET) UNPUBLISHED WORK ON PHILOSOPHY. AS WITH WRIGHT, MIES, AND LE CORBUSIER, WOODS IS LARGELY SELF-TRAINED AND HAS DESIGNED OVER 150 HOUSES AND BUILDINGS—ESPECIALLY SACRED BUILDINGS, WHICH ARE THE SUBJECT OF HIS NEXT BOOK.

HIS HOBBIES ARE READING THE CLASSICS, LISTENING TO CLASSICAL MUSIC, MOVIES, CHESS, KARATE, AND TENNIS. HE IS MARRIED TO AUTHOR JULIE KETTLE GUNDLACH AND LIVES IN THE POCONO MOUNTAINS OF PENNSYLVANIA IN AN EARTH-SHELTERED HOUSE OF HIS OWN DESIGN. HE IS INTERESTED IN PRACTICING WHAT HE CALLS "NATURAL ARCHITECTURE" WITH LIKE-MINDED CLIENTS.

MALCOLM WELLS IS A NOTED ARCHITECT AND IS KNOWN AS THE "FATHER OF UNDERGROUND ARCHITECTURE." HE IS A NOTED RENDERER, ARTIST, AND THE AUTHOR OF OVER A DOZEN BOOKS. HE LIVES UNDERGROUND IN BREWSTER, MASSACHUSETTS.

STONE SHELTER

A Mountaintop Retreat in the Arkansas Ozarks for Vince and Betty Van de Venter

This Earth-sheltered residence is to be called "Stone Shelter" since the "Earth" in this case is solid rock, and slopes steeply from the ridge down 400 feet to the White River Valley. The flint-like rock is to be "sulptured" out with dynamite by a "solid rock extraction" specialist, to form the space, with the exposed "living rock" as finished walls, with the roof hovering above the space with all glass to the valley view.

ARCHITECT VINCENT E. VAN DE VENTER IS KNOWN FOR HIS CREATIVE DESIGNS, QUALITY RENDERINGS, AND MODEL MAKING. HE IS A GRADUATE OF THE UNIVERSITY OF OKLAHOMA, WHERE HE STUDIED WITH BRUCE GOFF AND WAS INFLUENCED BY FRANK LLOYD WRIGHT, WHOM HE KNEW. HE ALSO STUDIED WITH NOTED SCULPTOR, ALPHONSO IANELLI AND WRIGHT-TRAINED ARCHITECT, DENNIS BLAIR. HE HAS BEEN ASSOCIATED WITH ARCHITECT CHARLES G. WOODS FOR THE LAST THREE YEARS. HE IS CURRENTLY BUILDING AN EXPERIMENTAL HOUSE, CALLED STONE SHELTER, NEAR FAY JONES' THORNCROWN CHAPEL IN ARKANSAS, FOR HIS WIFE, BETTY, AND SON, ANDREW.

STOCK PLAN SALES

($750 PER SET, $50 EACH FOR EXTRA SETS, $35 FOR MAILING/ HANDLING)

I HAVE TRIED TO OFFER STOCK CONSTRUCTION PLANS FOR THOSE WHO ARE INTERESTED, EITHER TO BUILD OR FOR STUDY PURPOSES. FOR THOSE PLANNING ON ACTUALLY BUILDING, I SUGGEST CUSTOM SERVICES, BUT IF STOCK PLANS REALLY FIT YOUR NEEDS, THEY ARE, OF COURSE, LESS EXPENSIVE. CALL OR WRITE FOR INFORMATION ON OUR CUSTOM WORK, WHICH COSTS 12 TO 15 PERCENT OF CONSTRUCTION COSTS, FOR FULL RESIDENTIAL SERVICES (WE DO WORK NATIONALLY WITH LOCAL ASSOCIATIONS). THE DRAWING STAGE OF WORK TAKES ABOUT ONE YEAR, AND BUILDING COSTS RUN $100 TO $200 PER SQUARE FOOT. WE ALSO DO COMMERCIAL WORK AND SACRED ARCHITECTURE. OUR PREVIOUS THREE BOOKS, WITH POSTAGE, ARE $100.

NAME: _____

ADDRESS: _____

PHONE NUMBER: _____ FAX: _____

PLAN NAME/NUMBER: _____

ADDITIONAL SETS: _____

VISA/MC NUMBER: _____

EXPIRATION DATE: _____

CHARLES G. WOODS, A.I.A., AND ASSOCIATES
REGISTERED PA ARCHITECT
65 COMMERCIAL STREET
HONESDALE, PA 18431

OFFICE: (717) 253-5452 PHONE/FAX
HOME: (717) 253-0891 (EVENINGS)

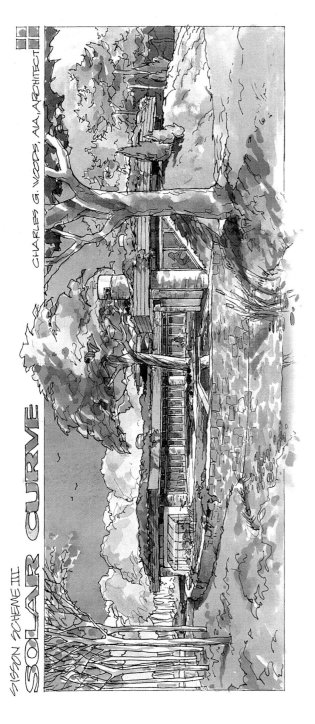

SISSON SCHEME III
SOLAR CURVE

CHARLES G. WOODS, AIA, ARCHITECT

FOUNTAINHEAD - A PROPOSED HOUSE OF RADIANT ARCS FOR MR. KEN WILBUR

CHARLES G. WOODS, AIA, ARCHITECT

COLOR
SAMPLES
OF WOODS'
WORK

"RED ROCKS" A DESERT HOUSE BY CHARLES G. WOODS, A.I.A. ARCHITECT

RED ROCKS   INTERIOR - LIVING AREA   CHARLES WOODS, A.I.A. ARCHITECT

SHARDS

AN EXPERIMENTAL PRIVATE ESTATE HOUSE

CHARLES GREGORY WOODS, AIA ARCHITECT

2.90

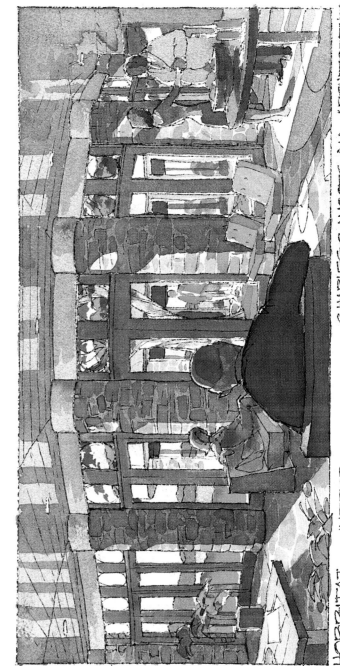

CHARLES G. WOODS, AIA ARCHITECT

HOBBITAT - INTERIOR

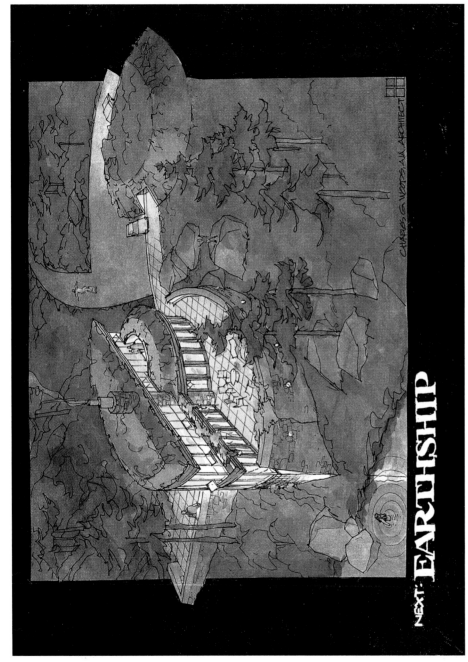

NEXT: **EARTHSHIP**

CHARLES G. WOODS, AIA, ARCHITECT

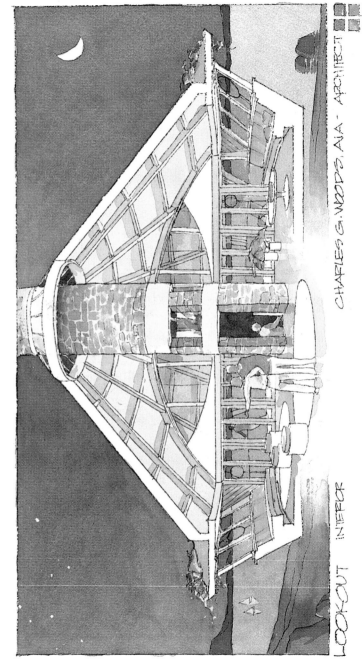

CHARLES G. WOODS, AIA - ARCHITECT

LOOKOUT   INTERIOR

CHARLES G. WOODS, AIA, ARCHITECT

"LOOKOUT" SAUCER VACATION STUDIO IN MEMORY OF JOHN LAUTNER

CHARLES G. WOODS, AIA, ARCHITECT

SPIRAL HOUSE

"CRYSTAL" - A BEACH HOUSE FOR BARRY/JANET KANDEL.

CHARLES G. WOODS, AIA, ARCHITECT

"CRYSTAL" - A BEACH HOUSE FOR BARRY & JANET KANDEL.

CHARLES G. WOODS, AIA, ARCHITECT

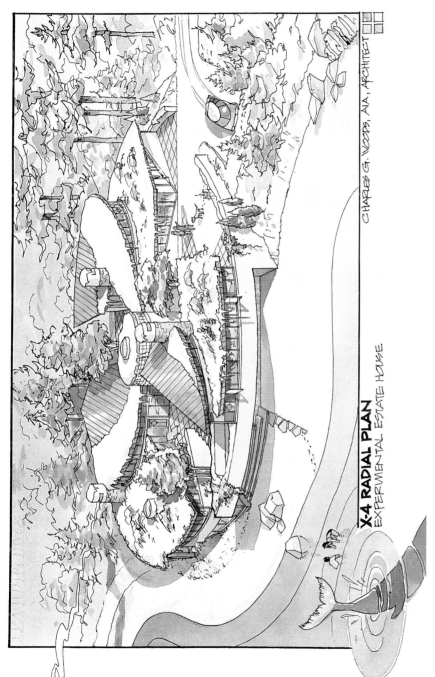

X-4 RADIAL PLAN
EXPERIMENTAL ESTATE HOUSE

CHARLES G. WOODS, AIA, ARCHITECT

SHARP CURVES

CHARLES G. WOODS, AIA, ARCHITECT '96

CHAOS

AN EXPERIMENTAL PRIVATE ESTATE HOUSE   CHARLES G. WOODS, AIA, ARCHITECT

CHARLES G. WOODS, ARCHITECT, AIA

DUTCH CIRCLE HOUSE

CONE HOUSE, A.K.A. THE CONE RESIDENCE

CHARLES G. WOOD, AIA, ARCHITECT

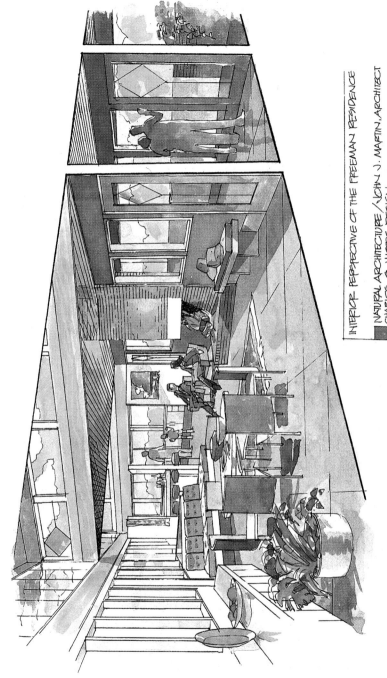

INTERIOR PERSPECTIVE OF THE FREEMAN RESIDENCE

NATURAL ARCHITECTURE / JOHN J. MARTIN, ARCHITECT
CHARLES G. WOOD'S DESIGN

"SNOWFLAKE"

THE SISSON HOUSE / AERIAL VIEW FROM THE SOUTH

CHARLES G. WOODS, AIA, ARCHITECT

Expressive Suburban "Prototype"

CHARLES G. WOODS, AIA, ARCHITECT
1996

CHARLES G. WOODS, AIA., ARCHITECT
A CALIFORNIA "SINGLES" HOUSE

A CALIFORNIA "SINGLES" HOUSE
CHARLES G. WOODS, AIA., ARCHITECT

OUROBOROS AN IRREGULAR HOUSE AT THE BEACH ON A REGULAR 8' GRID

CHARLES G. WOODS, AIA, ARCHITECT '16

"HARMONIOUS DISCONJUNCION" - DEDICATED TO MR. ROBERT ORLOSKI

CHARLES G. WOODS,
AIA
ARCHITECT

WILSON QUAKER DUPLEXES
ECONOMY-ENERGY EFFICIENT

CHARLES G. WOODS, AIA, ARCHITECT

THE RAMIREZ HOUSE at TINKWIG, PENNSYLVANIA

CHARLES GREGORY WOODS, AIA, ARCHITECT

1996

CRAGGED ROCK / FREEMAN HOUSE II...   CHARLES G. WOODS, AIA, ARCHITECT
...AN IRREGULAR HOUSE BASED ON A REGULAR SQUARE GRID

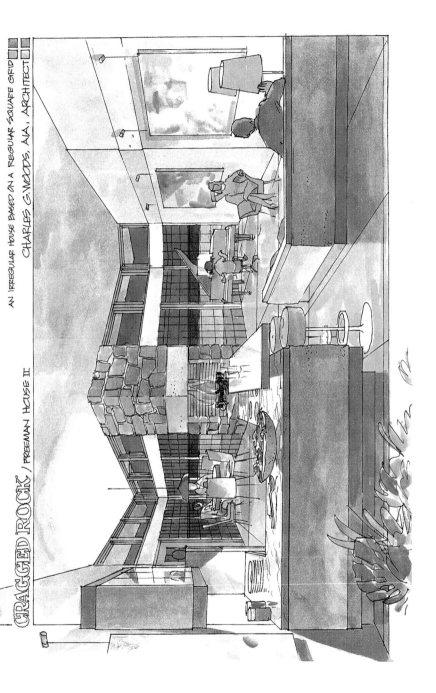

AN IRREGULAR HOUSE BASED ON A REGULAR SQUARE GRID
CHARLES G. WOODS, AIA, ARCHITECT

CRAGGED ROCK / FREEMAN HOUSE II

CHARLES G. WOODS, AIA
ARCHITECT

"WEBER HOUSE, SCHEME 'D'
SOLAR ARC."

NORTH/EAST FITNESS
AND HEALTH CENTER

CGW '93